WHY DIDN'T THEY TELL ME THAT WHEN I WAS YOUNG?

WHY DIDN'T THEY TELL ME THAT WHEN I WAS YOUNG?

Life Lessons Learned

JEAN SPALL

ANCHOR RECORDINGS

Copyright © 2015 Jean Spall
The moral right of the author under the
Copyright, Designs and Patents Act 1988 has been asserted.

First published in Great Britain in 2015 by
Anchor Recordings Ltd
72 The Street, Kennington, Ashford TN24 9HS

No part of this publication may be reproduced or transmitted
in any form or by any means, electronic or mechanical,
including photocopy, recording or any information storage
and retrieval system, without prior permission
in writing from the publisher.

Unless otherwise stated
Scripture quotations taken from the
HOLY BIBLE, NEW INTERNATIONAL VERSION.
Copyright © 1973, 1978, 1984 by International Bible Society.
Used by permission of Hodder & Stoughton Publishers,
a member of the Hachette Livre UK Group. All rights reserved.
"NIV" is a registered trademark of International Bible Society.
UK trademark number 1448790.

USA acknowledgement:
Unless otherwise stated
Scriptures taken from the
Holy Bible, New International Version®, NIV®.
Copyright © 1973, 1978, 1984, 2011 by Biblica, Inc.™
Used by permission of Zondervan. All rights reserved worldwide.
www.zondervan.com
The "NIV" and "New International Version" are trademarks
registered in the United States Patent and Trademark Office
by Biblica, Inc.™

ISBN 978-1-909886-88-9

Printed by Lightning Source

Contents

PART ONE
    INTRODUCTION   9
1. AIM HIGH   11
2. FEAR NOT   16
3. PRAISE   21
4. FORGIVE OTHERS – AND YOURSELF   26
5. READING THE WHOLE BIBLE   32
6. HAVE A GENEROUS SPIRIT   37
7. WATCH OUT FOR CURSED THINGS   41
8. THE MAJORITY IS OFTEN WRONG   46
9. THE MORE CELEBRATION THE LESS REALITY   52
10. A BAD CONSCIENCE IS A GOOD CONSCIENCE   55
11. LOVE LANGUAGES   59
12. LOVE AND MARRIAGE; EVOLUTION; COMMITMENT   63
13. OUR CULTURE   77
14. FAN INTO FLAME   85
15. IMAGINATION IS STRONGER THAN THE WILL   92
16. OCCUPATION IS ...   96
17. THE POWER OF INCONVENIENCE   102
18. LET'S TALK TO OUR FATHER   106
19. WHERE'S THE KEY?   110
20. INFLATION – BUT NOT THE KIND YOU'RE THINKING   112
21. EVIDENCE OF THE BIBLE'S AUTHENTICITY   115

PART TWO

INTRODUCTION	119
22. WHAT IS STRENGTH?	121
23. WORK ETHICS	124
24. WHAT DOES GOD THINK OF HOMOSEXUALITY?	127
25. BEAUTIFUL? HANDSOME?	133
26. WHERE ARE YOU?	136
27. IT'S PARENTS' JOB TO TRAIN THEIR CHILDREN	145
28. MISCONCEPTIONS	148
29. WHAT ABOUT A JOURNAL?	150
30. HYMNS OR SONGS?	152
31. YOU HAD A TOUGH START? SO DID JESUS (DON'T PLAY THE VICTIM)	155
32. NOT WHAT YOU CAN GET, BUT WHAT YOU CAN GIVE	160
33. DON'T UNDERESTIMATE THE VALUE OF SMALL THINGS	163
34. ARE YOU A REFLECTION?	168
35. DOES GOD HEAR EVERY PRAYER?	172
36. APPRECIATION	176
37. THE OLD ENHANCES THE NEW	180
38. DO YOU EVER FEEL ASHAMED?	193
39. THE LORD'S SUPPER OR COMMUNION	200
40. HAVE YOU THOUGHT ABOUT RETIREMENT?	206
41. THERE SHOULD BE A DIFFERENCE	211
42. MORE EVIDENCE FOR THE BIBLE'S AUTHENTICITY	216

PART THREE

INTRODUCTION	239
43. THE POOR	241
44. GOD IS A PRACTICAL GOD	245
45. TREASURE THE MOMENTS	253
46. FEARING THE LORD?	259
47. HOW SECURE IS OUR SALVATION?	264
48. OUR RESOURCES AND ENCOURAGEMENT AS BELIEVERS	268
49. GOING THROUGH A TRIAL?	277
50. WHAT DOES GOD WANT?	281
51. SMALL-MINDEDNESS	287
52. DO YOU HAVE A HERO COMPLEX?	291
53. RITUAL OR REALITY?	295
54. DO WE REALLY NEED RULES?	302
55. IS IT WRONG TO FEEL GOOD ABOUT YOURSELF?	307
56. WATCH OUT FOR THE MEDIA	310
57. ARE YOU SOARING WITH THE EAGLES OR PECKING WITH THE TURKEYS?	315
58. COULD GOD LOVE YOU?	319
59. WHAT KIND OF GOD DO YOU HAVE?	326
60. YOUR POWER OF CENSORSHIP	330
61. ANCIENT WONDERS	334
62. FURTHER EDUCATION	342
63. FURTHER EVIDENCE OF THE BIBLE'S AUTHENTICITY	347

Part Four

Introduction	349
64. Terror Alert	351
65. Jesus is Always Near	355
66. A Timely Reminder	360
67. Are You Minding the Supplies?	363
68. Do you Have Itching Ears?	369
69. Having Trouble with Prayer?	372
70. What Should I Pray for Others?	379
71. God's Secrets	382
72. What do His Laws Show us about God?	386
73. If at First You Don't Succeed	395
74. Hospitality	397
75. Another Look at Temptation	402
76. The Cups of the Lord	405
77. The Diamond	410
78. Humanistic Religion	412
79. Tracing Redemption Through the Old Testament	417
80. Knowledge to be Gained When we Fear the Lord	436
81. God-Incidence	439
82. Faith Means Risk	445
83. The Foreigner and the Kinsman Redeemer	456
84. Even More Evidence for the Bible's Authenticity	462

Acknowledgements

I would like to express gratitude for the following blessings in my life:

My parents, Sam & Doris Rafferty, for their sacrificial love
My husband John for his unstinting support and love
Our family for making our life so rich
J. David Pawson for faithfully teaching the Bible from God's eye view
Philip James for introducing us to life in the Spirit
Peter Bettson for his godly example and prayer support
Friends and relatives for 'being there'
And above all
God for being an anchor for our souls

PART ONE

Introduction

When we're young, we wish we had the wisdom needed for difficult issues. When older, we wish we had the energy of the young. As we age and have learned a thing or two, we wonder 'Why didn't they tell me that when I was young?'

We may not be able to do much about gaining youthful energy as we grow older, but at least we can pass on to the young the wisdom gained with ageing. That's my humble, simple intention with this book. If you take the time to read it, I hope you'll feel that I've accomplished that. Some of the life lessons came without my noticing, others were learned from fellow students in the school of life and yet others were found the hard way—by personal experience... By sharing them, I hope you may be spared some of the painful learning.

I am keeping the subjects brief because each of them could form a book in itself but I encourage you to go more deeply into them for yourself. I just want to give you a little nudge in the right direction.

1

AIM HIGH

Avoid mediocrity. Many of us seem to use up the gift of life we've been given in small thinking. Our personal world is dwarfed by insular thoughts—clothes, cars, food, fun, friends, complaining about things in our world we don't like but never doing anything constructive about them; taking the easy road to everything; giving no thought to building our character; avoiding anything which requires a bit of stretching. So we draw a line around our lives and imprison ourselves within it.

Aim at being proactive – easier said than done if you are not naturally inclined. *So let's begin with something minor*—is your room always messy? What are you doing about it? (This can apply to people young or old as some never learn the simple secret; and can relate to other jobs as well.) First of all, the best way to avoid a messy room is—don't put anything DOWN, put it AWAY—every time. If at all possible, before you walk from your room each morning, take a quick look around to see if anything is out of its place and fix it. That way, you will never *have* a messy room and never have the awful task of cleaning a huge mass of chaos. If you don't have this problem, just skip the next two paragraphs...

[If you already have that mess, follow this easy line... To look at the whole project may be too off-putting, so take it one section at a time, say your bedside cabinet. Place something old such as a towel or sheet on the bed, put on it everything from the bedside cupboard. Dust/clean the cabinet then put the things back in/on the cabinet, cleaning them as you go. This is a good time for culling—toss out or give away anything which you really don't need to keep. *The more you possess, the more your possessions possess you.* And that's a burden you carry with you all the time.

When the first section is completed, move to the next section until you have a room you are pleased with. If you are one who 'carpets' the floor with discarded clothes, etc. you can treat these things the same way; place them all on the bed then go through them one by one. When your things are in order, you will notice how light you feel. The burden has gone...]

That's just one of the compartments of your life but the pattern is the same for all parts. **Work on one bite-size at a time so you don't feel overwhelmed and give up.**

The main thing is to be aware of what's in your life and what needs changing; then setting about making the changes. Don't grunt and groan under the weight of things when you can feel light and carefree so simply.

Once you've brought all sorts of things under control, look at your life and ask yourself what your life goals are. If you are saying 'Goals?' then now's the time to decide on some. You can just allow life to happen or you can direct life events so that you accomplish good (and perhaps great) things throughout your life.

Firstly, you are probably capable of more than you expect. Most of us lack personal confidence and don't really see ourselves achieving much. And if we have no goals in life, then we will probably be correct about that. But why be satisfied with less than your best?

And before we go any further, *this is not about pride or being better than somebody else.* This is about being our personal best. In Little Athletics, the junior athletes are not encouraged to necessarily be the winner, but their performances are judged against their own previous performances. So in a way, they are competing against themselves. What a great idea. We each have a potential and that varies from individual to individual. So it's unfair to expect someone with a moderate talent to beat someone especially gifted. *That means that it's unfair to expect the same thing of yourself.*

Now, how to start? The first thing in every avenue of life is to pray about it. Ask the Lord to bring possibilities to your mind. He is very good at thought transference if we are listening. Secondly, where do your talents lie? If you have no idea, asking a trusted person can be helpful. It is usual that our talents will be used and we 'click' with goals which put our talents to good use. Of course the best way is when we have a sense of call from God and then a goal becomes a passion for our life. There is no limit to what can be achieved with God as our guide, and passion in our heart. I've found that it is easier for God to get us moving in the right direction if we are already moving. I don't recommend just sitting around waiting for God to direct every step in our lives. Ask his direction then begin to act on what SEEMS right. He will then indicate your further steps.

I recall a lesson taught in Bible College. We were looking at the exodus of God's people from slavery in Egypt and being led by God to the land of Canaan. When they came to the flooded Jordan River, there was no way for them to cross. God told them to have the priests stand in the water at the edge, carrying the sacred ark of the covenant. If God didn't do something on their behalf this was an action which made no sense. So it required faith for them to carry out this direction. But when they did, God miraculously caused the water flowing downstream to heap up to one side of them at a distance from them and the entire nation of Israelites were able to cross on dry land. (Joshua chapter 3) I believe this is one of God's principles: When we take a (sometimes tiny) step of faith, his power is unleashed on our behalf. So begin to move in expectation that God will act and we will find that we are on our way. Faith is simply expectation that God will do his part.

The Bible speaks about 'good works' so how about asking the Lord what good works He has planned for you? Of course, the good works aren't to earn our way to Heaven because there's only one way for that. But they are meant to follow our conversion. God has a plan for every life—isn't that exciting? - and He's ready to let us in on what ours is when we are asking and listening. Of course He may tell you only as much as you need to know at any one time.

[A caution here—sometimes in life we have to do jobs we don't like. That's good for our humility and character building. So, as Winston Churchill said, 'Just do it!']

Don't be limited by those in your family or circle of friends. Without offending those close to you, if they aren't goal-setters, reach beyond them to someone who is already proactive in a good work and learn from them. Some folk have been put down by family, friends or teachers who couldn't see what they would later achieve in life. Sometimes conditions like Dyslexia or Aspergers cause people to have learning difficulties although they may be very intelligent. Thus their abilities may be misjudged. So if you are one of these, ask the Lord to help you and to guide you into the achievements He means you to have. Don't allow yourself to be dwarfed by the words or expectations of others. It is said that the young Albert Einstein's father was told by his teacher that Albert wouldn't amount to anything. It is thought that Albert suffered from Aspergers but of course he went on to show the world his brilliance.

There is a picture of Albert often seen in publications where he has twinkling eyes and a huge smile on his face, and I think perhaps he was enjoying 'the last laugh'. If you've been put down by the words of others, why not join Albert in having the last laugh?

If you have real trouble being self-motivated, seek out a mentor, someone to whom you have to be accountable, who will check up on you, say once a week or once a month, to make sure you are keeping to your goals.

Aim high right throughout life. Aiming high and sometimes missing the mark isn't failure. **Fearing and not trying or just being too lazy—that's failure!**

2

FEAR NOT

Speaking of fear, as we were at the end of chapter one, there are so many occasions when God's Word, the Bible, says "Fear not" that there is one "Fear not" for every day of the year. There's no accident in that! It tells us that we need to make a habit of overcoming fear from every avenue of life. Often coupled with the word about not fearing is the positive aspect—"Be of good courage". How do we develop a courageous attitude? Well, the opposite of fear is faith so we look to encourage our faith in God...

Step 1. Learn what God is like by reading the Bible—not just a verse here and there but systematically (more about that later—chapter 5)...

Step 2. Talk things over with God. Ask Him to prompt you, to guide you, in all you do, especially in making decisions. And if you begin to go the wrong way, you will notice a 'check' in your spirit that is God's way of warning His people. Peace in your heart is one of His ways of guiding you to the right action. If you suddenly are aware of a sense of confusion you will know that you have departed from God's way. God never sends confusion to His children. In these ways you will avoid some of life's traps and this will grow your faith.

Step 3. Don't stop talking and walking with the Lord when troubles come. Troubles are part of life for everybody and it is in the most difficult times that we often really see the power of God and know His practical comfort. We are

growing more courageous as we get to know God better...
He IS reliable so there is no need to fear, even when danger is present. God will either protect us or go through the fire with us as in his promise to the Israelites via his prophet Isaiah. Let me quote a little chunk of the passage as it is so comforting and empowering...

Isaiah 43:1-3a: "But now, this is what the Lord says—he who created you, O Jacob, he who formed you, O Israel: 'Fear not, for I have redeemed you; I have summoned you by name; you are mine. When you pass through the waters, I will be with you; and when you pass through the rivers, they will not sweep over you. When you walk through the fire, you will not be burned; the flames will not set you ablaze. For I am the Lord your God, the Holy One of Israel, your Saviour...'"

Isn't that awesome? And if God could care for his people under the Old Covenant, how could we expect less under the New? ***If God didn't allow the hard times to come to us we would not develop character; we would be marshmallows that would melt when the heat is on.***

Let me share an episode from my own story with you...

Years ago I was living on a small island in Vanuatu with my hubby John and youngest daughter Angela when 13-year-old Angie was struck down with Dengue Fever. There are two strains of the fever as far as I know and one of them is fatal. The locals call it 'Breakbone Fever' because every bone is aching. Our house was tiny and of woven bamboo with thatched roof and only one bedroom and Angie was lying on a mattress on the floor. She would call me to please massage her back to ease the pain, night and day.

One day as I was praying—and worrying I confess as I didn't know whether we were going to lose our beloved daughter—I felt an urge from the Lord to go to a bundle of books I hadn't yet read. There were a half dozen of them and as I fingered one after the other I 'knew' that I should take a closer look at "Beyond Ourselves" by Catherine Marshall. So I began looking through the index and when my eyes met "The Prayer of Relinquishment", chapter 6, I knew that I was to read that chapter.

Chapter six told the story of a woman with a very sick daughter in 1870 in Rome (which was not their original home). So far the story related to my situation. The doctor held no hope for the daughter to live. The mother decided that as God was a good God she would go on trusting Him and prayed a prayer of relinquishment of her daughter to God. In that story the daughter recovered.

All I knew was that the Lord wanted me to pray a similar prayer regarding Angie, relinquishing my hold on my daughter to His will. I did so and was immediately flooded with a wonderful peace. I had no idea whether Angie would live or die but I knew that I had done what God required. I felt as though God had just a few words for me then "Now remember that she's mine." As it has turned out, Angela did recover but in the ensuing years she has gone through difficult times and I have had reason to remind God that she is his responsibility.

I don't fully understand why that transaction took place between my Heavenly Father and me, in the middle of a steaming jungle far from medical help or telephones. But I do know that if I ever have the tiniest doubt regarding the existence and truth about God trickle across my mind, I just have to hark back to that experience when the Lord supernaturally directed me wordlessly to the story of a woman with a sick child in the 19th century and any doubt is instantly evaporated. Nobody will ever be able to convince me that God doesn't exist or that He isn't personally involved with His people, because I have EXPERIENCED IT. And it is through trials that we experience most wonderfully the undeniable presence of God. When the sun is shining, the birds are singing, all is well with the world we might almost believe that we don't need God but when troubles and trials come, if we lean on Him we find Him powerful and ready to support and direct us.

A twin with faith is joy. The Bible tells us that the joy of the Lord is our strength and I had an experience of that in spectacular fashion in 2010. To cut the story short, I was diagnosed with breast cancer. The word which strikes fear into many people had absolutely no effect on me and I give God all the glory for that. I went on to have three operations over 3 months. The first op removed a tiny spot, but pathology testing showed that there were more affected cells in the tissue removed. My surgeon, Lisa Creighton, had 4 choices for me to decide on as the next step. The most radical one was to remove the whole breast.

John and I were both being constantly buoyed by the Spirit of God and when Lisa said that it is sometimes possible to reconstruct the breast by taking fat from the tummy area, we had a giggle as we were both thinking that that would return my figure without having to diet. We were joking of course. But Lisa became concerned and put on a stern face as though she was dealing with two naughty children. She said 'Cancer is a serious matter' which we well understood of course.

God immediately gave John and me the same leading: I should have both breasts removed. Lisa was a little taken aback as that was more radical than any option she had given. We agreed to give her our final decision at our next appointment and told her we would be praying about it. When we saw her again, nothing had changed. It was to be a bilateral mastectomy. We had asked trusted friends to pray for direction for us and they had come back with the same answer. Two days after that surgery Lisa rang and said 'Jean, your decision was spectacularly accurate' because there were cancerous and pre-cancerous cells scattered throughout both breasts though nothing of the sort had shown up in either my mammogram or ultrasound. During these weeks I had literally been picked up by the Lord and carried above the circumstances. I was not in denial, but the joy of the Lord was flooding my whole being and there wasn't enough room for fear. People who knew my situation kept remarking about how calm I was, how well I looked, one even said I was glowing.

Now let's get this straight. This was not my doing, it was entirely the Lord's support. I kept thinking of a verse in Exodus where God tells the Israelites whom He had brought out of slavery in Egypt "I carried you on eagles wings" and that was precisely my experience. *If we are faithful in the small things of life, the Lord will be there supporting us "on eagles wings" when the more challenging events present themselves.*

Why am I sharing these experiences? To illustrate that we need the difficult times to form us into the people that God can work with and to teach us that what God has told us about Himself works in real life. *He works in an atmosphere of faith so He wants and needs us to be people of faith.*

Some folk are fearful because they have been brought up with negative thinking. Negativity is a breeding ground for fear. Always looking for the negative side of things is shooting yourself in the foot. If you are one of those people always expecting the worst, begin today to change to being a person with a positive attitude. Thinking positively is part of the pathway of faith. Expecting good things from God is an attitude of faith that God loves to respond to. Mind you, I am not promoting positive thinking as a means in itself. It is in relation to our trust in the goodness and power of God that it is actually '*faith*'.

3

PRAISE

While the Bible is the most important book to read and study, there are also some (and I emphasize *some*) Christian books which are real treasures as well. [I will insert a caution here: It's important to know the teachings of the Bible before reading other books because then we can check the veracity of the book's teaching. If it contradicts the Bible in any point we know that it is not to be trusted. As my heart aches over much of the teaching in pulpits today I get the feeling that the speakers have been reading books rather than *The* Book. If you are just beginning, may I recommend a reliable Bible guide. It is titled "Unlocking the Bible" by David Pawson and gives an outline or overview of each book of the Bible, a great help as you navigate your way around God's Word.]

Many years ago, one book was a real turning point in my life: "From Prison to Praise" by Merlin Carothers. I was going through a really troubling patch and a friend lent a copy to me. Merlin Carothers had a number of points to make in the book but the main thrust was the one which made the difference—we are to praise the Lord in all circumstances, good, bad and downright rotten. Of course we are told to praise the Lord repeatedly in the Bible so I was on safe ground. As I began to put this into practice things began to change dramatically. The author explained that when we praise the Lord for our situation, sometimes our circumstances entirely alter and at other times our attitude/

capacity/mood are enhanced and we are able to handle our situation better.

Merlin wrote more books on the same subject. Two of them were "Power in Praise" and "Answers to Praise". "Answers" was comprised of letters written to the author after people had read his book/s and put his message into practice. Following each letter was a comment by the author. It was amazing to read of the miracles which transformed either people's situations or their own attitudes. So praising the Lord is not only obedience to the instructions of the Lord Himself but it results in blessings in the lives of those who are exercised by it.

One of the things I've noticed about living with God is that He is so essentially good that His rules for living actually put us in 'The Way of Blessing'. There is a way of life which attracts the blessing of the Lord. It doesn't mean life is always easy but there are definite compensations when we lay down our lives to His Will. God's Word says things like "Give and it shall be given to you" Luke 6:38; "A man reaps what he sows" Galatians 6:7; "Whoever loses his life for my sake will find it" Matthew 10:39b.

Selfishness drives us to hold our minutes, hours and weeks to ourselves. But as we open our hearts to the Lord and to others we fulfil His will and He opens the storehouses of Heaven and pours on us all we have need of. Please don't think I am saying 'Give to get'. I know that is the attitude encouraged in some of our churches but I prefer to see it as 'Give because that is what God desires'. But also trust that He will see to it that we receive what He knows is best for us. (We will develop this thought in chapter 6.)

For most of us it isn't hard to understand praising God for the good events of our lives but to praise Him for the other kind goes against the grain doesn't it? So why does God require us to praise Him in ALL things? I don't imagine I have all the answers to this question but at least I see the following:

Beyond every facet of life are God's presence and power. He is the Maker and Maintainer of the entire universe including its population of individual men and women, boys and girls. He has given us the very breath of life. In one sense He owns us because He was the instigator of our being. As He is in control of everything, including for instance the weather, if we complain about the weather we are saying that we are not satisfied with how He is running the world.

Do you remember when the Israelites travelling in the wilderness after being released from slavery in Egypt began to complain about their circumstances—about the lack of water, about the unchanging diet God was supernaturally providing and about Moses' leadership? Moses said they were grumbling against the Lord Himself. (Exodus 16:7 & 8)

Similarly in the New Testament book of Acts chapter 5, do you recall when Ananias and Sapphira lied to the fledgling church about the money they were donating to the work? They had sold a property, as many of the believers were doing, to pool their resources to provide for the needs of all. But they held back some of the money they received for the property for themselves. They had every right to do so. But they pretended that they were giving the entire proceeds of the sale. They received the ultimate punishment from the Lord who said they had lied "to the Holy Spirit".

These things may be hard to get our heads around. But let's face it, God is always right! He's the boss. He's the Lord!

Let's look at another example. Back to the Old Testament: King David sinned by committing adultery with the beautiful Bathsheba so we are surprised when we read Psalm 51:4 where he wrote to God "Against You, You only have I sinned". We would probably judge that David had sinned against Bathsheba and her husband as well but David (whom the Lord said "had a heart after God" despite his sins) saw that beyond the other players in the drama, it was God to whom he was responsible for his actions. If your brain rebels against this way of thinking, realise that we usually see things from a human standpoint. We are "man-centred". We need to have a God's eye-view. Take time to meditate on these things, asking the Lord to help you accept His take on things, because He is always right...

Many people rebel against the fact that God can forgive horrendous deeds in one person yet send someone else who has led a more exemplary life to hell. It is because they fail to understand that some people are born with a propensity to sin while others are naturally law abiders. If you stand back from the situation a bit and take a wide lens to it you will see that God would be unfair if he let the naturally 'better' people be acceptable and the others who struggle to be good were banished. Looking deeper, we see that God is utterly holy and it is totally impossible for *anyone* to be holy because "All have sinned and fall short of the glory of God" Romans 3:23. Let's look at the following verse to keep things in perspective: "and are justified freely by his grace through the redemption that came by Christ Jesus. God presented him as a sacrifice of atonement, through faith in his blood." Now, what could be fairer than that? God knew we didn't have a hope naturally so he made the way—and at a dreadful cost to Himself. It's almost too wonderful to take it in. *But those who refuse to accept God's way of salvation have already condemned themselves.* Maybe we need to find a quiet corner to meditate on all of this...

There are magnificent words in Romans 8:28, 29—"And we know that in all things God works for the good of those who love Him, who have been called according to His purpose. For those God foreknew He also predestined to be conformed to the likeness of His Son, that He might be the firstborn among many brothers." Isn't that enough to encourage you to trust the Lord and praise Him even when circumstances look grim? God is working those circumstances so they will do us ultimate good and in the process He is crafting us into the likeness of Jesus, our big brother. We might say that he is causing a '*family* likeness'. Wow!

Extreme weather events can shake people out of their complacency so that they cry out to God so let's not always pray prosperity upon people. Sometimes prosperity is the pathway to hell...

Just this morning I 'phoned a dear friend. In the course of conversation she related a recent event... One of her daughters who lives an hour away accidentally locked herself out of her house. As her husband was away for the weekend she and her two young children were stranded. So she rang her Mum to ask if they could stay at her home for the weekend. Of course she welcomed them and dried the wet clothes her daughter had taken from the washing line so they had enough to wear. On the Sunday morning they all went along to the parents' church where the sermon was on "Fear". It was just the word this young mother needed as she was about to begin five weeks of 'prac' for her University course and was feeling fearful about it.

When I finished the 'phone call I marvelled at how God causes all things to work together for our good. By the very anxious situation of being locked out of her house, God was able to corral this young mum into hearing a word from Him at the precise time she needed it. I love it!

So remember when anxiety knocks at your door, send praise to answer the knock and by the time the door is opened, anxiety will have fled.

4

FORGIVE OTHERS – AND YOURSELF

There is something which drives many people without their knowing it. It is the need for forgiveness. Some folk behave badly as they are so caught in a web of feeling unforgivable because of something they've done in the past. And the very worry of it makes them put on a tough front as though they are in control of everything while underneath they are quaking.

Forgiveness is freely available, no matter what our past, if we are willing to surrender to God and His way. The Bible makes it clear that none of us is righteous in His sight—until we repent of our sins and claim Jesus Christ's sacrificial death to cover them. Then God looks at us as part of His family and He lovingly guides us as we allow Him to do so. Just as Jesus took our sin upon himself, it is as though we put on Jesus' righteousness like a garment and in that garment we are acceptable to a holy God. If you doubt my word, here it is in Scriptural form: (2 Corinthians 5:21 'God made him who had no sin (Jesus) to be sin for us, so that in him we might become the righteousness of God.'

[A warning here: Please don't take God's love and righteousness for you for granted. There is much carelessness in this regard in today's church I'm afraid. Take warning from Romans 11:22 where Paul is teaching about how unbelieving Jews, who had been God's chosen people, had been largely cut off from God's blessing, and Gentiles (non-Jews) had been grafted into the family of God as they accepted Jesus as their Saviour and Lord. Paul has this to say 'Consider therefore the kindness and sternness of God: sternness to those who fell, but kindness to you, provided that you *continue* in his kindness. Otherwise, you also will be cut off. And if they do not persist in unbelief, they will be grafted in, for God is able to graft them in again.' I mention this because I want to bring balance to our minds. I want you to feel warmly and greatly loved by your Father God but I don't want you to under-value the Grace of God. It's *not cheap grace.* If you were to feel that it didn't matter how you live because God's grace will cover it, then you haven't understood the sternness of God. He has gone to great trouble and pain to enable us to be reconciled to him. But he expects us to respond to his love by giving him our hearts and lives in obedience to his will, not in obedience to the old Jewish laws but in obedience to what is revealed in the New Testament and the leading of the Holy Spirit within you if you are a disciple of Jesus.]

Now we move on to the next phase, forgiving others for what they do against us. Many of us struggle with this, particularly with someone who is a repeat offender. Why should we forgive them, especially if we've done so previously, only to be hurt again? Let's stand back from the situation a little and try to see the 'big picture'.

As I mentioned, none of us can ever be good enough for God's holiness—of ourselves. And even as Christians we still do wrong sometimes. God has already forgiven us once when we asked—by His own perfect Son's humiliation and dreadful suffering. Should God forgive us again when we slip up? We would hope so, wouldn't we? And we are assured of this forgiveness in His word as long as we remain walking with Him. So how can we withhold forgiveness when we ourselves need to be forgiven again and again?

This is such a vital point that it is found right in the Lord's

Prayer which Jesus taught his first disciples. Remember how it says "Forgive us our trespasses *as we forgive those who trespass against us.*" That means that our forgiveness hinges on our being willing to forgive others. Now that really is vital! Not only that, but if we look at Matthew chapter 6 we see at the end of the Lord's Prayer, verse 14 continues "For if you forgive men when they sin against you, your heavenly Father will also forgive you. But if you do not forgive men their sins, your Father will not forgive your sins." It can't get any clearer than that. Our forgiveness is linked with our forgiving others, is actually dependent on it.

Then we come to how many times should we forgive others. Well that's clearly stated in the Bible as well. The Apostle Peter had the same question. He probably thought he was being generous when he suggested seven times. But Jesus Himself came back with this reply: "I tell you, not seven times, but seventy-seven times." Matthew 18:22. Jesus goes on to tell an illustrative parable about a king who forgave his servant an incredibly large debt. Then it was reported to the king that the same servant had gone out and found a fellow servant who owed him a relatively small amount and utterly refused to cancel the debt. The king's anger was roused against the one he had forgiven especially as his debt had been so very large. Of course we can see ourselves in this story. Let's face it, our sins put Jesus on the cross. How dare we expect to claim forgiveness for our sins yet withhold forgiveness from someone else? And if we are to forgive 77 times obviously we would not be able to keep count so the figure is really meant to be infinite.

While it is so clear in Scripture, we sometimes struggle to forgive, especially if the person who has hurt us in some way doesn't repent. But even this is covered in God's word because we are told to bless our enemy, to give him food if he is hungry, etc. (Romans 12:19-21). So obviously we are to have a forgiving attitude even when there is no repentance on the other person's part *based on the fact that we all need forgiveness. We have no right to judge the other person. But we can be assured that he will front the Judgment Seat of Christ eventually and God has said "vengeance is Mine". So let's leave that to Him in His time.*

As is so often the case, there is a physical aspect to this spiritual matter. A little verse in the Old Testament gives us a clue: In Psalm 32, David is discussing struggling with his sinfulness. Firstly he announces that the man whose sins have been forgiven is blessed. Then in verse 3 he refers to the time before he had repented and been forgiven. He says "When I kept silent, my bones wasted away..." This intimates that our physical bodies are affected by our spiritual attitudes. And it is fairly common knowledge today that many cases of arthritis, for instance, are due to the holding of grudges — resentment, in other words the lack of forgiveness.

The association between spiritual attitudes and physical consequences is echoed in some of the Proverbs. Chapter 17 verse 22 "A cheerful heart is good medicine, but a crushed spirit dries up the bones." Chapter 18:14 "A man's spirit sustains him in sickness, but a crushed spirit who can bear?"

Now what's the next phase? Forgiving ourselves! Some of us find it difficult to forget our sins of the past even when we've asked forgiveness of God. The shame seems to dog our footsteps. What is the answer? It may be different for each person but here are a couple of things I would suggest. One of the reasons we can't forgive ourselves could actually be pride. We don't want anyone to know that we've been guilty of such a thing. Perhaps we are angry at ourselves because we see ourselves better than the deed we committed. But if we are going to be good representatives of God to our world we need to have the integrity to admit that we need God's forgiveness as much as anybody else does. It may help someone else to know that we had to bow the knee in humility before God to ask for forgiveness. This doesn't mean that we have to blab our sins to all and sundry but it does mean that we need to watch that we are not wanting glory for ourselves in the eyes of men.

Another reason for continuing mourning over our previous sins is that we may realise that our past will preclude us from certain forms of service for the Lord. For instance, if we could see ourselves doing much good by serving as a politician or other public figure, we may realise that our past would be bound to be dug up and paraded for the population to see and our reputation would be cut to shreds and people may then feel that they couldn't trust us to represent them etc.. Well, I'm afraid we may have to live with that. But we can comfort ourselves that God usually has a Plan B, or in fact, as He knew about your sin long before you confessed it to Him, His Plan A is still able to be fulfilled. Maybe it's just *our own* Plan A which has to be forfeited.

I will finish this subject with a couple of wonderful verses to remind us that we don't need to thrash ourselves because God's love is truly amazing. Romans 8:38,39 "For I am convinced that neither death nor life, neither angels nor demons, neither the present nor the future, nor any powers, neither height nor depth, nor anything else in all creation, will be able to separate us from the love of God that is in Christ Jesus our Lord."

And a postscript. If we continue wallowing in the shame of the past we will miss out on accomplishing the very purpose for which God saved us. So let us all live in forgiveness—the wonder that our forgiveness was purchased "while we were still sinners" (Romans 5:8), the brotherly kindness of sharing that forgiveness with those who hurt us and the victory of living in the reality of forgiving ourselves.

I will add that forgiveness of self is not mentioned

in Scripture. What is actually needed is to live in the forgiveness that God has made available to us when we have repented and surrendered to him. I hope that what I have said in this chapter will help you to move into that place of victory which God intends you to have.

5

READING THE WHOLE BIBLE

Why read the Bible is the first question. Because it is the Manual for Life. When we buy anything from a small kitchen appliance, a sewing machine or a power tool to something like a car they usually come with a manual to acquaint us with how to use them properly, how to use them safely, how to get the most benefit out of them. And the Bible is really much the same. The manufacturer of the world and of our incredibly complex, wonderful bodies/souls/spirits has had a splendid manual printed especially so that we can become acquainted with Him, know how to live life properly and how to dodge life's pitfalls. Some people don't read the manual that comes with an appliance until they run into problems. Then they flick quickly through the manual to see how to get out of trouble.

Does that sound familiar? Have you used the Bible that way? Ignore it, feel confident in your own intelligence until you run into a sticky situation then think that maybe the Bible can shed a little light? Well, as with an appliance manual, it really works out better if we read the manual first. God has gone to considerable trouble to put together the Bible. It is really a library of 66 books written over a period of centuries. There is no other book like it. And though the authors (under God's inspiration) have lived in different eras of time the same thread of story amazingly can be traced right through the 66 books. Of course it is because God is the author behind all of the men who put quill to parchment.

Some folk today feel that they need not read the Old Testament because we now live under the New Covenant. But the Old Testament is an absolute treasure house of events which give a deep understanding of what God was to accomplish under the New Covenant. Every piece of furniture in the ancient tabernacle spoke of an aspect of Jesus Christ. Every sacrifice the Israelites offered to God was a picture of His sacrifice and what it would accomplish. Every Feast the Israelites were instructed to keep also spoke of His ultimate work in the future. That is how God could accept these stipulations of the Law to allow the people to have a relationship with Him. Each thing was a 'shadow' of what was to be.

How to tackle the task of reading right through the Bible? There is no hard and fast rule but generally people find it tough going if they begin at Genesis and Exodus which are captivating because they are stories of our first ancestors, and keep ploughing through books about laws and good and bad kings etc. So I would suggest that there are two good ways of tackling the Bible for the first time. You could read through the New Testament first then go through the Old. Or, you could read both by beginning in the first books of the Old - Genesis, Exodus and Leviticus then switch to the New Testament for a change of pace. After a couple of books there, go back to the next book of the Old Testament. This way you are more likely to persevere. Remember, if you read 3 chapters per week day and 5 chapters each on Saturdays and Sundays you will finish the entire work in a year. That's not too hard, is it? And your reward will be that you will have a fascinating overview of what it's all about. Once you have read it right through you may then decide to take more time to read particular portions and digest them well.

If you consider any other book in the library, would you think it sensible to read a sentence, a paragraph or even a chapter at random when you have never read it right through? You wouldn't 'get' the plot at all, would you? You could even badly misjudge the work because you had read only snatches of it out of context. Well, it's just the same with the Bible. I guess that taking verses out of context is one of the reasons we have so many denominations in the Christian faith. It is in gaining an understanding of the whole book that we learn how to interpret the bits and pieces.

There are those who have claimed that the Bible contradicts itself but it is only when you haven't read the whole Word that you think that. The remainder of the Word explains the individual verse, shows us how to take its true meaning.

Years ago John and I bought Pentel pencils which had 8 different coloured 'leads' in each. We then chose a category for each colour and began marking our Bibles as we read them. For instance, there are lots of 'hinge' words which we marked in orange; words like *'if'*, *'but'*, *'and'*, *'therefore'* *'except'* *'then'*. So often God's promises rest on a condition. Just think of this one: "To the Jews who had believed him, Jesus said 'IF you hold to my teaching, you are really my disciples. THEN you will know the truth, and the truth will set you free.'" (John 8:31,32). So there we have two hinges, *if* and *then*. How many times do we hear people say 'The truth will set you free' without any qualification; but when we look at this verse we see that Jesus has a qualification — Obedience is needed to be a true disciple of Jesus and as an obedient disciple we will know the truth which sets free. Makes quite a difference, doesn't it?

It is so very vital to notice the conditions God has placed on things and colouring the 'hinges' helps with this. There are many illustrations but here is another: Romans chapter 4 finishes thus: "He (Jesus) was delivered over to death for our sins and was raised to life for our justification."

Then chapter 5 begins "THEREFORE, since we have been justified through faith, we have peace with God through our Lord Jesus Christ..." Now if you simply picked up your Bible and began reading at chapter 5 you would miss the important verses which preceded it. But the very fact that the chapter begins with a hinge word should make us look to see what came before. Highlighting the word reminds us.

One of the side benefits of colouring as you read through the Bible the first time is that you are not mindlessly running over the words but you are noting the content. This helps to keep your interest as well as providing help with quick comprehension when next you read the same passage.

It may be helpful if I share our code with you. **Red** denoted very important points (perhaps sermon points too). **Pink** noted things repeated. **Orange** coloured the conditional hinges—if, but, and, therefore, except, then. **Brown** was for moral codes or laws. **Deep Blue** highlighted things to be lived out in our daily lives. **Light Blue** referred to the Holy Spirit. **Green** referred to a new thought or something that required further study. **Yellow** was for verses which deserved to be memorised.

I don't know whether these multi-colour pencils are still available but if not, a set of coloured pencils will do as well, though not be quite as convenient.

I'll mention one thing which puzzles some folk about the Bible. They wonder why there are four gospels, Matthew, Mark, Luke and John which are basically telling the same story of Jesus' life on earth. But once you realise that each was written to a specific audience, it is easy to understand.

Matthew wrote to a Jewish audience presenting Jesus as their king and focussed on what Jesus *said*.

Mark wrote to Romans who were ruling over the Jews at the time. He showed Jesus as a servant and focussed on what Jesus *did*.

Luke wrote for Greeks and presented Jesus as the Son of Man. His focus was on how Jesus *felt*.

John wrote for everybody – the world – presenting Jesus as the Son of God. He focussed on who Jesus *was*—The Light, the Way, the Truth, the Life, the Word, the Door, the Shepherd, the True Vine.

This explains that when they are relating the same event, each sees his particular emphasis. It's the same with us in everyday life. If we are writing an account of some happening we may present a different emphasis depending on whether we are writing to our girlfriend or our grandfather, for instance. We tend to emphasize the aspects which will be meaningful to the recipient.

6

HAVE A GENEROUS SPIRIT

Have you noticed that some folk trudge through life while others almost dance their way through it? Of course there can be reasons of age or health that cause varying attitudes but much of it has to do with how we choose to view the world. And interestingly, if we adopt the right attitude, even with age and ill health we can sometimes be helped to cope - with a lighter heart.

We have had a brief look at negative and positive thinking in the light of having a faith outlook; what else is there to consider? It's surprising how a change of attitude in one avenue can afford us a change from a colourless existence to a rainbow-coloured life.

Firstly, we can check up on God's Word to see if this is indeed what God wants of us. Well, how about these verses from 2Corinthians 9:6-8: "Remember this: Whoever sows sparingly will also reap sparingly, and whoever sows generously will also reap generously. Each man should give what he has decided in his heart to give, not reluctantly or under compulsion, for God loves a cheerful giver." Paul here is speaking about a gift which is to be given for other believers who are in need. But the principle is the same in general living.

Surely we have all witnessed someone who has a mean spirit, won't part with a pin if it can be helped. Is there any true joy in that person? Of course not, because he/she is not living in accord with God's principles. Over and over we are urged to give to others: Luke 6 shows the principle in all its extent. Verses 27-31: "But I tell you who hear me (Jesus speaking) 'Love your enemies, do good to those who hate you, bless those who curse you, pray for those who mistreat you. If someone strikes you on one cheek, turn to him the other also. If someone takes your cloak, do not stop him from taking your tunic. Give to everyone who asks you, and if anyone takes what belongs to you, do not demand it back." And then *the Golden Rule:* "Do to others as you would have them do to you." (Luke 6:31)

Now some of this is hard to accept, isn't it? It is so opposed to the way we naturally feel and react. If we are bitten, we want to bite back. Isn't that right? But Jesus came to show us another way—God's way.

Have you ever imagined what kind of world we would live in if everybody adopted the Golden Rule as their attitude for living? It would be like heaven surely. Well, the least we can do is to make it *our* motto. Then that is one less person biting back. What if we could start a trend? What if it picked up more and more people? It won't be easy, but it will never happen if someone doesn't start the ball rolling. Imagine how different the world would be if even every *Christian* acted out the Golden Rule every day. Let's get on with it...

There is something about generosity of spirit that opens us up to the blessings and joy of the Lord. God responds to those who live his way. They recommend Christianity to those they meet. The blessing gets passed on and on. Can you catch a glimpse of the effect? Don't you want to expand your heart to those you meet?

One point—it must be genuine. You can't fake this kind of thing. It begins in your own heart when you start to see the heart of the Father who loves us so much that he made a way for us to be part of his family, that he gave us a life manual so we could walk the right way, that he is attentive to genuine prayers, and fashions an answer to them. That kind of God deserves only the best response from our heart to his. When we fully surrender to him (as much as we can comprehend to do so) we have begun on the road which will change us and change the world.

Generosity of spirit extends to much more than money and possessions. It gives a listening ear to others when they are old and infirm, young and uncertain, or when they just need to be heard. It gives them the benefit of the doubt when their behaviour is not all we would desire. It is willing to forgive when we are hurt. And we find that if we are willing to open our hearts to God to be made willing to be generous, he is only too ready to grant our desire. Philippians 2:13 confirms "For it is God who works in you to will and to act according to his good purpose." So be assured, God is working in co-operation with you. He's not against you. He's for you and will help as you reach out to co-operate with Him. Hallelujah!

A little postscript: Cultivating a generous spirit toward others can help to control jealousy. Instead of viewing others as rivals we welcome them as friends. If they have wrong motives, we leave it up to the Lord to deal with them.

Cultivating

Years ago, I bought a small plant in a pot.
I watered it every few days.
After 3 or 4 years, the plant looked just as it had when I bought it.
I was disappointed.
I dug a hole in the garden,
popped the plant into it, fertilised it,
and continued to water it.
That spindly plant began to grow and expand until it was huge.
It produced lovely red berries
and made me very pleased.
If we want to be successful at life,
we need to cultivate good habits.
We can't just let ourselves stay as we are.
We need to weed out bad habits
and cultivate good habits;
perhaps weed out bad friends
and cultivate good ones.
Cultivation is needed.
It doesn't just happen automatically.

7

WATCH OUT FOR CURSED THINGS

I mentioned pitfalls in life and now we must enlarge on one of those. It is the possibility of being affected by things which bring a curse with them. You say, is that possible? Won't God protect me automatically from something like that? No, not automatically. Remember that a life manual gives warnings. That's one of the ways God protects us. We follow the manual and we stay safe from these dangers.

Time and again God warned the Israelites to have nothing to do with the idols and practices of the pagan nations which surrounded them. The Bible gives us to understand that evil spirits inhabit items which are worshipped so that they receive the worship for themselves. Over the last few years in Australia we have undergone a plague - in the form of a rash of idols in many people's homes and gardens—buddhas and other exotic statues (and even gnomes) in various forms. Without realising it, people are inviting evil spirits into their lives.

When we were looking to buy our present home 5 years ago we called to inspect it. It was elegantly furnished but it was full of buddhas of all types—from magnets on the 'frig to a carved one about 40cm tall on the deck. The first thing we did when the time under contract was completed was to go round the entire house and yard removing any of the offending articles which had been left behind, smashing and binning them. Then a fellow pastor and his wife joined us as we prayed through the place cleansing it. We have had enough to do with deliverance ministry over the years to know we must leave no toehold for the enemy, the devil (also called Lucifer).

Does this sound too extreme for you? Well, don't make a judgment too quickly. Let me share some of our experiences with you so you understand why we feel so strongly about this matter.

A lady (let's call her Yolanda) came to our home years ago to get some help for her 10-year-old daughter (let's name her Jessie). Jessie's teacher had approached Yolanda asking her to seek psychological help for her daughter because she was spooking the other children by always talking about death and allied subjects. When Yolanda and Jessie sat in our counselling room and the situation had been explained, Yolanda was surprised when John turned his attention to her rather than Jessie. The Lord often gives John a gift known as 'word of knowledge' - that is John knows something about the person which he has no other way of knowing except that God has told him. John said to Yolanda 'How long have you been deaf in your left ear?' She said 'how do you know I'm deaf in that ear? It comes and goes.' John explained that the Lord sometimes tells him things so he knows how to help the person. (It also causes the person to realise that God is involved and interested.) Next John asked Yolanda if she had some jewellery with her. She said that she had some in her handbag. John asked to see it and asked where it had come from. It was of Burmese origin and had been a gift from a relative. John knew that it was the jewellery which had been cursed or had a demon attached to it.

He told her that the jewellery needed to be destroyed but when he tried to take it from Yolanda she began to hiss like a snake and would have struck John except that she was pinned to the seat by the Spirit of the Lord. John told her he was going to destroy the jewellery, he went into our back yard and smashed it with a hammer. When he returned, he prayed with Yolanda and she not only had her hearing restored but was set free of the vicious spirit which had revealed itself in her. John prayed for Jessie as well, knowing that the evil which had been haunting Jessie had been overcome.

You can see that it was important that the Word of Knowledge had been given by God on the matter or John could have gone on praying for the little girl when the problem originated with the mother and her jewellery. But I'm not so much wanting to share with you about Word of Knowledge but simply that there are evil beings of the spirit world which delight in living in everyday items so we need to be careful what things we allow into our homes, what we wear, etc. This is important to keep in mind if you buy second-hand items in particular but also new goods can be contaminated as you will see in a story later in this chapter. There is no need to be scared. Ask the Lord for discernment so you will know if something you have or are thinking of buying is not 'clean'. Also pray a prayer of cleansing in the Name of Jesus and his blood over anything you bring into your possession. It is good to know that God's Spirit is more powerful than any other spirit.

We need to be alert because, with so many people migrating from countries where other gods are worshipped and with so many Aussies visiting overseas countries, exotic goods and practices are being incorporated into our lives. The problem is that people are attracted by the exotic nature of things without realising that they are connected with or derived from these false religions. Yoga is so popular now as are many forms of self-defence like karate. But you need to know that they are connected with Eastern religions. With yoga, for instance, some teachers tell their students to "empty their minds". This is dangerous, don't be involved in it. It is too easy for something of the spirit world to penetrate an opened mind in these circumstances. We have had to help people who have been contaminated by involvement in yoga. I don't dispute that the stretches taught may be helpful physically but it is the risk of our becoming captive to an evil spirit which overrides these benefits.

A young Christian friend of ours years ago was progressing up the ranks of karate and believed that it was a harmless pastime. Then, as he was doing so well, he was invited to be in a special class with a sensei, a master from overseas. This visiting teacher revealed that when they make the 'grunting' sounds they are calling on a power to help them. It was then that our friend realised that there was more to karate than just self-defence and he withdrew from it.

Most people who are seeking God realise that Ouija boards are not to be messed with but sometimes young people think of them as games and take part without realising that they are joining in things which may affect them for the rest of their lives. Let me share another story, a more recent one:

(I will use assumed names in my stories to protect people's privacy.) Helen was recently married and had found that she had a cyst on an ovary so she asked for prayer. John asked the Lord for wisdom, as he always does. He then said to Helen that the Lord had said that she had a spirit of fear. She laughed at this and said that she was not a fearful person. John then gently said that fear comes in many forms. He began to give her an example of how a spirit of fear can come to a person. He said 'suppose a little girl of about 5 goes to visit her grandmother with her mother. Unbeknown to either of them the grandmother is about to take part in a séance. During this time the little girl sees a 'ghost' and from then on will not go to bed at night without the light being left on. That is a spirit of fear.'

When he had finished his example, Helen said 'you have just told me my life story. You can ask my husband; I will not go to sleep at night without the light on because of seeing a 'ghost' at my grandmother's séance when I was five.' Thus, Helen realised that she did indeed have a spirit of fear and was then pleased for John to pray for her to be set free of that which had plagued her for over 20 years.

These are not isolated instances. Though John didn't seek a ministry of deliverance he has been involved in many cases because once people are set free they recommend others to visit the one who has helped them. Please note that all the glory goes to the Lord because he is the ultimate and only one who has the power of deliverance. If you would like to read more on this subject, my husband John recommends the book "Unbroken Curses" by Rebecca Brown, M.D. with Daniel Yoder (her husband).

8

THE MAJORITY IS OFTEN WRONG

Many of us have either a 'tribal' or a 'herd' mentality—either the leader is always right or we just go with the mob. An example of the *tribal* mentality is what we found in Vanuatu. If you speak to a village assembly the people wait to see what the chief does then they tend to follow his lead. *Herd* mentality sometimes translates to gang mentality in human beings. Sheep will move as one, herding together to face the sheep dog for instance. Gangs have a strong sense of loyalty to the gang so that they will stick together even when their business is criminal.

A small example of herd or gang mentality was played out before me years ago. I was driving into the high school grounds to pick up our daughter and the students were streaming along the footpath. As I came to the place where the young people had to cross the road I was driving on, instead of waiting on the footpath for me to pass they continued to pour across the street and I had to stop the car and wait for them. One student would never have walked straight across the street alone for fear of being run over. He would have waited for the car which had right of way. But because they were in large numbers they 'took over' the road. That's gang thinking. It is sometimes seen at football matches etc. where supporters of one team will become violent after a game which hasn't pleased them.

Most of us fall into one or other of these categories. We feel secure in following a leader and perhaps don't examine too closely what his real motives are or whether wisdom is being applied. Or we look around us to see which way MOST of the people are leaning. Isn't that right?

Now let me say—there is a place for strong loyalty to a leader and there is a place for sticking with your mates. But each of us is responsible for our decisions in the long run so let's look at something the Bible has to say which may shed some light for us.

1Corinthians 2:14 says "..a natural man does not accept the things of the Spirit of God; for they are foolishness to him, and he cannot understand them, because they are spiritually appraised (discerned)."

What does this alert us to? It means that most people ('natural' people because they don't have a relationship with God) are basing their thinking, their ideals, their decisions and their actions on faulty foundations. It does not mean that everything they do or think is wrong but it does warn us not to follow others like sheep. Jesus said "I am the Good Shepherd". We follow him. And when we are new believers, we may be able to follow HIS other sheep if they are indeed following the Good Shepherd.

We have to conclude that, as most people are not walking with the Lord, the majority is often wrong. Voting in elections of any kind is usually based on the majority decision but as the majority are not thinking from God's point of view the results often bring bad government. I am not thinking only locally but globally also. Why is this so? One reason is that people often vote according to the promises made by a candidate. If those promises favour them they will choose accordingly. A current example is the country of Greece:

Greece is in an extremely bad economic position at this very time. If we probe a little it is not hard to understand how they came to this state. Seventy percent of the workforce is employed by the government. That means at the most, 30%

of the people are paying wages for 70%. On top of that, the retirement age is a mere 55 years old (that may be only the 70% in government jobs, I'm not sure). But it is easy to see that this is not a tenable position yet the government, or perhaps succeeding governments, have allowed this to occur.

Because the country is in such a financial mess, austerity measures have been called for by countries who are trying to help them to a more stable situation. But many of the Greek people have risen up against this idea. Now I'm no expert in economics but it is clear that things have to change or their economic position will flatline, if it hasn't already.

I have no wish to go into the politics of Greece or any other nation but it is clear that bad decisions have been made in the past. Why? Probably to keep everybody happy and to win votes, rather than to make wise decisions which would ultimately improve the situation for everybody, though they may cause some short-term pain.

All I want to say is 'the majority is often wrong' so don't automatically go with the majority. Think for yourself. Don't be afraid to stand alone on some issues. Seek the wisdom of the Lord before making small and large decisions. The New Testament book of James chapter 1 verse 5 invites us... *"If any of you lacks wisdom, he should ask God, who gives generously to all without finding fault, and it will be given to him."*

Let's look at an aspect of life which is entirely different: fashion. Fashion can be fun and can allow us to express our own individual style. It can enable us to show ourselves in the best light. But fashion can also be slavishly followed with rather odd or undesirable results. I remember when the mini skirt first came into fashion years ago. Suddenly every woman paraded in short skirts, and some of them really shouldn't have. I had to giggle sometimes as a girl with extremely thin legs walked down the street, looking rather like a bird with stick-like legs, certainly not a good look. With good sense, fashion can be chosen to cover our worse features and focus on our better ones.

More recently, waistlines were replaced with 'hip' lines. Skirts, slacks and shorts no longer went up to the waist but often placed a tight band round the hip. Now it was the chubby girls' turn to look comical with flab bursting forth from the top of the clothes. As you walk behind them you wonder 'why would they do this to themselves?' The answer is again the herd mentality. They must follow the trend instead of finding a more suitable one or creating one of their own.

Some of these things are simply cringe-worthy but others are worse to my way of thinking. In the last few years women have begun to have no shame in the clothes they wear. What only street women would flaunt themselves in years ago has become commonplace. (I sometimes wonder how street women manage to attract attention now when every third woman looks the way they used to?)

I actually feel embarrassed for women who bare their cleavages for the world as they don't seem capable of being embarrassed on their own behalf. What is disturbing me most of all is that this 'fashion' has extended to the church. There are women who love the Lord who have left modesty behind because they are following the 'majority'. I think there may be something other than herd mentality involved here sometimes. Are they feeling that men may not be attracted to them if they don't join the majority? So here we need a call to spiritual men to resist the attraction to women who don't dress with reasonable modesty. And to parents to encourage their children, particularly their daughters, not to look like 'walking pornography'.

So there you have just a few examples of how the majority is often wrong. There is a natural inclination for humanity to spiral downward morally and spiritually. This trend is dressed up as 'enlightenment' or 'progressiveness'. Those who buck the trends are made to look uncool if not downright stupid. It will take some courage to stand against the tide. All this is nothing new. We have examples of whole towns (Sodom and Gomorrah) which had surrendered to wickedness and who sought to involve others in their degradation.

Having called on men to look for the deeper qualities a girl may possess, I also want to challenge women to think very solemnly and seriously about the responsibility they have to the men of the nation. Women tend to set the tone of a nation. If women hold to high standards they tend to cause men to aim higher. If they become cheap, men tend to lower their standards as well. I want to say to all women, young and not-so-young: you can be rescuers to the men of your nation.

Men are attracted by what their eyes see more than women are. More than that, men are *turned on sexually* by what they see so it is vital that women don't provide temptation that men may find irresistible. There's a difference between dressing in an appealing way and dressing provocatively. Our people are fast sinking in the mire of immorality. Women could turn the tide if they will start to respect themselves enough to act with a little decorum. Yes, it's an old fashioned word because decorum—the art of being discreet—has largely been banished from our current behaviour patterns. But can I say to all women, you can make a difference in our whole nation. If you will begin to dress, think, speak and act with a little modesty, men will begin to recognize that they need to lift their game too. Generally speaking, men don't respect women the way they once did because women behave disgracefully in so many ways. How often has the TV news shown sad scenes of pretty young women staggering about streets, shouting to the camera, raising glasses of wine although they've obviously already had too much. I weep for the lives which are being thoughtlessly wasted and debauched, and without a hint of shame. At least bad girls used to have the decency to be ashamed of their lifestyle.

Again I would say to girls and women—you can be the rescuers of the males of society but to do so you will have to buck the trends.

Don't be a thoughtless follower. If I would leave this subject with one phrase to both genders, it would be *think for yourselves*.

9

THE MORE CELEBRATION, THE LESS REALITY

I've been noticing for some time now that there is a great increase in the outward trappings of celebrating events such as weddings, Christmas, Easter, etc. The strange thing is that the amount of money spent and the degree of celebration bears an equal and opposite relationship to the heart value placed on the thing being celebrated. What do I mean? Well, let's look at marriages for instance. There has always been a great emphasis on the bride and her gown. But because people were not usually wealthy their event was restricted to a certain extent. In other words, people lived within their means. They didn't invite every person they knew to the reception but usually pared down the invitation list a little. Perhaps they had volunteers help with the catering. They were content to go to a lovely spot within Australia for the honeymoon as well.

But now, the celebration often has to be such an over-the-top event with a honeymoon overseas that the couple live together for years saving up for it or begin married life with a huge debt. Man and wife used to respect each other and respect marriage itself enough to wait until they were wed to actually live together. The surprising thing is that marriages last such a short time comparatively now. The heart value isn't on the important thing itself, but rather on the outward show.

Let's take a peep at the way society sees Christmas now. Firstly, let me tell you a funny story which happened many years ago so that you know that I realise there have always been those who wanted the show without the substance. John and I were both born in Brisbane, capital of our State of Queensland in Australia. We lived there many years and at Christmas time some of the major stores in the city decorated their large windows with storybook scenes for the enjoyment of children. But they would have one window with a Biblical scene showing Mary, Joseph and baby Jesus in the stable along with animals, shepherds and wise men (although the wise men didn't actually go to Jesus until later when they went to a "house" according to Scripture). Families would travel to the city at night to see the illuminated window scenes.

One year our family was surrounded by others all keen to see all that there was to see. As we looked in on the sacred scene one woman said quite loudly 'Oh! They've got to bring religion into everything.' We were left pondering her ignorance. But there it was—the true meaning of Christmas was completely lost on that woman. All she wanted was the outward show, something to entertain her or her family.

But now, her clan has multiplied... The Christmas trees are so beautifully and expensively dressed, the parties abound, the gifts are chosen carefully and decorated with flair, but all they are celebrating is 'mas' because 'Christ' has been extracted from Christ-mas. There is an obese fellow in a red suit who gets all the glory of course.

It's the same with Easter. Children at kindy are helped to make Easter bonnets for their fun Easter parade, chocolate eggs are hidden in the home garden for children to hunt, a great fuss is made of a rabbit for some mysterious reason but God's great love for his creation—so great that he sent his own son to die to set us free from our sins—is hardly ever given a mention.

Have you noticed the correlation between the amount of

fuss made over a celebration and the utter cheapening of the fundamental reason for that very celebration? Amazing, isn't it? Let's get back to reality. Let's value the reason for the celebration rather than the celebration itself. Now, let's get the balance. I don't wish to be a killjoy. By all means celebrate—weddings, Christmas, Easter—all these are worthy of celebration. But let's not lose sight of the real value of the event itself.

10

A BAD CONSCIENCE IS A GOOD CONSCIENCE

I've often noticed when listening to speakers on TV or radio, or when reading advice in magazines that they want to free people from guilt. A sense of guilt is seen as an enemy. Now, let's face it, nobody likes to feel guilty. But if we examine the subject a little more closely, we realise that a guilty conscience is usually a conscience doing what it was designed to do.

Why do we have a conscience? A conscience draws a line in the sand and says don't go any further than this; if you cross this line you'll be guilty of something. Now to be truthful, sometimes we don't notice our conscience until we've already crossed that sandy line. Then the feelings of guilt assail us. But is this a bad thing? I think not. It's a sign that we have a healthy conscience which is doing its job. Without an active, working conscience we could be like psychopathic serial killers. So, a bad conscience is a good conscience, isn't it?

So what's the answer? It is simply to be thankful for that working conscience and to respond appropriately when it is pricked by our behaviour, or even our thoughts. The appropriate response is to put things right: if we've done something against someone, we apologise. And we need to remember that an apology in itself is only the beginning. Once we've apologised, we need to take measures to see that we don't repeat the bad behaviour.

This leads us on to the subject of anger. Often it is anger

which causes us to be hurtful in our speech or to go too far in what we say or do. Someone has said something which is worth repeating: *whatever makes us angry controls us*. (That includes *whoever* makes us angry controls us too.) And who of us wants to be controlled by something or someone else? Let's say at the beginning that anger is not *necessarily* wrong, but most times it is wrong. For example, we can be angry at *injustice* or *cruelty*. God gets angry about those things. He has spoken about it a number of times in his Word. (See Isaiah 58 for instance.) But to be honest, most of the times anger strikes us it's all about *us*. We are offended because we haven't received the attention we wanted for ourselves, we are enraged because someone cut us off on the road or we didn't like having to wait to be attended to. In these instances, it's our self-centredness which is offended.

You'll probably have noticed by now that my approach is usually to step back from the individual situation so we can take a look at the big picture. So here I go again. We can look at this two ways; firstly we can widen our lens to look at the whole world; secondly we can look down the telescope of our whole life. Both of these views give us a better perspective on an individual circumstance in our life. To look at the whole world brings into focus the great needs of many of the world's citizens, both young and old. I have witnessed boys as young as 10 or 11 living on the streets of the Philippines, spending their days on median strips in the middle of the road hoping to sell bottled water to passing motorists, especially when they have stopped at traffic lights. I have visited a 'rubbish village' in Cairo where families live among the stench of rotting animal carcases and mounds of miscellaneous trash, where young children drive carts pulled by donkeys and collect the rubbish from their allotted suburban area. The rubbish is then taken to their homes to be separated—the plastic pulled from soiled nappies, cans opened up and flattened, hard plastic ground into 'beans' for recycling. And their homes are hardly worthy of the title. They are cardboard crates or loose structures of corrugated iron often without full walls, etc. The floors are the rising levels of leftover rubbish containing nothing worth recycling.

The saddest thing of all was that the reason for this great poverty and the hopelessness of a future for these poor, uneducated children was the gambling habits of their fathers. And in the midst of this squalor were some truly beautiful people. One was a priest of the colourful, clean Coptic church right there in the village. He hadn't been trained as a priest but he felt the call of God to go to that rubbish village to share the good news of the gospel with its inhabitants. Because nobody else was likely to put up their hand to lead a church in that situation, he was specially ordained for the job. And when we went to a Sunday morning service in the church, there was such joy in the people who attended. The other group of people were an order of Lutheran nuns in light grey habits who had made their home in the middle of the village in order to teach the children. They wanted to show them that there is a better way of living. They knew that the men of the village probably wouldn't respond but their hope was for the next generation—the innocents who had been born into this wretchedness through no fault of their own.

Now those are just a couple of examples in two different countries but they could be multiplied untold times all over the world, even in our own country. But my purpose is to put into perspective how insignificant are the things in our own lives we often allow to rattle us.

Let's take that other view: looking at our entire life. What I have often said to myself about something that was bothering me is *'Will it matter in fifty years' time?'* It just helps to shrink our concept of the matter to a size which is more realistic and more manageable. So often when people are upset with each other, it is bickering over something which is *so* unimportant that someone watching them could be thinking that they are crazy. Yet to them it can be consuming. My take on it is that they need to stop right there and alter the lens they are looking through, changing it to the wide world view or the long life perspective. They could save a lot of wasted energy, build a quality relationship, and become people with bigger hearts.

Of course, once you are hot under the collar it is difficult to turn the heat off. So we need to form a habit of putting matters into perspective *every day* so that we don't get to the boiling point when something irritating occurs. Once an angry word is spoken even an apology doesn't erase it from the mind of the one who is hurt by it. They may forgive you but the heart has still been bruised.

So maybe next time you are thinking of your blessings, you can add a *thank you* for a healthy conscience.

11

LOVE LANGUAGES

There are some great books written about *love languages*. So I won't go into great depths here but I will say that when I read 'The Five Love Languages' by Gary Chapman some years ago I dearly wished that I had been given the information long before. So I can't leave this subject out of this book altogether, can I?

The whole point of being aware of these love languages is that each of us has our own way of expressing love. Some people (like myself) are always speaking out their love but not all use words to say *I love you*. Some (like my husband John) offer acts of service as their expression of caring deeply while others like to give presents to feel that they are showing love. And so it goes on....

That may seem rather insignificant until you realise that what a person's love language is determines how that person needs to be treated to *feel* loved. So you can have a husband expressing love in *his* love language yet his wife is left feeling empty because she doesn't speak *that* language of love. I can't do justice to this subject in a few words so if you are interested you really need to read the book to have the full impact of the significance of it. It is *so* important, not only for the relationship between spouses but between friends, family, etc. I believe many marriages could have been saved if the partners had understood the working out of these principles.

While we are on the subject of love, there is something

I want to drop into your thinking. It is about how we love those who are a little (or a lot) different from ourselves. Especially if they have been born with a lack intellectually or physically.

I have come in contact with mothers of children who have a small or large deficiency mentally. I see the yearning of their hearts that people will treat their darling children with love. Can you for a moment try to step into their world, into their shoes? Your child is very slightly autistic which means he has some learning difficulties. You see the struggle he has with trying to keep up with the others in his class. He is always that little bit behind them. But he is a loving child, a thoughtful child, one who likes to be helpful. As he grows he enjoys engaging with others but he doesn't notice that he is standing in their 'personal space'. He lacks the intuition to distinguish between when 'mates' are laughing *with* him or laughing *at* him, in fact he always mistakes those two things. Relatives his own age are brought into close contact with him at get-togethers but they seldom *choose* his company because he's that little bit *different*. At school he is bullied relentlessly. His frustration brings him to boiling point and he explodes in strange ways, leaving onlookers not understanding the reason. But he is still a young man with many interests and dreams of what he will achieve in life. He sees himself achieving much.

What is the ache of this mother's heart? That there will be enough people in his life who will see the lovely person he is at heart and be able to overlook those small quirks he has no way of overcoming, though his mother's tireless care and gentle advice will possibly curb to some extent. He is capable of working hard and, with a little understanding, could hold down a satisfying job. Her heart dares to hope that one day a young woman will come along who can appreciate this fellow with the tender heart, and who can overlook the small inadequacies. Is she hoping for too much? Only if we fail to look at all people with a little love in our hearts.

If you have been ignoring those in your circle who are lacking in some way, won't you begin to see them through their mothers' aching hearts? Won't you allow them a little leeway? After all, what does it matter if someone in conversation slightly invades your personal space? Does it really matter if he is a little different in some ways? Doesn't that add to the wonderful patchwork of humanity?

I think I can leave it to you to think through the heart of the mother of the child who is profoundly challenged intellectually—or physically. She lives with her burden for her child's welfare 24/7. Surely she hopes her child will be given some kind attention; and yes, there are some people who give up lots of their time to interact with such needy ones. But if only a larger percentage of the population would regard them with gentleness and understanding, especially when the frustrated child has a public meltdown because she just can't cope with the noise and bustling of so many people around her, many hurting mums—and dads - would heave great sighs of relief.

....

Let's look at another aspect of love. Have you ever thought that it is possible to love *too much*? How could that be? The Bible says that there are three great things—faith, hope and love—and that the greatest of these is love. We are also told that God *is* love. So is it really true that we can love *too much*? I believe that we should love generously, so that we have enough love to overlook hurts and make up for lack in those we mix with. But there is an order about how we should love. Our *first love* should be toward God. He must have the *first place* in our affection. He is the one we are to please, to obey, to give our *first loyalty* to. Then, flowing from that basis, that foundation, his love can ripple out to others through us.

If we love our boyfriend/girlfriend/spouse more than we love God we are out of balance. Loving God first gives us perspective. It helps us to see our 'significant other' through God's eyes. It helps us choose wisely. We won't follow their desires if they are at variance with God's ways, for instance. So, if you are finding that you would do *anything* for the one you love, perhaps that should be ringing a warning bell in your brain right now. Yes, it is wonderful if we love that one extravagantly.... but not recklessly. How many girls have become pregnant because they loved *badly*? By all means love bountifully, but not desperately or dangerously. Loving someone means that we want the best for that other person. If your special one demands something of you which is not your desire or not in your best interest, he/she does not really love you in that instance at all. How many times have young fellows told naïve girlfriends that *if they loved them* they would have sex with them? Hello! Wake up before it's too late....

Loving someone should lift them up, not pull them down into sin and shabby lifestyles. So let's love wholeheartedly, but with our eyes wide open.

12

LOVE AND MARRIAGE

While chatting about love in various ways, let's look into another aspect. Many of us enter marriage with unrealistic expectations. In what way? We expect our significant other to be like us. We love them so much we want to spend our whole life with them, they love us to the same extent so why wouldn't they act and react the same way we do? I hit my head up against a wall on this one for years (not literally) until eventually I realised that a man cannot think like a woman and a woman cannot think like a man. I am speaking generally of course. On rare occasions we do come across a man who's very much in touch with his feminine side and vice versa.

It has been shown that a man's brain is simply wired differently from a woman's. Why would that be? Simply because *they were created to play different roles in life*. It has been illustrated like this: a man's brain is like a set of pigeon holes or compartments, one part kept separate from other parts; whereas a woman's brain is like a bowl of spaghetti with all parts touching—and affecting— many others. Wow! Can you see how that makes such a tremendous difference to how each one perceives situations and reacts to them?

If one part of a woman's life is in chaos it is very difficult for her to entirely detach herself from that to concentrate on another part. Her emotions tend to spread themselves over all parts. This is because God created us women to play mainly a nurturing role. Emotions are important in nurturing—

caring, hurting when others hurt, thus empathising, etc. etc. And of course a female's monthly rollercoaster of hormones mean that at times she may be more affected by circumstances than at others.

A man, without even trying, can concentrate on the job at hand without being hampered by some trouble in his life. That's how his brain is made. He tends to be more logic based. I'm not saying that women lack logic, but their emotions play a pretty large part as well. Now, to be fair, can you see how a man's ability to disengage is a good thing? Until recently, who over all the centuries went to war? Males of course. Who had all the hefty decisions involved in running a business or a country? Again, males. Would you truly want a woman to be fighting in a war or making life-and-death decisions while her hormones were raging out of balance?

I know I'm treading on really explosive territory here. But I've lived long enough to have seen women happy in their roles as care-givers more than rulers. And men facing the world in their quest to be the breadwinners. And I've seen women who have perhaps been hurt by men decide to take over a man's roles and prove that they can do better. Yes, that's right; they weren't satisfied to be equal with men, they wanted to have the upper hand. And they've convinced many young women that they'd be better off if they fought *for their rights* too. Books have been written on the subject and now we have a gender war which quietly smoulders... To be honest, this is not entirely new *but it has been made more extreme by those who are activists*.

Have I put you off-side with me now? Well, all I ask is that you will at least give me the benefit of the doubt. Don't write me off entirely. Put it on the backburner and let it tenderise in your mind for a while. Do I have some points worth pondering? Am I not old enough to have seen things which you may not have experienced? (And recall that when God created our first mother, Eve, his expressed intention was that she would be *a helpmeet* to her husband. What is a helpmeet? It is an ancient term but it is pretty self-explanatory really. Her purpose was to *help* her mate to *meet* his potential, to support him in his role in life. And haven't we heard so many men express their thankfulness to their spouse for her support, saying something like 'without her support I couldn't have succeeded'. And what about the saying 'behind every great man is a great woman' or 'the hand that rocks the cradle rules the world'?) Women can exert great influence without ruling the roost.

Let me interrupt this subject for a moment: *Single people* often feel left out as subjects are mostly addressed to those who have married. As I haven't been single for 50 years I would rather leave the subject of living a single life to someone else, and there are books written specifically for singles. However, most things under discussion in this book apply equally to single people as to marrieds. Even most of the things in this chapter can be applied to help single people in their relationships.

Enough of that! What I really wanted to say was that because of the radical differences between male and female brains it is self-defeating to expect your boyfriend/girlfriend/spouse/boss/colleague to behave as you do yourself. Therefore in the day to day experiences you share, you may be greatly disappointed in his/her responses, even in their reactions to something you say or do. We think they are without feelings perhaps, but it is simply that it is *impossible* for them to think as we do. What a relief it is once we are aware of this. We stop expecting things we will never have the delight of experiencing. So we can then begin appreciating other things about them instead, and looking forward to their differences. After all, with regard to a spouse at least, we chose them because they were different from ourselves in the first place, didn't we?

Someone has wisely said that we fall in love with someone's strengths but then we have to live with their weaknesses. If you haven't yet found your Mr. or Miss Right, try to be aware of the weaknesses as well as the strengths in him/her when the time comes. That way, once married, you won't feel that you've made a big mistake. It's not always easy because in the early days each is trying to make a good impression and weaknesses may be well and truly hidden. I think it helps to watch how the person acts toward animals, children and the elderly. That could give some measure of their character. They don't need to absolutely love dogs, for instance, but we would hope that they would not be cruel toward them.

While still quite young I decided that I would only marry the man God showed me was the right choice. And I can recommend this as your measuring stick. My man is not perfect but knowing that he was God's choice for me has meant that I found it easier to stick with him during the rough patches that all marriages strike from time to time. And of course, need I mention that I'm not quite perfect myself? (Giggle)

And if you are already married, good advice is to not so much be looking for your partner to be a good spouse, but rather concentrate on *being* a good spouse yourself. What we are focussing on can make a large difference in a relationship.

One thing my husband John speaks about to couples when giving premarital counselling is the need to be a whole person. We often hear people speak of their 'other half' or their 'better half'. It's an old fashioned phrase and often meant in jest. But the fact of the matter is that folk often go into marriage looking for their mate to complete them. They are hoping that he/she will make all the difference in their life, make up for what's missing, what's longed for. They may have a poor self-image and they think that marriage will be the magic wand to change all that.

That kind of thinking is a recipe for trouble. Two 'half people' don't make a whole person. Yes, the Bible says that when people marry "the two shall become one flesh", that's how binding God sees marriage and how close the relationship can become. But it doesn't mean each will supply all that is wanting in the other one. It is quite unfair, actually, to expect your marriage partner to make up for what is lacking in you. The ideal situation is when two whole people come together to become one whole person. What do I mean by 'whole'? We all have needs and weaknesses of course but we need to work on becoming a whole person before we bind ourselves to someone else.

A whole person accepts who they are and makes the most of what they have in the way of talents. A whole person is not seeking to hide because they feel bad about themselves. A whole person doesn't keep looking back at some hurt they've endured, seeing that as an excuse for their behaviour. How do we begin to become whole people? Well a good start is to see ourselves in relation to God. God says that nobody is good. You say that that doesn't sound like a good beginning? It's the best beginning there is because then we seek further to find our value as a human being. God also says that our hearts are deceitful, even to ourselves. You say, that sounds worse! No, no, it means that every person is in a sense equal. They can never be good enough for God. So where can we find value? Firstly, in the awesome fact that God loved us, even when we were outright sinners; and loved us enough to send his own precious Son, Jesus, to pay the penalty for our sin so we could be right with him and become a part of his family.

That fact makes us Important. And then we go on to

realise that God didn't just leave it there but he provides his own Spirit to indwell those who become his children. Thus a true Christian isn't just somebody who goes around doing good deeds. Rather, a true Christian is one who has a relationship with their Heavenly Father. They have checked up with the Lord to see what the Lord's plan is for their lives and then set about fulfilling it; but not in their own strength, in the strength of the Holy Spirit living within them as a result of their accepting the death of Jesus on the cross for the forgiveness of their sins. They find confidence in the fact that they are much loved by the God of creation and that he has a purpose for their life. *Purpose* is extremely important for a healthy self-image.

Can you see how this transaction between the person and God makes so much difference? It doesn't automatically make the person perfect, but it provides a basis for wholeness of thinking, speaking and living.

Now we need to acknowledge that many folk are the walking wounded. They have been bruised—and perhaps battered—by the circumstances of their lives. They may have had a broken home as children, they may have been neglected or worse, been abused. These things may leave their scars. Perhaps they make it difficult for them to trust anyone, truly trust them. So that isn't a good start to marriage, for instance. What's the answer? They can take their problems to the Lord but they may also need to talk out their sadness and problems with a good Christian counsellor. I stress the need for a Christian counsellor because other counsellors may have advice that is ungodly. For instance, we have heard about marriage guidance counsellors who suggest having an affair to improve a struggling marriage. Enough said!

So please try to do all that is needed to become a whole person before marrying. Having said all this, a good match should help both spouses to find comfort and improvement in confidence because of the support of their mate. The main problem lies in expecting too much from your mate if you are a very needy person.

Evolution

While this may seem a complete departure from our subject of love and marriage, I feel I need to mention evolution here because it relates to how we view ourselves. When I was at school many years ago, evolution was never taught. Then it began to be presented as *'a theory'*. But for the last couple of decades it is accepted and taught very widely as fact. While it is clear to see that there is a certain amount of evolution *within a species (adaptation)*, there is no evidence that we all came from some little blob in a muddy pool as was told to John and me as we were travelling around Australia. The guide was virtually presenting the isolated, boggy area as the cradle of the world, and pointing out that the organisms present give off oxygen which allows us to live.

I am not a scientist so I can't present academic credentials but there are **many scientists** who dismiss evolution as nothing more than *'a theory'*. I take my stand, firstly and foremost, on the Bible. God not only created the different animals, for instance, but it says each was made 'after its kind'. So there in the first book of the Bible, Genesis, we have the clue that one kind has not issued forth from another kind. It's possible that God created only a few dogs, for instance, and from those, many different types of dogs have been bred. But they are still dogs.

The second point of reference I have is that hybrids are generally sterile. For instance, lions and tigers (both cats by the way) have mated—when isolated from other lions and tigers—but their progeny are sterile, that is infertile, so cannot continue the line. It's the same in the plant world. It is possible for horticulturalists to produce a new variety, a hybrid plant, but they don't produce fertile seeds. You need to buy more young plants from the company who owns the patent, more evidence that one kind doesn't change into another kind and continue to do so...

My third point of reference is the very cosmos itself. Creation in every part is so delicately balanced, so very complex, so inter-related that it couldn't possibly have happened by chance. A drop of water is like a little world within itself. And as for the human body! How amazing, how awesome! So complex, so wonderful! Just one tiny instance — we have in our stomachs such strong acid for the digestion of our food that it could burn other parts of our bodies. But it is kept contained in the area where the lining is able to withstand the caustic quality of the acid. That just happened by accident?

Need I mention the male and female bodies, sex and reproduction — perfectly designed and a miracle we often overlook.

Next we look underground at the humble termite. Living underground, it needs neither eyes nor wings so has none. But when the time comes to move on, the hordes of tiny creatures break out of the mound, grow eyes and wings and fly until they locate a suitable place at which time their wings fall off. Can you truly believe that these things 'just happen'? Someone has said that to believe that this universe came about randomly is like believing that an explosion in a printing press could result in a dictionary. I think I could believe that before believing in evolution.

The reason I'm mentioning evolution at all is that I believe the teaching of evolution has been responsible for much of the downward spiralling of society. Does that sound like a huge claim??? Well, what are the implications of teaching evolution to children in schools? It says that there is no powerful God who created their first parents, no loving heavenly Father who listens to prayers AND no purpose to their lives. There is no other life to look forward to with our Creator in heaven. They are just one big mistake in the cosmos with no meaning. Look at the younger generation now and we find for many it is a matter of "Eat, drink and be merry for tomorrow we die". Why not go out and get drunk on a regular basis? Why not blot out the realities of life by taking drugs? If you have no idea that there is something more than what you can see with your eyes, why reach for something higher, something noble? I'm not saying that this applies to all young people of course, but I've lived long enough to know that society's values and attitudes have changed dramatically and not for the better, generally speaking.

So let me reiterate—your life *has purpose*. *You are important to God*, partly because he loves you but also because he has chosen to use your mouth, your hands and your feet to perform his works on the earth. When Jesus left earth to go back to heaven, he dispatched his very own Spirit to live within us so that we could go on doing his work here. More than that, he actually said that we would do *greater works* than what he had performed himself. (I'm not sure just what Jesus meant by 'greater works'. It's hard to think of something *greater* than raising the dead or walking on water. John and I have witnessed several folk raised from the dead but haven't *yet* walked on water. Some folk say it may be the fact that the multitudes of Christians can multiply the work done.) So please be encouraged to seek out your purpose. Each of us is so unique because of our particular DNA, our personality, our life experience, that no-one else can do the work *we* are meant to accomplish.

Having said that, I should add that it is important that

we don't just put our hand up every time there is a need. Perhaps it is meant for somebody else to help in that particular circumstance. Check it out with the Lord to see if he wishes you to be involved when anyone is asking you to do something or you hear of some need in the community or worldwide. If you are trying to fill every need around, you may miss out on God's special mission for you.

Commitment

As we are on the subject of marriage, and all around us marriages are crumbling, may I offer some basic advice on the subject? There are many reasons why marriages fail, but it is also a fact that many more would have failed if one ingredient had been missing from them. We still hear of people celebrating 40, 50, 60 and yes even 70 years of marriage (and John and I celebrated our Golden anniversary last year). These couples weren't perfect. How did they stay together? I believe there are many facets to these relationships but one basic ingredient is Commitment to the Marriage. Note carefully, I didn't say commitment to the other person, though that is important. But commitment to the marriage, commitment to the vows made.

Why I make a distinction is this: Most couples face their wedding day believing that their marriage is going to last a lifetime yet a high proportion of them break up and go separate ways. They usually understand that they are making a serious commitment. But I believe that most of them are making a commitment to their partner rather than to the marriage. Why is that important? Living as husband and wife is vastly different from life before marriage. After a time, each partner (or at least one of them) begins to see that the one they have married is quite different from what they thought. As mentioned, weaknesses become prominent, weaknesses that the person had not even suspected. They may try valiantly at first to adjust but when added pressures are brought to bear, such as children, work commitments, illness and financial struggles, good intentions are sometimes stretched very thin. And let's face it, people often begin to think that they've married a jerk, or someone completely self-centred, etc. etc. They then move on to thinking that this person doesn't deserve the commitment made to them.

And so we have the setting for separation. And the party/parties feel quite justified in separating, even more so today when friends and relatives have been divorced. John and I went on a tour of Italy a few years ago and formed a friendship with four young American women who were fellow travellers on the tour. We were told that one of the women had recently been divorced and I commiserated with her but she quite brightly said "Oh it's alright, all the others are divorced too". It was as though she had just simply joined a club. My heart cried for the modern marriage. I am quite sure that many young people these days don't even have a strong commitment to their mate let alone their marriage. It's a matter of — 'as long as it feels good, we'll stay together'. And if that is the level of commitment, we can kiss the marriage goodbye in a very short time.

So, let's look at the other attitude: Commitment to the Marriage. If we make a serious commitment to the Marriage rather than just the Person, when things get tough, we can see the problems as challenges to be overcome. If we find that the person is not quite what we were expecting, we look for ways to adjust and cope. Can you see the difference? I truly believe that it does make quite a difference to how we respond within the marriage and the relationship.

When John is officiating at a wedding he sometimes speaks of the Biblical word of 'yoking'. Yokes are usually for a pair of animals who have to work side by side hauling a burden together. Jesus, as a carpenter while on earth, would have shaped many a yoke. And as the animals changed in height or size, he would have shaved off some of the wood here and there to keep it just right for them. This is in some ways a sweet picture of marriage. Two similar beings willingly yoking themselves together, pulling the same load in the same direction, taking time every so often to adjust their relationship to suit their changing circumstances, perhaps sickness, loss of a job, etc. etc. But recognising that they are part of a team pulling the same load in the same direction, not tugging in opposite directions.

If you are already married, it's not too late to make a fresh Commitment to your Marriage. If your mate has seriously disappointed you, look for ways you can improve the situation; pray for him/her; look for ways you can show love and tenderness. Seek to respond rather than just react. Responding comes with care whereas reacting brings the tit-for-tat type of situation which doesn't benefit anybody, you or the other person.

Can I share with you that I have prayed that God would make me the type of wife my husband John needs. This kind of thinking takes the spotlight off what *I* want and onto what I can do to bring blessing instead which is pleasing to the Lord. The Lord loves to answer that kind of prayer. If we are honest we will admit that if we look at any person through the lens of criticism we will find flaws in them. And the longer we look that way, the worse those flaws will seem; they will get right under our skin. But if we look with love, we may be surprised how understanding we will become of the person, and how we will begin to discover that there is a reason for the way they think or speak or act. Then as we pray for healing for them, we become actively involved in building them up instead of tearing them down.

We have witnessed many broken marriages mended, even

after the couples have been divorced for some time. John, as a Pastor, has had the happy privilege of remarrying some of them.

The Bible says that God hates divorce and Jesus reiterated that marriage was meant to be insoluble so we need to have really generous and healthy attitudes to both ours and those of others.

Perhaps I should mention another little matter. I think that many people feel so much in love when they marry that they can't imagine being attracted to anyone else. But that's not realistic. I should think that most human beings experience being drawn to someone other than their spouse. And if things are a bit rocky in the marriage relationship that attraction may be even more tempting than ever. Knowing that this will probably happen helps to arm us against the temptation. We can recognize that this is what it is—a temptation. And what a temptation it can be. It can so overwhelm us that it feels as though we're no longer in love with our spouse. Being attracted to someone else is not the problem so much, rather it's what we do with the temptation.

We need to resist the urge to draw closer to the attractive person. If the temptation is very strong we may need to remove ourselves from the situation that brings us into contact with him/her. And we needn't worry about our feelings for our spouse. They can be rekindled as long as the other person is not allowed to be a regular part of our life.

Let me say again that marriage relationships (and relationships of all kinds) are multi-faceted. I don't mean to over simplify the difficulties faced but I do know that our attitude is vital—it can make so much difference to the welfare of the relationship and the outcome for both our self and the other person. May the Lord lead you in whatever relationships you may have in your life. One little proverb from the Old Testament is relevant and touches my heart. I hope it will yours too. Proverbs 3:3. *"Let love and faithfulness never leave you; bind them around your neck, write them on the tablet of your heart."* The mental picture of wearing love and faithfulness like a necklace and engraving them on my heart speaks to the deepest part of me.

13

OUR CULTURE

Wow! Now we approach another big subject, one that is hard to get our head around sometimes. If we are to please God we need to comprehend that we have not only entered a new family, the family of God, but we now have a new culture. What do I mean? We are citizens of a *heavenly city.*

It is clear when somebody from another country has different ways of dressing, of eating, a different language, a different religion, etc. that they have a different culture from ours. What we don't always notice is that we have a culture of our own. We have a culture of our country and we have a culture from our family. We may have a culture with our peers. These are ways of dressing, ways of speaking, food we eat. But perhaps, so ingrained that we hardly notice them at all are also *values and attitudes*. We've grown up with them from Day 1 so it seems there is no other way to dress, speak, eat, etc.

Let me say that your culture may be a very good one. But is it pleasing to God? You've probably never thought of this before so take it easy. Jesus talked about culture. He may not have used that word but he talked about the *'traditions of men'* which is the same sort of thing. And he warned that if we raise the traditions of men ABOVE the Word of God there will be serious consequences. What consequences? The Lord will not hear our prayers for one. AND we will worship God in vain. Now that's serious isn't it?

I will speak only about my own country, Australia, in this book. But overseas readers will readily identify cultural attitudes for themselves. What are some of the cultural ways and values for Australians in general? Well, they usually worship a god, the god of Sport. They may eat all sorts of food but for many of them they MUST drink beer or wine, and lots of it. Again, generalising, an Aussie will be kind to his mate, but he may lie to or cheat his boss. And the tax man? Hide as much of your earnings as you can, mate. When driving, he will generally ignore the speed limit. That's only for idiots and old ladies, mate.

Can you see what I'm getting at? Many, many Aussies live this way and have no bad conscience about it at all. Why? Because it is the culture they've grown up in. That's simply the way we Aussies do it, they think.

But if we are to be people of purpose and nobility of thought, we must look at our culture—in particular, the parts we've adopted as our own—to see if the traditions of men are at variance with God's Word and ways.

Dare I look at the items I've listed for Aussies and weigh them up against the word of God? Let's have a go... Firstly, Sport, the great god. Can we deny that this is a god? It is given first place; we as a people are downright passionate about it. Not only will we wear our team colours in public but we will stand and shout to encourage our team or boo the others. We will even do the arms-raised-and-bow worship action toward our 'sports idols'. If that's not worship, what is? And, dare I whisper it? Some players are absent from the bedside when their wives give birth because they put the game first and foremost. [Let me say that sport can be harmless, healthful and a lot of fun as well as helping us meet other people with like interest. And while I'm at it, I would say that many things, of themselves, are neither good nor bad. It is how they are used or indulged in that determines whether they are being used well or badly. **See note at the end of this chapter.]

Now let's check it out. The Word says not to have any other God beside the Lord. And would you get many of these red blooded males wearing something that tells the world that they belong to God, would they be outwardly passionate about their love of God? Would they raise their hands in worship to the Lord? I leave the answer to you...

We move on to beer and other alcoholic drinks. The Word of God does not forbid having a moderate amount of alcohol but it does say that drunkards *will not enter the kingdom of heaven*.

An Aussie will stand by his mates. Good on him. But the Bible says even pagans do good to those they love and who can return the favour. The Bible says that we are to love even our enemies, to turn the other cheek if we are struck, to invite the needy to our home for food even though they will not be able to return the favour.

Regarding the boss, the Bible has a word for slaves which applies. It says that the worker should work well for his master as unto the Lord, not only when he is being watched but all the time.

And as for the tax man, Jesus provided the perfect example. He said to render unto Caesar (government) the things that are Caesar's and to God the things that are God's. (Matthew 22:21). Jesus paid the poll tax of the time. As he had no belongings he sent the disciple Peter to catch a fish and to extract a coin for the poll tax from its mouth to pay his tax. If this seems farfetched, when John and I were in Israel we had a meal at a restaurant on the shore of the Sea of Galilee. The meal was fish and each fish had a coin in its mouth. Of course the coins had been specially placed there at our tour leader's request but we were informed that these particular fish often hold a stone or something similar in their mouths. There was a reason for it, but I must confess that I've forgotten what it was. The little P.S. to the story is that God will provide some way or other if we trust him (and if we are willing to work).

What about the speed limit and other road rules? We find that the Bible tells us quite clearly that we should obey the laws of the land, and that they are there for our good. I always say that God's angels travel at the speed limit so if we are wilfully exceeding that we can't expect them to protect us.

Now we can see that there are everyday habits which don't stack up against the Word of God and we need to examine our habits to see if they are the same. But it's not only in matters of national or family culture that we can trip up. Some of the worst are within the church. As a matter of fact, Jesus was speaking to religious men when he challenged them about their traditions. Many people in pulpits are teaching a version of the Gospel that is not in accordance with the Bible. So what's the best way to escape this trap? Of course, it's by knowing the whole of the Bible as we spoke of earlier. But not only knowing it, but THINKING about what we read. It's possible to read the Bible with our *culture spectacles* on. What do I mean? Well, our culture is so deeply entrenched in our psyche that it's possible to not notice that what we read in God's Word is at variance with our ways of doing things. So again, the word is *think!*

Perhaps I should share a little story with you at my own expense... Years ago I used to drink about nine cups of tea per day. It was my drink of choice. I was having some trouble with my heart rhythm. My heart would beat fast and sometimes skip beats and would make me feel weak. My doctor encouraged me that it was no real 'heart trouble' but rather the electrical part that was out of rhythm. One morning as John brought me my early cup of tea in bed I felt an impression in my mind *'don't drink tea'*. I wasn't sure that it was the Lord speaking to me. I certainly didn't hear a voice. And I thought to myself 'I suppose I should cut down on my tea consumption. I am drinking rather a lot.' So I began to drink less over the following 3 weeks at which time it occurred to me that, if it was the Lord instructing me, he hadn't said to *cut down* my intake of tea but to *stop drinking* it.

I immediately cut tea out of my diet and found, to my surprise, that my heart began beating in correct rhythm. Now the Lord hadn't mentioned my heartbeat in relation to tea and I hadn't connected the two either. But the thing which shamed me was that I didn't actually obey the word, *but gave it my own interpretation.* And that was when it began to dawn on me that it is very easy for us to think we are doing the right thing when we have actually filtered the situation through our own way of thinking. So it is really needful to examine our thinking to check whether we are fooling ourselves and disappointing our God.

I should add that I am not suggesting that you become very introspective, always looking inward as this is not healthy or helpful. We would become very self-centred if we were always looking inwardly. But every now and again, it is necessary. I am also not suggesting that everyone should give up drinking tea. It obviously was not good for *me*.

Now I know that I am likely to really upset some of you with what I say next but it has to be said. Baptism is one of the things that many Christians have adjusted to their own understanding, or culture. Why do I say that? The disciples were told to go into all the world teaching and baptising. Baptism is the sign of being dead and buried to our former life and as we are raised from the baptismal tank or the river as the case may be, we are symbolising being raised to new life in Christ. The word baptism comes from the original

Greek *baptizo* which means to dunk, to saturate, to sink. We had a friend who went to the local Greek fish and chip shop owner and asked him for the real meaning of *baptizo*. With that, the shop owner took his basket of chips, sank it deep into the hot oil and said "I *baptizo* the chips". And when a Greek liner sank at sea the Greek newspaper's headline was something to the effect of "Ship *baptizo* at Sea".

When the Bible was translated into English, the English church of the time had already been sprinkling babies as a form of baptism so they exerted their considerable influence on the translators and had them *transliterate* the word instead of translating it. Do you know the difference? To transliterate means to use the equivalent English letters for the Greek ones whereas to translate means to give the *meaning* of the word. Thus they hid from the people the true meaning of the word baptise.

This has resulted in hordes of believers never being truly baptised in the way God intended. I mean no offence to those this may have affected. I hope it means that you will now go and have the kind of baptism that God meant you to undergo. In fact, many people of different Christian denominations who discover that their sprinkling as a baby—when they had no way of exercising faith or of repenting of sin—is not really fulfilling God's Word, then go to a pastor (or even a Christian friend) who will baptise them by immersion.

If you think that baptism is not all that important, especially however it may be done and to whom, I should mention that miracles have occurred during baptism for many people. So it is not just a symbol but God is active in it as well.

Years ago, after baptising a man of 80 years of age who had only recently come to faith in Christ, John dressed in one of the dressing rooms at church and returned to the pulpit to give his message to the congregation for the evening. Bill, the old fellow, dressed a little slower and when he returned into the church, he rushed up to John and interrupted with excitement. John soon understood that Bill had had a clawed hand from being a boxer in his early days—if he made a fist he couldn't open it again except by using his other hand to prise it open. But there he was opening and closing his hand at will. The Lord had healed him right there in the baptismal tank.

A friend of ours has related another story of marvellous work done by the Lord during a fellow's baptism. It related to a young man who had been a bikie and keen on tattoos and because of his previous atheism had a large tattoo of the devil on his chest. He wanted to be baptised but was horrified that everybody would be able to see this awful blot when his shirt was wet after baptism. Have you guessed what God did? That's right, when this man rose from the tank, there was no tattoo on his chest. So please don't think of baptism as just something we do as a symbol. God is very interested and involved in our doing it and it was his instruction that we follow.

On another occasion, a terminally ill man named Don made a journey from Sydney to Brisbane to say farewell to his old navy buddy. His navy buddy happened to be a Christian attending our church and he talked to him about becoming a Christian. Don accepted Jesus as his saviour and was soon after baptised. Don found to his delight that he was healed of his 'terminal' cancer and never returned to Sydney to live but continued as an active member of our church for another 20 years or so until he died an old man.

Now that's just one of the ways in which the traditions of men are raised above the Word of God in this day. I don't want to go into more ways, but I would warn you that if you hear someone say "But we've always done it this way" you're probably being faced with a tradition. It isn't necessarily wrong, but check it out against the Word of God to see whether it is legitimate or not. Okay, it's over to you...

**On the subject of things being neither good nor bad of themselves, television is a prime example. When it first came on the scene when I was a teenager, it became the focus of some harmless family fun as we watched comedies or family situation shows as well as viewing the day's news. It has been the means of great teaching via documentaries. Christians provide godly programs sometimes as well. School programs are helpful. But over the years the tone of the content has headed south and now there is little which can be innocently watched. More and more lurid scenes confront those who watch into the night, including unprotected children, and we can rightly deduce that it has become largely a means of encouraging sinful attitudes. And the insidiousness of the situation is that, as people become involved in relating to the characters in shows, they hardly notice that they are being encouraged to accept attitudes, words and values which would have been abhorrent to them years earlier. So is TV good or bad? It depends on how it is used. Use it wisely...

14

FAN INTO FLAME

Romans 12:3 speaks about the gift of faith given by measure. And we find that some people have great heaps of faith while others find it more difficult to step out on a limb for the Lord. We can take heart from a couple of things: Firstly, that the Lord said that faith as small as a mustard seed could lift a mountain and thrust it into the sea; secondly there is another encouragement I want to draw your attention to... 2Timothy 1:6 says "For this reason I remind you to *fan into flame* the *gift of God,* which is in you by the laying on of my hands."

The Apostle Paul was writing to his younger 'apprentice' in Christian things, Timothy. He had laid hands on Timothy, probably for him to receive the baptism in Holy Spirit, for this is usually how we receive the Holy Spirit's special power to equip us to do the Lord's work. So it is clear that Timothy had received a gifting from the Lord. But that wasn't the end of it. Paul is urging him to now *fan into flame* that gift.

[*For those who want to study a little deeper, <u>in the original text of the New Testament</u>, when Holy Spirit is mentioned, sometimes it is preceded by the definite article 'the' and other times not. When the text says 'the Holy Spirit' it is referring to the Person of the Holy Spirit. When it says only 'Holy Spirit' it is referring to the Power of the Spirit as received at the baptism in Holy Spirit. Unfortunately, in English translations the definite article has been added where it was absent in the original text. An extremely important example is in Matthew chapter 1 verses 18 and 20. It is referring to* *the conception of our Lord Jesus and says that Mary was 'found to be with child through holy spirit', in other words by the power of the holy spirit, not by the person of the Holy Spirit.*]

Let's step back and look at the larger scene... When we become a member of God's family, God becomes our Father. If you were born with a less-than-good dad, don't compare him with God, and certainly don't compare God with him. God is a pattern for earthly fathers, he is how dads ought to be—a balance of love and discipline; we could say love that is sometimes demonstrated by his discipline and discipline that is birthed in love. Some dads are too harsh in their discipline whereas God tells fathers not to be too harsh or they will discourage their children. Some dads are too soft; they let their children get away with anything. This is not true love because it is neglecting its duty. God arranged families so that children would be not only nurtured but also trained. What happens when children aren't disciplined? They run the risk of becoming selfish, self-centred brats who grow up to be lawless. They haven't learned to obey and respect so it is more difficult for them to respect those in places of authority over them, and also the laws of the land. I am particularly speaking about fathers because the Bible lays the *main* responsibility for discipline into the hands of our male parent. Of course, in single parent families the mother may have to take over what God intended as the *mainly-male* role. Ephesians 6:4 puts it this way... "Fathers, do not exasperate your children; instead bring them up in the training and instruction of the Lord." And from my experience I can tell you that, while a child may run to Mum for comfort when they skin their knee, they will listen more carefully when Dad is speaking.

Enough of that. What I want to establish in your thinking is that as a loving Father, God doesn't just give us everything we want but He *interacts with us*. The best kind of family is a team. Each person plays a part in the success and smooth running of the team. Little ones are given jobs which they are capable of performing. This helps everyone and gives the little one the concept of being useful and a real part of the family. They are being trained to work so work won't be such a difficult thing as they grow up. They have a more realistic view of life. [***This will be developed in Chapter 16.] But it also means that the parents are interacting with the child, forming a stronger and stronger bond with him/her.

In a similar way, God continually interacts with us. He doesn't just 'give birth in the spirit' to us and then leave us to our own devices. In each stage of our development He is there guiding us, training us, teaching us and disciplining us if we are willing to receive. Otherwise we won't 'grow up' and mature. We will stay immature. Immaturity in an adult is embarrassing to witness isn't it? When we see an immature person we wonder if perhaps his parents didn't train him well. It's the same in a Christian who has been a believer for years. We expect that person to be more mature than a new believer.

So to achieve this, God does some of the work and leaves some of the work to us. We spoke much earlier about looking for the gifting within ourselves. What are we equipped to do? Well, God has given the gifting but it is up to us to *fan it into flame*. How do we go about that? There are a number of avenues to do so. Firstly we can talk to the Lord about it, ask him for his guidance. Then we can watch someone else who has the same gift but is further along the Christian road than we are. To make this easier to explain, let's take the gift of teaching for instance. If I feel that God has given me the gift of teaching (and I'm referring to teaching Spiritual truth in this example), I can take note of a leader or pastor at my church who is a good teacher. I will think about how he presents a lesson or a sermon or an illustration so that it sinks into people's minds and hearts (and hopefully their spirits too). I will note how he can teach a difficult lesson without being too harsh. I can learn from his example.

Of course, to become a good teacher I have to be very familiar with my subject. So I will be diligently studying the Word of God and perhaps reading good books to help my understanding. I may keep a journal of things I have learned, especially if God draws my attention to some particular point. It may be a good thing to do a Bible College course where I will be challenged to step up to a higher level of study and understanding. Thus I am working with God to make the best use of the gift he has given. But I will not become a clone of somebody else. God has made me unique and I want to be what I was made to be.

I see a great goodness and kindness in the way God works with us. He is sharing the responsibility and the achievement with us. For instance, on an everyday level, I think of those who have a job or a hobby involving breeding something. It may be dogs or it may be roses. Now they have a choice of reproducing what is already there or they can take part in a kind of creating. They can go on breeding the one breed of dog, or the same kind of rose, or they can interbreed to improve or simply alter. With dogs, sometimes a breeder will mate two differing types of dogs to gain an animal with a good nature and a coat that doesn't shed all over the place. This would be good as a pet for a child with allergies. Thus it is almost as though God has shared his creating ability with man. What a kindness.

With roses it is a similar situation. Breeders are coming up with new varieties—they are sometimes looking for a bloom that combines a lovely perfume with a shape which holds for a long time—doesn't open up fully too quickly; or they are after a particular colour combined with a beautiful perfume.

What a thrill for these people to be able to present a new variety to the world. I see this as God's generosity. He has provided all the essentials but man is given the opportunity of working out the result.

We need to recognize that that is how it all works. If we wait around for God to do it all, we will be waiting a long time. He wants us to have the thrill of being a part of the result.

Another reason I need to speak to you about fanning into flame is that we are all surrounded by attractions, distractions, temptations and I guess ignorance. It is so easy to be drawn from the 'straight and narrow' pathway God has for us. We need to be encouraging ourselves to keep following the Lord closely. Perhaps we should interrogate ourselves every now and again.

Am I spending time with the Lord regularly?

Does he have the first place in my heart and life?

Am I following any leading he has already given me?

Am I putting into practice the principles I've read in the Bible?

(I should mention here that God usually doesn't take us on any further until we have put into practice what he has tried to teach us previously. Sometimes people hit a barren place in their lives and they feel as though heaven has closed to them when it is simply that God is waiting on them to be obedient. Thus the person is responsible for their own difficulties.)

Am I running with friends who will pull me down?

Am I showing God's love to those around me or have I become self-centred?

Then, once you've decided that things could improve, you do something about it. Thus you are *fanning into flame* what God has given you. You're doing your part. You're part of the Christian Heavenly Family Team. Good on you!!!

I should enlarge on one of the items mentioned above, our friends. Certainly we don't want to run with friends who pull us down. But the positive thing to do is to make sure we make some good Christian friends so we can be mutually encouraging. You may have to join a group at church or an inter-church activity to develop these friendships but it is worth the effort. The Bible speaks about light and darkness. Belonging to God brings us into the Light and out of the darkness. If all our friends are still walking the dark path it will be more difficult for us to continue to rise higher in our daily walk. Of course we need non-Christian friends as well or we won't have the opportunity to influence anyone for God.

Before we leave the subject of fanning into flame, let's look at a few Scriptures. In each of these instances, we are being given instruction on things we must do for ourselves. Ephesians 5:19–20 *"**Speak** to one another with psalms, hymns and spiritual songs. **Sing and make music in your heart to the Lord**, always giving thanks to God the Father for everything, in the name of our Lord Jesus Christ."*

1 Peter 4:1 *"Therefore, since Christ suffered in his body, **arm yourselves** also with the same attitude, because he who has suffered in his body is done with sin."*

1 John 5:21 *"Dear children, **keep yourselves** from idols."*

2 John 1:8 *"**Watch out** that you do not lose what you have worked for, but that you may be rewarded fully."*

Jude 1:20–21. *"But you, dear friends, **build yourselves up in your most holy faith** and pray in (the) Holy Spirit. **Keep yourselves in God's love** as you wait for the mercy of our Lord Jesus Christ to bring you to eternal life."*

This world is a war zone. We have an enemy who roams about looking for anyone he may devour (1Peter 5:8). Therefore we must be alert and guard our minds in particular as that is mostly the arena of the skirmishes. There is a rather lovely little line by the Old Testament character Job. In chapter 31:1, he reveals "I made a covenant with my eyes not to look lustfully at a girl." Now that's one of the ways Job *built himself up in faith*. And though he poetically called it a covenant with his eyes, the decision, the impetus, was made *in his mind*.

Let's finish this segment on a most positive note. Let's recall that very encouraging Scripture, 2 Chronicles 16:9... *"The eyes of the Lord range throughout the earth to strengthen those whose hearts are fully committed to him."* So there we have the balance: you do your part and the Lord will be doing his.

15

IMAGINATION IS STRONGER THAN THE WILL

As I was an only child I lived largely in my imagination. My Dad had been injured during the 2nd World War and was chronically ill as a result. He forced himself to go to work every work day but as he was in continual pain we tended to keep largely to ourselves. Our weekly outing was to the movies which in those days were pretty innocent and we walked about a kilometre to get there. As a 4-year-old I was sent to Sunday School which provided me with the basics of Christianity and I accepted Jesus as my personal Saviour and Lord at 13. When I finished Sunday School round that time I then became a teacher to the youngest children. The church service began soon after Sunday School finished so I took myself to church as my parents didn't attend.

I had friends at school and would sometimes have them over to my house after school to play or occasionally go to their house. But there were lots of hours when I was alone in our home with just one or both of my parents. So I acted out my own stories and had a lively imagination. This is pretty normal for children, or at least it was in the days before television, computers, mobile 'phones and other distracting gadgets. We didn't have a home 'phone or a car during my growing up years though we lived in the city. As with other things, our imagination is neither good nor bad of itself. It is a God-given ability to see things as they could be so *what* we imagine determines whether it is being used wisely or badly. It is also a matter of *how much of our time* we spend in our imagination as we grow older.

Now here is the reason we need to discuss this subject: **The Imagination is Stronger than the Will**. So you can see that it is extremely important where our mind wanders. There's a passage in the 15th chapter of the book of Matthew which touches on this: Verses 18-20a— "...*the things that come out of the mouth come from the heart, and these make a man 'unclean'. For out of the heart come evil thoughts, murder, adultery, sexual immorality, theft, false testimony, slander. These are what make a man 'unclean';*"

Imagination springs from the heart. Deep desires fire the imagination to think on possible things. And we must guard our hearts from desiring base or sinful things. Our hopes and dreams come from this area of our being. They may be high and noble aims and we would not wish to be rid of those. But if we are not very aware and careful we may begin on the downward staircase of sin which could even lead to crime. Why do I say that? Because every action begins as a thought and unless we keep a rein on our thoughts we *will* eventually put them into action. 2Corinthians 10:5b has this to say: "...we take captive every thought to make it obedient to Christ." Why is that necessary? Because our thoughts can run away with us.

I mentioned a downward staircase because if we allow ourselves to get away with sinful thoughts the next time we steal away to that secret place the thoughts will have worsened. A man doesn't usually commit adultery because he suddenly meets an attractive woman. It's because he has entertained thoughts of having a secret lover. A woman doesn't usually steal an item from the shop on a whim. Prior to that, she has been imagining herself with more than she can afford, or with something she has admired on somebody else.

It is so easy to begin indulging in small naughty thoughts

and to enjoy them. So easily it can become a habit and as I said before, eventually thoughts develop into actions — sins and crimes. So you can see that Jesus drew attention to where sin really begins. In Matthew 5:28 he says "...I tell you that anyone who looks at a woman lustfully has already committed adultery with her in his heart." Earlier in the chapter we read: again, Jesus speaking "You have heard that it was said to the people long ago, 'Do not murder, and anyone who murders will be subject to judgment.' But I tell you that anyone who is angry with his brother will be subject to judgment." Jesus tore away the external covering of sin, he unwrapped it and laid it bare. Sin is in the heart, in our thoughts. And it emerges as action sometime later. But God sees the heart. We may fool people but the Lord is aware of our thoughts, our imaginings.

James 1:14 & 15 has this to say: "...each one is tempted when, by his own evil desire, he is dragged away and enticed. Then, after desire has conceived, it gives birth to sin; and sin, when it is full-grown, gives birth to death." That's very picturesque isn't it? And serious!

My husband John has had young and not-so-young men come to him for counsel who have become addicted to pornography. It haunts them. It spoils their marriage relationship. One man became a victim innocently. As a young child, if his father was drunk and angry, he would scuttle under the bed to hide. And this was where his father's stash of pornographic magazines was. The boy began to take a look and fascinated, continued to look. You can imagine that pornography became associated in his young mind with the comfort of a hiding place from danger and punishment. And so it became entrenched and if he had not had a loving, understanding wife later in life, his marriage would have been broken.

So many young fellows ogle these lewd pictures as part

of their 'growing up' experience. Their mates sometimes encourage them to begin and it seems 'normal'. But it isn't normal. God shows that the naked body (or nearly naked as the case may be) is nobody's business but your own (and your spouse's). We only have to visit the Old Testament to see that Noah's son was severely punished by the Lord for laughing at his father's naked body. In this modern age, many folk don't think it matters to parade naked or nearly so before others, but God doesn't change his values. So we need to align ours to his.

These are some of the traps of life. Imagination needs to be used for higher purposes or we may become so entangled that we will be led into situations we never expected or truly wanted.

The Bible clearly states that "the fear of God is the beginning of wisdom". You see, many people are clever but not so many are wise. So don't be tricked into being simply clever when, by reverencing the Lord and his values, you can be truly wise. Cleverness knows some things but wisdom understands the most important things.

16

OCCUPATION IS...

Have you noticed how once in a while you hear or see something and it stays with you for a lifetime? One of those things for me is a small thing but immensely significant. Over 50 years ago, (yes, I really am that old though it's hard for me to believe) I was working in an office. On a desk was one of those old fashioned calendars with a small page for each day. At the end of the day you simply slipped that day's page over the heavy wire frame to reveal the following day's date. And on each page was a quotable quote. I must have read many of them but just one has remained with me over all the years. I don't know whose quote it was, but it read *"Occupation is the armour of the soul."* That sounds simple enough doesn't it? But I thought on it deeply to understand it and I have recalled it quite a number of times over the years. Why? Because it's true.

We have just been discussing the problems with imagination and where it can lead. And we have so much more leisure in this day and age than we did when I was young. This quote can be part of the solution. Keeping ourselves occupied with vigorous work is one way we can not only be productive but safeguard our minds from idling into unproductive thoughts. Perhaps I shouldn't call them unproductive thoughts because all thoughts produce something but not all are helpful.

There is an old saying that goes something like this 'Idle hands create mischief'. So that goes hand in hand with my calendar quote, doesn't it? For many young folk, life has much leisure time. They may fill it with computer games, texting friends, posting on Facebook, watching movies, shopping, hanging out with friends, going to nightclubs or just lying in bed 'til late in the day. These things aren't necessarily evil, and can be good in that they keep up communications with friends but they mostly are self-centred time fillers rather than productive occupations. I long to see young people gainfully occupied; firstly with earning their own living by regular work and secondly with hobbies or volunteer work which employ their creativity or help those who are in need. Of course, some young people are doing these very things and I congratulate them. But one only has to go around the neighbourhood or to a shopping centre to see the evidence for lazy or even damaging activities. Languid youth are just *hanging around* without purpose. This simply is the breeding ground for negative happenings and dwarfing of the personality.

I believe that *everyone*—no matter their age—needs to be involved in something bigger than themselves. Anxiety, depression and mischief of all kinds largely derive from pre-occupation with self. And unfortunately, for the last few years we have been faced on TV with advertisements for anything from cosmetics to banking assuring us we are Number One or that We're Worth It or that they're Doing It Our Way. This emphasis on self-gratification is not helpful to the individual or to society in general. I am not Numero Uno! I am important to God and valuable for all I can contribute to others (including simply loving them) but so is every other soul. Don't be influenced by advertisements because the bottom line is that they are after your money and flattery is simply a tool to that end.

So, as much as possible, leaving self behind, let's look for the call of God upon our lives so we can be immersed in a greater purpose. Nothing is so enjoyable or so fulfilling as being a blessing to others and knowing we are fulfilling the reason for our being on Planet Earth.

I have always been a little curious about the **Amish** people in the United States. (You know, the folk who still dress in very modest clothes and ride in horse drawn buggies). I had never heard much of them and thought it a little strange that they refused to use modern conveniences such as electricity and cars. Then a few years ago a man went to one of their little schools and shot several children dead. The world was horrified at such an atrocious act. But I was also impressed when it was reported that the Amish adults of that community said that they forgave the murderer.

The seed of curiosity about them was still lingering when John and I recently went to the U.S.A. We had a number of friends/contacts to visit so after drawing breath for 3 days in New York we hired a car and drove around for our appointments. At one place we visited a shop which had rejects or 'end of line' items. I discovered a novel written by a Christian. It was a love story involving Amish people so I avidly read it to garner some more details about their thinking.

Toward the end of our six weeks there we had a few days to spare so we drove to Lancaster, Pennsylvania, which has a large population of Amish folk. We took a ride in an extended buggy drawn by two heavy horses and driven by one of the 'plain people'. This is the term used for themselves by not only Amish but also Mennonites and Brethren. All three groups had originated from the Anabaptists of the 1600's in Europe and had migrated to America to escape persecution for insisting on obeying the Bible instead of the traditions of the church.

Our buggy driver was a young woman who was brought up Brethren. She gave us some insights into the Amish ways and reasons for rejecting things which most of us take for granted. It wasn't easy to get to know any Amish in the one day we spent in Lancaster. For instance we shopped in a large Amish health food shop where several Amish women were working but only spoke to the cashier about the products. And outside the shop I spied a young woman and her little boy in his typical straw boater getting into their buggy. I asked if I would offend her if I took their photo and she shyly said that they don't usually pose for photos so of course I didn't get my shot. However in a Mennonite Information Centre there were videos to watch and books and postcards to buy which had photos of the Amish going about their activities.

Imagine our surprise on our return to Australia to find that there were a couple of small series of programs on the Amish on the SBS channel. So I avidly followed these programs and piece by piece we are completing our picture of these people called after the name of their founder, a Mr. Amman.

The main reason I am relating these things is this. The Amish don't put emphasis on the individual but rather the community. Their lives are spent in devotion to the Lord and following to the best of their ability His ways. They live in families, not like monks etc. But the name 'plain people' comes from the fact that they have virtually no decoration in their homes or their clothes or on themselves. No jewellery, the women don't even have buttons on their dresses which are fairly long and with sleeves at least down near the elbows. The emphasis is on not drawing attention to yourself or your body or anything that is yours. I should mention that there are differing groups of these folk who have slightly different rules for their communities.

The other point I wanted to emphasize is that their lives are ones of work. They rise early, have breakfast and are off to work and work hard. Most are farmers but as farmland is increasing in value and they generally have large families it is not possible for parents to continue to divide land or buy land to provide for the next generation. So those who don't farm mostly work with wood making furniture or barns or build buggies or make saddles for the horses which every family has for riding or to pull their buggies or old-fashioned ploughs.

In the TV programs I have watched, I haven't seen any self-righteousness which might be expected in people who choose to follow the Word of God extremely literally. Rather they are sweet and welcoming of those who have a different way of life. They train their children to be workers (members of their team) early in life. Young boys are out on the farm learning from their fathers. The girls are learning to keep a clean home and provide healthy, tasty meals. They work long hours and love it because they have been trained with a good attitude and work ethic. Their older children work with them fulltime usually once they've finished 8th Grade at school as they don't educate their children beyond that point. They provide the schooling for their children in one-teacher schools. Their education is to equip them to be capable and skilled members of the community. Family devotions round the Bible are a daily practice. They seem to marry young.

They don't have television, some don't have electricity and if they do it is usually powered by a generator. But they work hard and get together for a visit or to help one another. (Especially with barn raising. This is a real feature of the Amish. When somebody needs a new barn, the whole community get together for it. The wood has been cut ready and parts of the frame have been constructed then maybe 40 or more men gather on the barn raising day to lift the huge, heavy pieces into place and to connect them by driving in wooden pegs instead of nails or screws. The women meanwhile have been busy producing loads of food to feed the builders. The roof and boards for the outer walls are then attached. Because of the plethora of workers the barn is standing complete the day they begin. And much happy fellowship has been enjoyed.)

The general rule is that they don't have a house telephone because they don't want to encourage gossip but some have a phone in the barn, etc., for emergencies or business. I am not for one moment suggesting that we should adopt the Amish way of life but we can certainly learn from some of their attitudes and habits. They appear to be very content and that's something that can't be said for most people who live more affluent, leisurely, self-centred lives. Don't you agree?

17

THE POWER OF INCONVENIENCE

I mentioned in the Introduction that these life lessons had come to me in various ways. Some I just seemed to know. I guess we all have understanding of certain things as we develop as young people. But I can tell you that as long as we don't harden our hearts and minds we will go on learning until our last breath. This subject—The Power of Inconvenience—is hot off the press. Yes, I knew it in experience over the years but it came with fresh impact just yesterday encapsulated in the Sunday sermon. The speaker was a young pastor, Dave Dawkins. I asked him for permission to share his message with you so here are just the bare bones of what he had to say....

We enjoy convenience: Online shopping where we can click the items we want while involved in other things in our lives, and in a couple of days the goods are delivered; Gold Class Cinema where we don't have to jostle for space to rest our arms; an indoor café with a playground for the children. Today, we could live in a Cocoon of Convenience.

But Dave reminded us that life begins in Inconvenience. Our mothers put up with quite a bit of inconvenience bringing us into the world.

Next he drew our attention to a Scripture where the Apostle Paul describes some of his experiences as a missionary to the Gentiles. (1 Corinthians 6:4-10) "...As servants of God we commend ourselves in every way: in *great endurance; in troubles, hardships and distresses; in beatings, imprisonments and riots; in hard work, sleepless nights and hunger;* in purity, understanding, patience and kindness; in the Holy Spirit and sincere love; in truthful speech and the power of God; with weapons of righteousness in the right hand and in the left; through glory and *dishonour, bad report* and good report; genuine *yet regarded as impostors;* known, *yet regarded as unknown; dying* and yet we live on; *beaten, and yet not killed; sorrowful,* yet always rejoicing; *poor,* yet making many rich; *having nothing,* and yet possessing everything." (The italics are mine.)

Well you can see that Paul didn't live in a Cocoon of Convenience... And what he achieved is still echoing around the globe, is still impacting lives.

Dave reminded us that if we follow after Jesus Christ, we WILL have inconvenience. Then he said Inconvenience is the Gateway to Impact. Can I repeat that because it certainly made me think: Inconvenience is the gateway to IMPACT! People are won to the Lord by the power of inconvenience.

Dave spoke about the incident in John 4:5-42, where Jesus took the time to speak with a Samaritan woman at a well. Jesus was tired from his journey and sat at the well. So it wasn't *convenient* for him to bother with this woman but he was *willing to be inconvenienced*. There was general ill feeling between Jews and Samaritans and they didn't usually speak to one another. But Jesus took time out and that woman's life was impacted. As a result of this interaction the men of her town also believed in Jesus as the Son of God.

Dave told the story of a woman he knows who lived in a very remote area of Western Australia. She was one of 9 children in her family. Every so often there was a married couple who took it upon themselves to travel hundreds of kilometres to visit this family. They had to travel in their old car over rough dirt roads in excessive heat to hold a little church service—not for thousands, not for even hundreds but for the 11 family members plus their couple of workers. As this woman, then a child, heard the stories of the Bible from this couple, the messages took root in her heart. The couple who had been willing to be *inconvenienced* had made an impact on her.

But she also endured some abuse during her childhood and as a result developed the eating disorder, anorexia. In this remote area of Western Australia they knew nothing of anorexia so there was no help for her there. But a relative in South Australia was in contact with the family and sensed that this young person needed loving help. She invited the girl to come and live with her and her family. Now it wasn't *convenient* for this relative to have her move in with them because they didn't have a spare bedroom. But they were willing to be *inconvenienced*. And so this woman was healed by love and prayer.

Yes, her life was Impacted. And as a result her son's life would eventually be Impacted too and he is now a pastor of a church. And he now has a young daughter and her life is being Impacted because she is being brought up in a Christian home. So it was so worthwhile that the married couple who travelled to the remote WA region were *willing to be inconvenienced* and it was so worthwhile that the relative living in SA was also *willing to be inconvenienced*.

At this point, you could be wondering if you could put up with a lot of inconvenience to benefit others. Dave informed us that it is a matter of attitude. If you have the right attitude you can endure inconvenience.

Then he spoke about what he called *'Attitude through Altitude'*. Moses, for instance, had a difficult job and certainly not convenient. He was called by God to lead a mob of moaners for 40 years. But Moses would go to the mountain. He would ascend to spend time with God. You notice from a high point everything looks different. God changes our perspective, shifts our focus onto where we are heading, *not on the inconvenience*.

Dave reminded us of William Carey's life. William went to serve God in the wilds of Africa where the hardships and illness eventually meant the loss of two wives and several children over a number of years. Still he persevered. When he was on his deathbed, a young man came to take his place and William shared his experiences with him. You would think that Carey would have liked his suffering to have been recorded so that at least he would have a little consolation but his last words to the young man were something to the effect 'when you speak about this, don't speak about William Carey but speak about William Carey's Saviour.' Carey had been *willing to be inconvenienced*.

And in the Ultimate Act of Inconvenience, Jesus left his glory behind and came to earth as a baby, accepted the limitations of humanity, suffered the beatings and railings from men and allowed himself to be hung on a cruel wooden cross. ONE MOMENT OF INCONVENIENCE CAN CHANGE A LIFE FOREVER.

Thank you Dave for challenging us to refuse the moulding of our modern age. We will 'buck the system' and be willing to be inconvenienced to make a difference.

18

LET'S TALK TO OUR FATHER

I ask for your patience with this next matter. At first, it may sound as though I am just being pedantic. But I think you will understand if you 'listen' to my small chat about it.

When I took myself to church when I was young, prayer was always addressed to God the Father in the name of Jesus Christ. But for the last 2 or 3 decades I seldom hear our Father God spoken to, except by folk of the older generation. It's all about Jesus. We pray to Jesus, we thank Jesus, we praise Jesus. Why the change? That's one question I can't answer because Scripture says something different...

Now I'm certainly not saying that relating to Jesus is wrong. He is our Saviour and he said that the Father is in him and he is in the Father. But I am concerned that relating only to Jesus, rather than the Father, is resulting in our taking a warped attitude to God the Father. I don't ever want you to take my word for anything I say without being able to back it up with Scripture, so let's consider some Bible verses...

Romans 5:10a—*"when we were God's enemies, we were reconciled to him by the death of his son..."* This indicates that Jesus' death on the cross was to reconcile mankind to God the Father.

Again in Romans chapter 5, the first verse—*"Therefore, since we have been justified through faith, we have **peace with God** through our Lord Jesus Christ..."* We see that we have gained access to the Father via his son.

Bear in mind that the ENTIRE Old Testament is a history

of God the Father's people relating to him. Although the feasts, the sacrifices and the very furniture of the tabernacle represented aspects of what Jesus would accomplish later, thus ushering in the New Testament or Covenant, both Covenants were between God the Father and his people.

What light did Jesus shed on this subject? When he was asked to teach the disciples to pray (Luke 11), he showed them a pattern of prayer which we've titled The Lord's Prayer (Matthew 6:9-15). It is immediately addressed to the Father—"Our Father who art in heaven". It goes on to pray that the Father's name would be kept holy, that the Father's kingdom would come, that the Father's will would be done on earth as it is in heaven. It beseeched the Father to provide food, to forgive our sins, it asked that the Father would deliver us from temptation and the evil one and it acknowledged that the kingdom, the power and the glory belonged to him for ever and ever.

John 17:25 & 26. This is part of the beautiful prayer where Jesus was speaking with his father about the disciples and those who would believe through them. *"Righteous Father, though the world* (unbelievers) *does not know you, I know you and they* (believers, disciples) *know that you have sent me.* ***I have made you known to them, and will continue to make you known*** *in order that the love you have for me may be in them and that I myself may be in them."*

Let's take a look at a passage in the book of John—chapter 16 from verse 23b. *"I tell you the truth,* ***my Father will give you*** *whatever you ask in my name. Until now you have not asked for anything in my name. Ask and you will receive, and your joy will be complete. Though I have been speaking figuratively, a time is coming when I will no longer use this kind of language but will tell you plainly about my Father. In that day you will ask in my name. I am not saying that I will ask the Father on your behalf. No, the* ***Father himself***

loves you *because you have loved me and have believed that I came from God."*

Jesus had been spending time with his disciples and had been gradually showing them the Father by his own life and ways and words. Now he was virtually handing them over to the Father. Now they would relate to the Father in a new way. They would use the "password" of the name of Jesus who would soon become the sacrifice to pay for their sins so that there would no longer be an impediment between them and the Father.

After Jesus was raised from the dead, spent several weeks amongst the people then ascended to the right hand of the Father, we have a record of a prayer by Jesus' followers (Acts 4:24-30). It is addressed to 'Sovereign Lord' and we know that it was directed to the Father because it mentions 'your holy servant Jesus' twice. It asks the Father to stretch out his hand to heal and perform miraculous signs and wonders 'through the name of your holy servant Jesus'. So they were now following the directions Jesus had given them.

Why am I bringing all this up? Well, in the words of an English man, in our churches these days God has become "All-matey" instead of "Almighty". I feel that by relating solely to Jesus, because he is a human being, we are bringing God down to our level rather than looking up to God as almighty, all-knowing, everywhere-at-once, righteous, holy, truly Awesome (in the full strength of that word), meaning striking us with sacred awe.

When Daniel, a righteous man of the Old Testament met with a spiritual being and was given a vision of the future, he turned pale and needed several days to recover.

Men of old were so in awe of God that they believed that if they were to see God they would be struck dead because of their sinfulness.

God loves us but it is not a mushy, emotional kind of love.

He expects us to respond to his offer of reconciliation by loving him with all of our heart, with all of our mind and with all of our strength. That is some kind of commitment, isn't it?

To balance the picture of the Father, we look back at the Old Testament and find that he longed for his chosen people, the Jews, to follow his ways. He loved them and he sent his messengers, both human (the prophets) and heavenly (angels) to each generation of them, pleading with them to obey him and know his love for them. He also gave them warning that if they chose not to obey him they would suffer badly.

So here we see we have a truly awesome Father God who loves us enough to send his own son to suffer on our behalf—*now that is some kind of love, isn't it?* – but who also cannot bear wilful sin, who loves righteousness. We should also add that the Father loves the son so it would have caused the Father great anguish to know the suffering of his son Jesus on our behalf.

Now that I've shown you just a sprinkling of Scripture verses and a short explanation, can you begin to see where I'm coming from? I simply ask you to talk to the Father because Jesus has made the way for you to do so and read his word with this in mind and you will gain an appreciation of the majesty and wondrous qualities of our Father God who deeply loves us.

19

WHERE'S THE KEY?

Do you hear the words "where's the key" in your house as someone—maybe yourself—is hunting for the pesky little piece of metal while ready to head off on the next journey?

I'd suggest that you think of those words next time you find yourself in a state of confusion or anxiety or depression. You'd like to move on in your journey of life but for some reason you are stricken with a black mood or maybe a simple lack of purpose. Whatever it is this time which has descended upon you it is paralysing you and certainly not a welcome visitor.

What has a key got to do with it? Just this: there is always something which lowered the gloom around your head and your heart and your spirit. What you need is to find that something. It will be your *key to freedom*.

If someone comes to my husband John and says they have lost their peace, he always counsels them to look back to the last time they were at peace, when things were humming along nicely. So I'm saying to you when you have a hiccup in your life, cast your mind back to the last time you remember being at peace. Now, what did you think/say/do that could have changed your atmosphere? Or was it that you reacted to what someone else said or did?

Once you figure that out, deal with it. If you sinned in thought, word or deed, apologise and put it right in whatever way you may need to do. Put it right with God and with the person involved (if there was someone involved). If you indulged in something you knew wasn't godly, turn yourself around 180 degrees and decide that you are not going in that direction again.

If someone else has said something cruel or perhaps said nothing at all when you had hoped they would, mark it down to experience and look for the lesson in it. Had you put too much hope in that person? Become wiser through the experience rather than dwelling upon the hurt it caused you. That way it becomes a positive event instead of a negative brooding experience. Some people carry a hurt all their life as a victim when they could have grown by it, becoming a victor.

If you're searching for the key without finding it, you need to ask the Father. He's good at revealing hidden things. Do you know that he found a diamond for a friend of mine years ago? Let me tell you the story...

Sylvia was working as a house cleaner for a wealthy lady. As Sylvia is a Christian she always gives of her best, does a good job and cares about and prays for the people she works for. On this occasion, her employer realised that the lovely diamond was missing from her ring. She searched for it fruitlessly. Sylvia said she would pray about it and the Lord directed her downstairs to the driveway. The employer had been out in the car that morning and Sylvia found the diamond. Guess where? In the tread of the car's tyre. Nobody would have thought of looking there and the gem could well have been lost forever the next time the car had been driven out. But the great Revealer of Hidden Things showed a humble lovely daughter, Sylvia, where to look.

So remember next time you are wanting to go forward in life but something is stopping your progress, say *'where's the key?'*

20

INFLATION...
But not the kind you're thinking

We hear a lot about inflation these days but it's usually of a financial kind. I want to chat with you about a different—but just as important—type of inflation. And we'll mention deflation as well...

There's a song called The Wind Beneath My Wings which is telling a good friend how, though they didn't know it, they helped make their friend the success she was. They were there when needed. They stayed in the background but made all the difference though they were unaware of the huge impact they were having all the time.

Now that's the kind of inflation I'm talking about today. Providing the wind to keep someone soaring. Now I don't mean to say that someone should be entirely dependent on us or our words. Of course not. But the truth is that our words of encouragement can make an enormous difference to those around us; not just one special person but all with whom we come in contact.

The Bible says that the power of life and death are in the tongue. Wow! That's a mouthful! (Pardon the pun.) We know of course that in the days of emperors and pharaohs that was easily understood. The Roman emperor didn't even have to use his tongue. When watching those in an arena from his 'throne' he could just raise or lower his thumb to signify if the person was to live or die. What power! Even today I guess, criminals can give the word if a person is to die at the hand of a hit man. But the Bible is not referring to these extreme means. No, the tongue has great power to inflate a person or to deflate them, to bring life or a kind of death.

There are people who are the walking wounded. You may not be able to see the scars of battle but they are just as injured because of words that have been spoken over them. Wounding Words! Have you heard of the Battered Wife Syndrome? Some wives are told so often that the violence they suffer is their fault that they believe it. They submit to the continued battering as though they deserved to be punished. They have become a victim not only of physical suffering but of the words spoken over them.

But I'm not speaking so much to the wounded in this chapter. I've done that in chapter 1. *Now* I want us to make sure we are not injuring people with careless words. Recall that the tongue has great might. It is just a small part of our bodies but is capable of inflicting the greatest damage. That's quite a statement but it is true in some circumstances. When we injure by words, it can begin a train of thought that takes someone down a very dark, hopeless road.

I first thought of talking this over with you when someone recently said just a few words to me and I literally felt my lungs deflate. My shoulders slumped and I felt like having a whinge. It didn't take me long to realise that I was in danger of becoming a victim mentally. So I gathered a fresh intake of air into my lungs, straightened my shoulders, and mentally cast off the offensive words. My world was not going to be brought low because of a few annoying words.

The corollary of this of course is that well-chosen words can inflate the life force within us. Now I'm not talking about the ego. Stroking the ego brings a false sense of importance. But our self-esteem is important. Perhaps I should say self-respect. If we are living the best way we know how we have a right to have a sense of wellbeing within. We respect ourselves and we expect similar respect from others. So when someone affirms us in some way, it assures us that we are respected and appreciated. That's how things ought to be. But sadly, they aren't always that way.

So let's make a considered decision to watch our tongue, to edit our thoughts before they become words that may leave a friend/colleague/whoever walking away with deflated lungs and slumped shoulders, even if only mentally.

21

EVIDENCE FOR THE BIBLE'S AUTHENTICITY

As Christians, we are sometimes overwhelmed by the brash criticisms made by unbelievers about the Bible. We may shrink back, feeling we have no answers for such allegations. Over the years I've found evidences in the Word of God that it is not a book of myths but a volume of Truth which can be backed up in several ways. In the last chapter of each of the 4 Sections of this book, I present such evidence...

In Revelation, there is a description of Heaven and God's throne which says "A rainbow, resembling an emerald, encircled the throne." (Revelation 4:3b). I used to feel a bit pensive at that one... emeralds are green so where does the rainbow effect come from except perhaps the arch shape (thinking of the word 'encircled')? Then I heard a marvellous message from Rev. David Pawson, a great English Bible teacher who happens to be a friend of John's and mine. He recalled that there are **12 gemstones** including the emerald mentioned in Revelation and it has been found that out of the 28 stones which are regarded as precious, there are 12—and only 12—which, when sliced finely and viewed in pure light, are vividly multi-coloured, as is a rainbow. Surprisingly, when a diamond is viewed in pure light, it is coal black as are some of the others which are highly valued here on earth. And I might add, the light in heaven will be pure light. I believe David's information on the gemstones came from the old book "Gemstones from the City" by W

H D Woodward—(from our memory).

The 12 gemstones which are rainbow coloured are the very 12 which God has chosen to have with Him in heaven. They are the same 12 stones which were worn by the Israelite High Priest on his breastplate. You may like to share this truth with someone who is doubtful about the veracity of the Bible. This fact about those 12 stones was not generally known and it's been there in God's Book for centuries.

This could be called **EXHIBIT A**. But this is not the only piece of evidence. Let's play sleuth to find another clue...

The Old Testament book of Job is believed to be the oldest written record of any kind on earth. Although Moses' record of the origin of creation in Genesis obviously pre-dates Job's life, Moses wrote what God told him about creation. Moses wasn't around at the time his forefather Adam was brought into being. It is believed that Job was alive before Moses.

In Job 38:31 we have these words spoken by God to Job. "Can you bind the beautiful Pleiades? Can you loose the chains of Orion?" Pleiades is a star cluster in the sky and Orion is a nebula, in case you're not into astronomy. The quote sounds quite poetic and we find that most of Job is written in poetic form.

[You can usually tell what is Jewish poetry in the Bible by the way it is printed. In most Bibles, the main body of Scripture is in prose and is printed like newspaper columns, with justified (straight) sides. But when it is in poetic form the lines are done in free print with the lines of poetry separated. If you thumb through your Bible you will see the difference as most Bibles do it this way. Take a peek at Genesis 2:23 as an example. Before this verse, you have the newspaper type of printing then in verse 23 Adam's words about Eve are recorded and they form a little poem and the lines are centred in the column...

> 'This is now bone of my bones
> and flesh of my flesh;
> she shall be called 'woman',
> for she was taken out of man.'

Don't bother looking for rhyming words as Jewish poetry doesn't have them, and even if it did it would change when translated into English. It is more the rhythm of the words which constitutes Jewish poetry.]

Getting back to Job 38:31, here we have a chunk of evidence in the case for Biblical authenticity. We might call it **EXHIBIT B**. How come? Well, let me explain. My husband John is an amateur astronomer and he has taught me a little of what he has discovered. A star cluster normally has a static form, it stays the same. But Pleiades, also known as The Seven Sisters because there were 7 main stars visible to the naked eye, is spreading apart. Now mankind has only been made aware of this fact since the Hubble Telescope has been sent into space to have a closer look at what's actually going on out there. How long is that? I'm not sure, but only around a decade or so. Yet here we have it in the most ancient text in the world that God, *who made the stars and flung them into space,* knew all the time that this star cluster was different from the rest.

But there's more... as they say in the TV ads. What did it say about Orion the nebula? You may know Orion as The Warrior by the way. The verse said 'who can loose the chains of Orion?' What's special about that? Just this. Nebulae are usually expanding, but you've guessed it, Orion is as if it had chains around it. Only God could have known about this. Men certainly didn't until the last decade or so.

So if we encounter someone bad-mouthing the Bible, we have a couple of pieces of evidence to counter their arguments.

Well, there you have it. Exhibits A & B to arm you for debate with those who don't realise that the Bible is genuine. Look for the exciting Exhibit C in Section Two...

PART TWO

Introduction

We begin our lives with no knowledge or understanding at all. Gradually we form a framework of understanding about what life is about and how to live it. Whether we live it well or badly will depend, not only on what education we have but also whether we gather wisdom as well as knowledge for the journey. I am grateful, first of all to God, and then to those who have passed on their wisdom to me. Where would I be if not for the teaching I have received—from parents, friends, pastors and authors who wanted to pass on wisdom they had received? Why always learn from our mistakes when we can avoid many mistakes by imbibing wisdom from those God provides in our lives?

It's about a year since I wrote the first section and I keep on thinking of things I want to say to you, so here goes again… I have been encouraged by some responses. For instance, with Section One, while it was still in draft form, one of my granddaughters read the first chapter, "Aim High", and as a result decided she would sign up for a University course to make the most of her life. Another young woman read a few chapters more and told her mother "I need to get back to church". A reader in England showed her son's fiancée what I had said about relationships between males and females. What more could an author desire than to know her words have been a blessing to those who read them? I certainly hope it is so for you.

I certainly don't wish to tell you how to live your span but simply to give you a nudge in the right direction…

Wouldn't You?

Wouldn't you think that once a human being of standard intelligence reached a certain age he would realise that this life he was using up each day was a gift?

Wouldn't you think that he would consider that Someone greater than himself must have given this life?

Wouldn't you think that it would then become the first passion of his life to discover this Personage to find out how he was intended to spend this life?

Wouldn't you think that he would suspend all major decisions in his life until he found out the answer?

Wouldn't you think it was madness to neglect such a search?

Wouldn't you think it was presumption to go on using up this gift of life without even trying to find the answer?

Wouldn't you think it was downright dangerous to risk using up this gift without making sure what was hoped or expected of him?

22

WHAT IS STRENGTH?

Are you one of those who regularly go to the gym to build your muscles? Or do you pound the pavement to improve your endurance? Are you looking at your abs in the mirror? Are you aiming at running a marathon or competing in a triathlon? Or just running on a treadmill?

So many people have become aware of ways to improve not only their appearance but their core strength. They regulate their diet as well as exercising regularly. This can be very helpful in gaining a healthy lifestyle. Of course it can also become obsessive which is self-defeating as it merely traps us in a never ending round of activity like the mouse on its running wheel. I have a dear friend who has spent years going to the gym every day no matter where he is in the world. In earlier years he was heavily into body building and has continued to deliberately consume lots of protein in his daily diet. He was shocked to find that for a time he became ill as a result of the lack of balance in his food intake and has had to moderate his diet.

Whatever our activity level, our diet or our goal in this regard, what is true strength? Have you ever stepped back to take a look at the subject objectively rather than just gobble up the hype being served out to us from every television channel and glossy magazine?

The ideal being handed to us for generations is that the well-built male (it mostly applies to males) is stronger and preferable to the more puny one. But is that an accurate assessment?

As human beings we live in a body, that's obvious. And it is mostly our bodies which are presented to the world (clothed hopefully) rather than our minds, souls or spirits. As we get to know someone we sense more of the other aspects of course. So it isn't surprising that it is our bodies that can get people's scrutiny is it? As a result, the emphasis for so many folk is on how they look. But is that where true strength lies?

We sometimes marvel at the feats of physical strength a strong man can perform. But that is only *physical* strength. As we've said our physiques are only one aspect of the real us. What about strength of character? What about moral strength?

*I believe that true strength is demonstrated not so much by what we can do but in what we **don't** do.* I'm speaking about *self-control*. Many physically strong men throw their weight around (not all of course). Some of them actually are show-offs. Some strong men are violent which is not a sign of real strength at all. It shows that they have no self-control so are actually weak men.

So let's begin acknowledging truly strong people, male or female; those who have the strength of character to control the urge to lash out verbally or physically when it would be easy to do so. Let's make a point of aiming, first and foremost, at strength of character in ourselves and praising it in others. This is not to say that it is wrong to train our bodies, to build physical strength, or aim at stretching ourselves by competing in events. But let's remember that we are far more than bodies, that our bodies are really just the temporary 'tent' we live in which will eventually wear out no matter how much attention we give it. Let's concentrate more on building our characters, on resisting the temptations of life so that we will be *truly strong*.

You may be a young person with a lot of your life before you. The decisions you make in this regard now will make the difference between whether at the end of your life you look back with a sense of fulfilment or with regret.

A good physique may win some admiring glances but a good character will win trust from those who know you and eventually more than an admiring glance. A good character is looked up to, is relied upon, and achieves worthwhile goals in life. It's the difference between just looking good and actually doing good. That's not too hard a decision is it?

[I would urge young people to apply themselves to learning to express themselves well. I have noticed that those who can debate with others are less likely to use their fists. Frustration builds in those who cannot communicate well with words. Then they let their fists do the talking. Parents, you could help your young ones by teaching them to become clever with words. Play with puns so that they get to love words and to see how much better life is when they can make themselves understood without having to shout or hit. There is more to the subject of violence of course. Many resort to violence because of a poor self-image for instance. But I believe having facility with words can help some folk.]

TOSS IT! Some people find it helpful to physically act out offloading past sin or anxiety. For instance, you could write on a sheet of paper whatever sin or worry you are having trouble forgetting even though you've asked for forgiveness. Ask the Lord to handle it for you, then screw up the paper and actually throw it in the air, 'to the Lord'. Then bin it or burn it. 1Peter 5:7 "Cast all your anxiety on him because he cares for you."

23

WORK ETHICS

Most of us will spend a good part of our lives working for an employer. Perhaps you are doing so right now. Have you ever thought about what you owe your employer? Have you ever considered how different his life is from yours? You may be thinking 'Yes I work and he takes home the profit'. But there's more to it than that.

My husband John ran a number of businesses in our earlier years of marriage. As well as owning a Christian book shop he also had music shops under the name of The Music Makers. These sold electronic organs, pianos, guitars, music CDs, sheet music, etc. He worked very hard and ran them successfully for a number of years. He travelled a lot throughout our State of Queensland as his stores were very widespread in a large State. Of course he had managers in each store and was dependent on their skills and honesty. But there was much responsibility on his shoulders and ALL the risk was his. So we had a lot of money coming in and going out during that time. He travelled to America every year to visit their Music Merchants annual show where new models of organs and guitars were released at discount prices. He had to decide how many of these expensive items he should import, etc. etc. As well as this, back home, he was out on service calls at night though he employed servicemen.

I can tell you that he *earned* the profit that came in. Because he was still building the businesses we didn't spend much of the profit on ourselves but poured it back into the business coffers. And at one time we lost thousands of dollars because one of the managers employed a worker with a gambling problem. Then when the floods hit Brisbane in 1974 we lost thousands more. But our workers were not affected financially. All the risk was on John as employer. So I can see employment from both sides, as an employee from my own experience of working in an office before marrying and as the wife of an employer.

We hear plenty from unions about the rights of the worker and certainly they need to be acknowledged. But how about the employer and his rights? Have you ever heard anybody speak of these? I don't think I have. But look at it this way... An employer pays you for x number of hours. That means he is buying your time, your skills and your actual output. So in a sense he owns your time for those hours. They are no longer yours. Therefore you have no right to be talking lengthily on personal phone calls during those hours, do you? (Unless they are urgent of course.) You have no right to be slipping out for a cigarette either, do you? You have your allotted breaks for morning tea and meals. But outside of those, your time is not your own. It has been purchased by your employer.

Is that a new concept to you? I believe it will be to many people. But it is a fact. Therefore you should be giving your best during those x hours to your employer and his business interests. Considering these points, are you a good employee? If you were an employer, would you employ someone like yourself? Now come on, be honest, would you? So often we think of the boss as our enemy, wanting his pound of flesh but we must realize that he is paying for it so it is our duty to use our time and skills to benefit his business. It is not a kindness but our duty. Otherwise we are stealing from our boss. Isn't that right?

And if you consider yourself a Christian that is all the

more reason to do your best by your employer. I'm sorry to say that some Christian employees expected a Christian boss to be generous to them because he is a Christian rather than seek to give him their best effort because *they* are Christians. Have you noticed that about some Christians? They expect other Christians to be generous toward them without having the same expectation of themselves. A mystery!

This subject can be related to the previous chapter about building a good character because our work ethics reveal whether we have a good character or a poor one.

So have a think about what I've just said and decide whether you are all your employer could desire in a good employee. Good on you!

Here again is that word to slaves which shows the attitudes which surely apply to all of us: *"Slaves, obey your earthly masters in everything; and do it, not only when their eye is on you and to win their favour, but with sincerity of heart and reverence for the Lord. Whatever you do, work at it with all your heart, as working for the Lord, not men, since you know that you will receive an inheritance from the Lord as a reward. It is the Lord Christ you are serving."*

Colossians 3:22-24

24

WHAT DOES GOD THINK OF HOMOSEXUALITY?

Firstly, let me ask you 'what is wisdom?' As I've mentioned, it differs from cleverness. Being clever has to do with your brain's ability to understand and use abstract facts. These facts may be important to gain a diploma to hang on your wall or to enable you to earn a lot of money, but they may be quite useless to help you live a useful life, a wise life or a noble life. So while it's nice to be clever it is much better to be wise so why not be both? So what is wisdom? We could say it is to see beyond the obvious, to understand the consequences of actions, to find the higher way in life. Sometimes it means we have to swim against the tide of popular opinion. But to boil it all down it is really to see things from God's perspective rather than from the human viewpoint. He is the fount of all wisdom.

God is looking at the entire universe, He is comprehending where everything is leading, He has the answer to every question and at the end of time, He will be the victor over every power which has raised itself up against him and his ways and his people. So please seek wisdom in every avenue of your life. This is why it is so important to read right through the Bible as I discussed in the first section. Now let's get on with this chapter's subject...

In many countries around the globe there is much discussion and concern about the subject of homosexuality and whether laws should be enacted allowing homosexual couples to marry. Opinions of politicians, celebrities and the man in the street are aired on the media virtually every day. There is a great push for the legalisation of marriage for gay couples. What is happening in the lives of many young people is that they have girls or guys within their circles of friends, relatives or acquaintances forming such alliances. What with the media making it appear to be intolerant to disagree with the right to marriage, and being surrounded by a growing number of practising homosexuals, young people begin to feel as though it is normal and acceptable to be homosexual.

Aside from remarking that human bodies are obviously designed for heterosexual relationships, I will refrain from offering my opinion on the subject. However, what is of paramount importance is what God's opinion is on the subject. And who is publishing that? I haven't heard many voices on that issue at all amid all the clamour. Do *you* know what God thinks?

What has highlighted this for me is a recent event. A young relative of mine, let's call her Katy, goes to a church high school and loves the Lord. One of the boys in her class recently announced that it doesn't matter about homosexuality because it's alright with God who just wants us all to be happy. I'm glad Katy was on the spot because she was able to tell him that he needed to read Romans chapters 1 and 2 and that God doesn't say that he wants us all to be 'happy'.

This reminded me that there are crowds of young people — and older ones too for that matter — who have no idea what God has to say about the subject of homosexuality. What my opinion is doesn't *really* matter to you but God's opinion *should*. For this reason I am printing here the relevant verses from Romans chapter 1 on the subject. The book of Romans is a long letter written to Roman Christians by the

Apostle Paul, the chief teacher sent by God to the Gentiles (non-Jews) after the death, resurrection and ascension of Jesus Christ. Of course you have the freewill to decide for yourself what your choices in life will be, but at least after reading this you do so in the light of God's Word. I hope you will make the *wise* choices.

Romans chapter 1 verses 18-32 "The wrath of God is being revealed from heaven against all the godlessness and wickedness of men who suppress the truth by their wickedness, since what may be known about God is plain to them, because God has made it plain to them. For since the creation of the world God's invisible qualities—his eternal power and divine nature—have been clearly seen, being understood from what has been made, so that men are without excuse.

"For although they knew God, they neither glorified him as God nor gave thanks to him, but their thinking became futile and their foolish hearts were darkened. Although they claimed to be wise, they became fools and exchanged the glory of the immortal God for images made to look like mortal man and birds and animals and reptiles (that is, idols).

"Therefore God gave them over in the sinful desires of their hearts to sexual impurity for the degrading of their bodies with one another. They exchanged the truth of God for a lie, and worshipped and served created things rather than the Creator—who is forever praised. Amen.

"Because of this, God gave them over to shameful lusts. Even their women exchanged natural relations for unnatural ones. In the same way the men also abandoned natural relations with women and were inflamed with lust for one another. Men committed indecent acts with other men, and received in themselves the due penalty for their perversion."

If someone wants to challenge me for sticking with the Word of God, my challenge to them is this: Homosexuality is so obviously not 'normal' and has been decried as immorality for centuries; what has changed to make it seem 'normal'? Also, if you are seeking to normalise something so horrendous to previous generations, what next will you 'normalise'? Paedophilia? Euthanasia? Theft? Murder? Rape?

All these practises give pleasure or relief to those who want to do them. But pleasure or 'happiness' should not be a reason to legalise, sanction or normalise anything. We need to recognize temptation for what it is. Temptation is the desire to do something which ought not to be done. Legalising it does not make it right. And when we legalise something which is wrong (sinful), we nudge the door open to make the next wrong acceptable.

The way this is done is that people push for something to be recognized as normal. There is an outcry from those who are rightly outraged by the suggestion. So there is a lull for a while then the subject rears its ugly head again, there are demonstrations in support of it, the media gets on the bandwagon so it is discussed round the water cooler in countless offices etc. Meanwhile there are young people who hear the persuasive arguments and—because they lack experience and wisdom and they (usually) like to push the boundaries—they join the voices in favour of the push. A politician, wishing to curry favour with his constituents, introduces a bill into parliament for legalisation of whatever it is. The bill is defeated but just wait a while and you will see it reintroduced down the track; and in the meantime there have been even more noisy demonstrations and more young people have been encouraged to seek liberty in the matter (and need I mention that vulnerable University students will be targeted) and this time there is a good chance that the politicians will pass the bill. Wise hearts will be heavy at these changes but the majority will go on with their lives hardly noticing what has happened in their midst.

If you think I am exaggerating, I can tell you that I have inside information and I *know* that this is how things are often accomplished. I know that University students, notoriously always short of money, have in times past become a rent-a-crowd as part of demonstrations. That is they have been paid to turn up for the demonstration to march in the street and make it appear that there is more support for the cause than there actually is. (I am not referring to the current debate as I have no personal knowledge of current methods.)

So *wise up* and see what is happening all around you, whatever age you are now. Perhaps it would be a good idea to join the Christian Lobby group who stand up for godly principles within our laws; and remember to pray about those laws which would accelerate the downward spiral of society.

For those whose consciences are not yet seared, I draw your attention to the Israelites of old who allowed themselves to be tainted with the views of the countries around them and the Bible records "Are they ashamed of their loathsome conduct? No, they have no shame at all; they do not even know how to blush." (Jeremiah 6:15). In other words, their consciences were not in good working order any longer because they had gradually slipped into evil ways. The following verse goes on to say: **"This is what the Lord says: *'Stand at the crossroads and look; ask for the ancient paths, ask where the good way is, and walk in it, and you will find rest for your souls. But you said, 'We will not walk in it.'"*** What was the result of this rebellion against the Lord and his ways? Verse 19 reveals *"Hear, O earth: I am bringing disaster on this people, the fruit of their schemes, because they have not listened to my words..."*

Do you want to see blessing on your life? Then stick

with the ancient paths where the good way is. God doesn't change...

25

BEAUTIFUL? HANDSOME?

Some people are thought of as beautiful or handsome. They have symmetry of features, marvellous eyes, good bone structure, well-shaped hair to frame the face, etc. etc. For others they understand the art of makeup which, if used well, draws attention to their best features and minimises the rest. But I want you to think a little more deeply about beauty. (We'll use the word 'beauty' for male or female as it is a somewhat generic term and a really handsome man is sometimes said to be beautiful.)

Do we have to have drawn well from the gene pool to be beautiful? I have seen people with great looks but cold steely eyes and to me they are not beautiful. Others are so laden with makeup that you feel you are looking at a mask rather than the person.

I remember being at a shop in Fiji years ago and was so struck by the great beauty of the Indian girl serving me that I could hardly take my eyes off her face. But it wasn't just her face which held her beauty. She had a lovely quietness of spirit, a gentleness, which made her truly lovely. On the other hand, the male Indian store owners all stood at the doors of their shops or even on the footpath trying to draw you in to buy their wares. They were almost dragging you in to their cash registers. And I don't know whether they were good looking or not because their brash manner repulsed me. I'm sure that if the beautiful girl had simply stood quietly at the door of her shop people would have gladly gone in to look around...

So what is true beauty? And can a plain person ever be considered beautiful?

As I've mentioned, I went to Sunday School from when I was 4 years old until I was 13. And in my final year I had a middle aged female teacher whom I considered the most beautiful woman I had ever known. She was not at all beautiful in the way we judge beauty queens but she had such a gentle and loving way toward all she met that when she gave her shy smile it was as though she bestowed a gift on everyone around her. She radiated love, joy and peace. When she spoke I was glued to her every word. As a matter of fact, though I had believed in God right from when I had first heard about Him, it was Miss Evelyn Brier who taught me that I needed to *accept* the sacrifice of Jesus to cover my sin, it didn't happen automatically. So I was born again there in her class that Sunday morning and have been grateful for that beautiful woman ever since.

Years later, with my mother I was visiting a family living in my home town of Brisbane. I had never met the family and when I saw the lady of the house my first impression was of a quite plain woman. But as I was introduced she smiled at me and suddenly became beautiful right before my eyes and ever after I could not see why I had ever thought of her as plain.

Then there are men and women who look very attractive but they open their mouths and their attitude turns them ugly.

So what is beauty really? True beauty comes from within. What is in a person's heart is usually revealed in their eyes. Love or hate, vivacity or apathy, even selfishness or generosity are mirrored there. Of course people can sometimes feign attributes but eventually the truth is revealed. So I would say, especially to younger people, look beneath the surface to find whether the person you find attractive is really a beautiful person. I have a sneaking suspicion that some people who don't feel adequate in themselves look for an outwardly attractive spouse to make them look good to others. I suspect that this is more of a trap to men. They sometimes have that 'trophy wife' to hang on their arm as though she is their stamp of approval to the world.

So if you want to be a beautiful person spend more time with the Lord. Realise that with the Lord's Spirit within, you are adequate in any circumstance. The Bible, God's manual for life, tells us that if we have the Spirit of God living in us we will produce certain fruit in our lives. Those fruits are listed in Galatians chapter 5 verses 22 and 23: love, joy, peace, patience, kindness, goodness, faithfulness, gentleness and self-control. Now fruit takes time to grow on trees and it's the same with the fruit of the Spirit. But over time, as we walk with the Lord and meditate on His wonderful Word, these life-shaping fruits should grow in us and begin to give us true beauty.

26

WHERE ARE YOU?

You know as well as I do that where we are bodily is not always where we are mentally. I often notice family groups or even groups of friends. They may be talking seriously or laughing and joking but one (or more) of them is not really 'there'. They are texting someone else in another place or playing a game on their 'phone. So in effect, they are really in that other place as well.

I must admit that I feel a little sad when I witness this especially when it is in a family group. Generally speaking, families have precious little time together and when one or some of them spend most of their time in cyber space they aren't really together at all.

But what I would like to tackle in this chapter is the fact that no matter where our bodies are, we are really where our minds are. That's where we live. It's where thoughts begin and actions and attitudes issue forth from thoughts.

I actually feel sorry for today's youth in some ways. Life was much simpler when I was young. We didn't have the myriad attractions and distractions to draw our minds away. And it is only in the last century that we have had more and more leisure time. In Bible times, there was a 6-day working week and the 7th day was a day of rest. Even now, Israel still has a 6-day working week.

Now the serious bit. We have an enemy, the Devil. He is our enemy because he is God's enemy and he greatly desires the worship that belongs to God. He has set his sights on human beings and targets them. You see, it is a fact that we always serve someone during our entire lives. If we are not serving God we are serving the Devil. We may not think we are serving him but if we are holding our lives to ourselves we are fulfilling his plans and plots. He has us in his grasp. The Bible informs us that the Devil roams through the earth **like a raging lion seeking whom he may devour.**

Our first forefather Adam was given a command from God that he was not to partake of the fruit of one particular tree in the garden where he lived. All other fruit was for his taking but just not this one. However the devil came along to his wife Eve with his insinuations and inaccuracies and at his sneering suggestion Adam and Eve took the forbidden fruit. I think you and I will relate to Adam and Eve here as surely there is still something inviting about that which is forbidden, at least before we belong to God fully. Well, in obeying the devil instead of God, Adam gave the Devil claim to rule his world.

If the Devil is roaming throughout the world seeking people to 'devour', what gives him the right to do so? Well, firstly because Adam handed over to him the right and then, if we despise God's will and live to please ourselves, we affirm that right.

So what is Satan looking for? He is looking for his toehold in each life. Jesus said to Simon Peter (Luke 22:31) **"Simon, Simon, Satan has asked to sift you as wheat. But I have prayed for you, Simon, that your faith may not fail."** Wow! This is so helpful for our insight. Satan is looking for those who are not living by faith. The Bible reinforces this in Romans 14:23 **"...Whatever does not come from faith is sin".** Now let's look at another interesting verse, this time John 14:30 where Jesus is speaking about the Devil **"...the prince of this world is coming. He has no hold on me,**

but the world must learn that I love the Father and that I do exactly what my Father has commanded me." So Jesus acknowledged Satan as the prince of this world but he also showed that, because Jesus loved God and obeyed his will, the Devil had no toehold in Jesus' life. He could bring temptation to Jesus, but he could not control him.

When we put these pieces of the jigsaw together we see that the Devil knows that if he can find faults in our everyday walk he can claim dominion over us. It doesn't mean we must be perfect or none of us would have any hope. No, it is plainly seen from Luke 22 above that Jesus intercedes on behalf of his people when they are honouring him in their ways. But if we are double-minded, seeking our own way while pretending to follow Jesus, we may as well paint target circles on our backs.

Let's get back to our minds. This is where we really live so that is the battle arena in Satan's war. If he can get our minds on dark things he has us hooked. If we are constantly thinking self-centred thoughts we've lost the battle already. And of course if our brains are sozzled with illicit drugs or too much alcohol, he's laughing. We're in his camp. His aim is to rob us of all that's good and eventually to destroy us.

The Scriptures reveal that Satan's ultimate destination is hell. And let's not fall for that foolish idea that Satan is enjoying himself in hell, having an eternal party. No way! Hell has been created for Satan and his demons as their punishment. There won't be any partying. And the saddest part of all is that if people are in the Devil's camp, they will end up suffering in hell along with him.

God doesn't want that to happen but the choice as always is ours. The Bible tells us plainly that **"God is not *willing* that any should perish"**, meaning it is not God's will that we should suffer pain and anxiety in hell. Can you imagine a place of endless pain and anxiety—anxiety so bad that we would gnash our teeth? Well God has warned us very plainly that that is the result of refusing His way of salvation through Jesus Christ. You see, just as I mentioned that the fruits of the Spirit of God are admirable things like love, joy and peace, if we are totally separated from God and His rule, there is a complete absence of those things. Can you picture a place where there is no love, no joy, no peace, no patience, no kindness, no goodness, no faithfulness, no gentleness and no self-control? It doesn't bear thinking about, does it? Well, please make sure that you don't have to go there. God is not wanting you to go so he has made a way for us to be reconciled to him. And Jesus is the ONLY WAY to God the Father according to John 14:6.

God always has a way to help us in the difficulties of life and in this instance we can look up Philippians chapter 4 verse 8: *"Finally, whatever is true, whatever is noble, whatever is right, whatever is pure, whatever is lovely, whatever is admirable — if anything is excellent or praiseworthy — think about such things."* So there are the places our minds need to go.

So here we have God's good advice. When men are preparing for battle they check their equipment. They arm themselves. In our case, as the battle arena is our mind, we furnish our minds with wholesome thoughts so we are not attracted to those things of darkness or distracted from our purpose.

So, I ask you, where are you? Where is your mind? Don't let it visit the gutter. Keep it on higher things. It is your protection. It is not to make life more difficult, but rather to keep you from being devoured by that roaring lion.

The Armour of God

I really cannot finish this subject without sharing with you something the Lord has provided for us in our battle with the enemy. Let's look up the book of Ephesians in the Bible. This is really a letter written by Paul the Apostle to Christians in Ephesus. In the centuries since the last book of the Bible was written two men decided it would be helpful if the entire Bible was divided into chapters and verses to help us find individual sections and subjects. So even letters now have chapters and verses. So we look at the last chapter of Ephesians, chapter 6 and verses 10-18. *"Finally, be strong in the Lord and in his mighty power. Put on the full armour of God so that you can take your stand against the devil's schemes. For our struggle is not against flesh and blood, but against the rulers, against the authorities, against the powers of this dark world and against the spiritual forces of evil in the heavenly realms. Therefore put on the full armour of God, so that when the day of evil comes, you may be able to stand your ground, and after you have done everything, to stand.*

*"Stand firm then, with the **belt of truth** buckled around your waist, with the **breastplate of righteousness** in place, and with your feet fitted with the **readiness that comes from the gospel of peace**. In addition to all this, take up the **shield of faith**, with which you can extinguish all the flaming arrows of the evil one. Take the **helmet of salvation** and the **sword of the Spirit, which is the word of God.** And **pray in the Spirit on all occasions** with all kinds of prayers and requests. With this in mind, **be alert** and always keep on praying for all the saints."* (In the Bible, 'saints' refers to all believers, not just those with statues with halos around their heads.)

Now what do we have here? What are the parts of the armour with which we should see ourselves equipped? Firstly the **belt of truth**. If we have placed ourselves on God's side in the battle, we need to recognize that we have been given the authority that Jesus gave the disciples when he sent them out 2 by 2 to speak to people, to heal and to cast out demons. In the Name of Jesus we can withstand the onslaught of the Devil. As we have identified ourselves with Jesus as our Saviour and Lord, we stand in his authority. That's the truth. This is incorporated in the belt that holds together the various parts of our armour. So when the enemy tries to tempt us or to bring up old sins of our past (or even more recent ones which we've repented of) we can remind ourselves that the truth of the gospel is that we are right with God via the sacrifice of Jesus.

Secondly, the **breastplate of righteousness**. A breastplate covers the vulnerable chest like the flak jackets our police wear on dangerous jobs. This is a protection for our hearts. We've already looked at Romans 3:21-25 which shows that our righteous standing with God is based on his righteousness, not our own which sometimes falters. So our hearts need not fail us for fear because we are viewed as righteous by God and that's all that matters.

Thirdly, we have our feet shod with the **readiness that comes from the gospel of peace**. Our feet take us through all kinds of terrain in life. There may be difficult climbing, sharp rocks, barriers of some kind but we need to remember that we walk in peace. We come from a place of peace and we aim to bring peace into every situation of our lives. We don't fight with fists, we don't kick with violent feet. We walk in the peace of God which has entered our hearts and minds and spirits. How comforting to be able to face all kinds of situations without anxiety and fear because of the peace of God in our walk.

Fourthly, the important piece of equipment called a shield, and this one is the **shield of faith**. This doesn't need much explanation, does it? Whatever situation comes our way we can face with faith in God. We don't always understand how and why we encounter some opposition but we counter it with faith that God filters out everything which he doesn't mean us to have to face. Also, we have faith that he is able to turn bad situations into blessings. We can look back to Joseph (in the book of Genesis) who was betrayed by his brothers who sold him into slavery in Egypt. He had been given dreams by God which suggested that he would be in positions of power yet he soon found himself as the lowest of the low, a slave. Then, after a number of challenging scenes which even resulted in his imprisonment, he was eventually able to face the very brothers who had sought to be rid of him and tell them that what they had meant for ill God had turned to good. And when he was telling them this, he was now in the position of being second in charge over all the land of Egypt. Who could have foreseen how God would manage such a desperate plot? But dear Joseph had kept his faith through it all.

Why is faith a shield? Well for the answer to that we just have to look at those who have no faith. What do they do when a challenge comes to them? There are many reactions depending on the person, but so often people become anxious or depressed or seek to hide from their problems in alcohol, etc. We look at the person who has faith to shield them and they often shine, they rise to the occasion because they have a firm foundation for their life. Without faith, we stand in quicksand. With faith, we are founded on the Rock which doesn't move.

Fifthly, our **helmet of salvation**. Now we look at the protection for the head, or the mind. We've talked about the importance of the mind and how we think. Salvation brings with it a transformation of the mind. We think along different tracks now, we see possibilities where once we may have seen problems, we have purpose in our lives where once we were wasting our lives in sinful or pointless pursuits. Praise the Lord for the helmet that protects our vulnerable minds.

Sixthly, the vital **sword of the spirit**. Every soldier has his weapon to bring him victory and we are no different in that. But our weapon is very different indeed. We have a sword and it is the old fashioned double-edged sword. This was a shovel shaped weapon, sharpened all round and used both for offence and defence. A man with this weapon would hold it in front of him and swing it back and forth so that he could cut down several enemies at a time. This is so much a picture of the Word of God. We use it to proclaim to people how they can be saved from the power and penalty of sin to live a good and productive life pleasing to the Lord. We can also use it for our defence against the lies which we encounter from time to time, such as the lies of evolution as the beginning of life for mankind. We have an answer to those lies as already dealt with in Section One. And when the attack is of a more personal kind, we defend ourselves by quoting what the Word of God has to say about us. We are loved by God, we are righteous in Jesus, we are gradually developing the fruits of the Spirit, etc.

Lastly, we are to **pray in the Spirit** always. To do this of course we need to be baptised in Holy Spirit, that is Holy Spirit power. Then we are able to pray for the exact will of God. Prayer is not something we do as a last resort. We are to pray about everything. And note that it mentions 'with all kinds of prayers and requests', so it isn't always to be a 'shopping list' of requests but also intercession on behalf of others, prayer for the leaders of our country, thanksgiving for blessing received, etc. Prayer doesn't have to be a formal thing. We are speaking with our 'Abba', father. Isn't it spectacular that the God of the universe looks upon us as his beloved children and wants us to look to him trustingly as our Daddy? It changes the whole complexion of the relationship, doesn't it?

There are some Bible teachers who would probably draw out much more meaning from this passage of Scripture, but

I hope the small amount I've brought to the table will be helpful to you.

Some believers actually rise from their beds each morning and mentally don each piece of the armour which the Lord has provided. It helps them to muse on each facet and also to be prepared for whatever the day may hold. You may find this useful too.

27

IT'S PARENTS' JOB TO TRAIN THEIR CHILDREN

Most young people hope to eventually marry, settle down and have a family. This is a natural yearning in the heart. But I've noticed a subtle difference in the parenting of today from that of yesteryear.

There is a great emphasis on fun in this age. Sportsmen being interviewed on TV often speak about aspects of their game and finish by saying that they are 'having fun and that's the main thing'. These are professionals being paid huge amounts of money yet their main aim is still to be having fun.

Years ago people hoped to have fun at a picnic or a party but they took their jobs more seriously. Perhaps they wanted to be happy but they weren't so much looking for fun.

This attitude seems to have seeped into every aspect of life, including parenting. Parenting can be the most wonderful experience of our lives but it is also at times quite difficult. Children aren't automatically wonderful little beings. They are basically selfish usually. Of course, they have to be in the beginning as they are totally dependent on their fathers and mothers. If they are hungry, thirsty, hot, cold or have a soiled nappy, their only way of notifying their need is to cry. And it sometimes is difficult for parents to decipher one kind of cry from another. But as time goes by and children begin to communicate via language they then need to be shown the boundaries of life.

Manners need to be taught and habits like sharing. And

because the little ones are not much more than babes they need to have these principles reinforced time and again, gently but firmly. Once out of the high chair they need to know that they must sit at the table until their meal is finished. And so it goes on...

But what I have observed over the last decade or so is that some Mums and Dads don't seem to recognize that their job is to *train* their children. It is wonderful if they can make the teaching fun but I believe that the child needs to understand that their parent is more than a playmate. They will most likely become brats if boundaries are not put into place, again *gently but firmly*. There was an experiment done some years ago with a class of young children at play time. The children played happily within the fenced area allotted to them. Then the fence was removed and the children's reaction was to crowd together in the middle of the usual play area. They no longer felt secure without a recognisable boundary.

So although it is hard work to train a child, we will do our children a good turn by gently insisting on the rules of the household for them. Even though they may try pushing the boundaries they will be more secure if they know where those boundaries are. And we will have children we can take to other people's homes without causing those folk to groan when they see us coming.

By all means have fun with your children but know when to be a little more serious so that they can move through life making friends rather than have others shun them.

Another aspect of child rearing is that of offering choices. I have been surprised to see mums asking very young children what they want for breakfast. I would suggest that it is better to set nutritious, tasty food before them to educate them in eating right. Then as they get older and have some understanding we can introduce choice. But when we offer choices all the time to very immature little beings they think

IT'S PARENTS' JOB TO TRAIN THEIR CHILDREN

they have the right to rule. Don't you agree?

"Train a child in the way he should go, and when he is old he will not turn from it."

Proverbs 22:6

"Wives, submit to your husbands, as is fitting in the Lord. Husbands, love your wives and do not be harsh with them. Children, obey your parents in everything, for this pleases the Lord.

Fathers, do not embitter your children, or they will become discouraged."

Colossians 3:18-21

28

MISCONCEPTIONS

In Chapter 5 I mentioned something of the Devil and hell and the misconception people hold about the devil being in charge there, perhaps thinking it wouldn't be so terrible being able to be bad and enjoy rugged partying. Well there are lots of things we've absorbed misconceptions about...

Take heaven for example. Have you noticed that no matter what kind of life people have lived, they are usually still given a Christian funeral and spoken of as being in heaven? It's not for me to say who may and may not go to heaven but as I've said the Bible makes it clear that there is only one way to the Heavenly Father and that is through belonging to Jesus his Son. Another thing people often speak of is that their dead loved one is looking down on them from heaven and orchestrating things in their lives. There is nothing in Scripture to indicate that once people have left this life they have any power to direct circumstances here on earth. It's a nice thought but without foundation. It is God Himself we need to call out to for any kind of help and guidance.

Another fanciful image we have is of angels. They are usually depicted as nude cherubs, perhaps with a bow and arrow to shoot at a lover's heart; or as a womanly being with long hair. And yet consider that every angel active in Scripture is masculine and powerful and when people have recorded visitation by angels they are always very tall and masculine. There seems to be a desire in some human beings for a feminine representation of God. But let me assure you that God our Father and Jesus our Saviour are capable of being extremely tender with those who are bruised in any way as well as harsh with those who are not fair dinkum ('genuine', for non-Aussies). There is a lovely Scripture written about Jesus who was yet to visit earth, Isaiah 42:3: "A bruised reed he will not break, and a smouldering wick he will not snuff out. In faithfulness he will bring forth justice." And again, when the haemorrhaging woman touched the hem of his garment and was healed, Jesus called her "daughter", surely a loving, tender touch. (Matthew chapter 9)

A dangerous misconception is that life is like an exam at school and 50% is a pass mark - If we keep God's commandments more often than we break them, we're home free. But the truth is that we are incapable of being good enough for a perfect God. Unrighteousness (sin) cannot live with righteousness. So God has provided a way for us to be righteous in his sight, and be reconciled to this righteous God. One of my favourite portions of the Bible: Romans 3:21-25 "But now a righteousness from God, apart from law, has been made known ... This righteousness from God comes through faith in Jesus Christ to all who believe. There is no difference, for all have sinned and fall short of the glory of God, and are justified freely by his grace through the redemption that came by Christ Jesus. God presented him as a sacrifice of atonement, through faith in his blood. He did this to demonstrate his justice...., so as to be just and the one who justifies those who have faith in Jesus." It is so simple but so profound. God has made a way for us to be right with him and to be able to live the life he planned for us. If that's not good news, what is? Yet so many people feel that they can *earn their salvation* and they are wasting their time. Good works should come as a *result* of salvation, not as a means of gaining it.

29

WHAT ABOUT A JOURNAL?

Here's a simple little idea which may be helpful to some of you. Many Christians keep a journal, a kind of diary. In it they keep a record of their journey through life, especially as it pertains to God. Every time you have a question for God, make a note of it and then also write down the answer God sends. God's answer may come from the Bible, you may just *know* an impression from the Lord or perhaps it will come up "co-incidentally" in conversation with someone.

All sorts of episodes can be recorded. If you find a great promise in the Word of God and you want to remember it, jot it down. If you pass through a really difficult time and you learn something about God via the experience, keep a record of it. And please understand that some of the most precious times in our lives are those that take us through great difficulties and sorrows. It is out of suffering that we develop a deep well of compassion, understanding and humility. We can move from being shallow people to those who can cry with those who are sad and rejoice with those who are celebrating, and do so from the heart.

Why journal? Well, for one thing, many of us forget things, even things which have been quite important at the time. Also some of us slip back and become lax in our walk with God and it's good to have a record of God's faithfulness in the past to bring us back to our faithful Lord. And let's face it sometimes doubts tiptoe across our minds and there's nothing like being able to refer back to a time when God's presence was so tangible that we felt as though we could reach out and touch Him.

Well, it's over to you. For some people this is a means of enriching their lives and keeping the really important things in their consciousness.

30

HYMNS OR SONGS?

I want to have a small chat about something which you may not have thought of. Over a period of centuries congregations of believers have worshipped God through the singing of hymns. Now—and for say 3 or 4 decades—we have largely replaced hymns with songs or choruses. Is this a good thing or not?

Quite honestly I enjoy some of the great old hymns and I love some of the modern choruses. But this subject has become somewhat divisive in many churches. Why? Because music is a kind of language to us and we tend to relate to the music language we grew up with rather than one introduced to us later in life.

I'll mention one difference between hymns and choruses. The old soaring hymns tended to proclaim theology, that is they speak of the many facets ABOUT God—his majesty, love, salvation, forgiveness, goodness, power and his suffering. Then there came a time where we moved into a more intimate relationship with God and our worship songs became more love songs TO God. And I have to say that while *some* of them lift us into the presence of the Lord, others have very little content except love and blessing, rather subjective aspects. I believe there is a place for both expressions of faith and relationship toward the Lord. So what is the problem?

Our congregations are usually composed of people from young to old and this is where the problem emerges. Remember that it is not just about content of the songs but also the form of music. As an example, my husband and I like 'middle of the road' type music because it's easy listening and easy on the nerves. Thus we choose to tune into certain types of radio stations for instance. Our children, themselves adults, obviously grew up a generation later so their taste in popular music genres varies from ours and some of them would prefer those stations which have more modern 'exciting' music. And then of course there is the extreme music. Do you know that I so dislike heavy metal music that I will not go into a shop playing it even if I would have liked to browse there.

Now place this situation into a church setting and we find there may be three generations of people all wanting to express worship to the Lord via music. There is no one type of music that they will all relate to. So we are dealing with not just the music we prefer but music which actually repels us.

What is happening in the majority of churches today? Hymns have been entirely dropped and only modern songs are used. What effect is this having? It is possibly pleasing the younger generation but alienating the older ones. Now once in a while it would not be so bad but when this is the order of every service, is it a good setting for worship? I realise that one of the reasons for dropping hymns is that musicians often cannot play the music because they read only chords. But I also know that there are some worshippers sitting in the pews who *could* play the hymns but they are not even considered.

I believe that the rationale is often that the church leaders don't want young people being turned off by having to sit through a hymn. But I ask you what kind of church society are we breeding if each generation cannot be taught to treat the others kindly and with consideration? I know some 'oldies' who attend week day meetings at churches other than their own just so they can enjoy the good old hymns as well as the fellowship. Is this situation satisfactory? I think not.

I certainly would not advocate a return to hymns exclusively. But I would strongly suggest that every church would do well to include one hymn at the very least monthly so that the older members (who have usually been faithful to the Lord for decades and are often the ones who spend more time in prayer for the welfare of the church) feel that they are still considered valuable members. I have been in churches that hardly ever use a hymn but when a worship leader includes one the singing is much more enthusiastic than when the usual modern songs are sung. And some of the younger generation just might find that their spirits are fed and charged with some of the marvellous theology they hear in the hymns.

On one occasion, at a church we attended previously, my hubby John and I put on a hymn night especially for the older folk who felt they were really missing out. The pastor of the church felt that hymns were outdated and he admitted that the usual musicians couldn't play them. But he was quite happy for us to have the hymn night and graciously attended with his wife. We had a great night—we imported an extremely good organ player and pianist, gave the interesting background to some of the hymns, featured an extract from a DVD of professionals singing a couple of hymns in Jerusalem, even showed a beautiful rendition of 'It is Well with My Soul' by the Three Tenors. At the end of the night the pastor and his wife were in tears as they had been so moved by the impact of the words and music.

So now I have unburdened my heart about this matter. It's over to you. Do you have any influence in your church to suggest that the oldies be given the occasional opportunity to sing something which resonates with every fibre of their being? Won't you think about it?

31

YOU HAD A TOUGH START? SO DID JESUS
(Don't play the victim)

We are all aware of people from 'the other side of the tracks', those who've had a rough start to life and struggle to make something of their lives. Or maybe they don't struggle at all and live a life which really doesn't amount to anything good. Many use their poor start to life as an excuse for living a less than ideal lifestyle. Are you one of them? I'd like to draw your attention to the start Jesus Christ himself had.

Firstly he was conceived out of wedlock which probably caused lots of rumours to circulate. Of course his parents were engaged but this was not a promiscuous era. We know that there was no immorality on their part because, as the angel informed Joseph, Mary had been impregnated by the power of God's Holy Spirit. Let's understand there was no sex act involved in Jesus' conception. I've spoken to you about the fact that in some places In the Bible there was no 'the' before 'Holy Spirit' and this refers to the *power* of the Spirit, rather than the person. In the case of the conception of Jesus it occurred by 'Holy Spirit' in other words by the *Spirit power, not involving personal action.* Perhaps we could compare it to creation when God created all things, not by fashioning them with his hands, but by *speaking his powerful word.* So we can understand that there was no immorality involved, but Mary and Joseph's neighbours would not necessarily have believed their story.

Next we can observe that Jesus' parents were poor people. How do we know this? Joseph and Mary took the baby Jesus to Jerusalem to present him to the Lord in accordance with the law of God. An offering was made. And we note that their offering was the one designated for poor people—"a pair of doves or two young pigeons".

On top of this the king, Herod, had heard that a child had been born who was destined to be king of the Jews. Fearing for his power, Herod called for every male child under two years of age to be killed but Jesus escaped because an angel had appeared to his earthly father in a dream warning him to flee with Mary and the child to Egypt which they did. Presumably this journey would have been funded by the gifts brought by the Magi (wise men). So Jesus was a refugee.

So we have 'illegitimacy', poverty, a price on his head, not a good beginning we would think. Things didn't ease as his life went on. His agenda was always different from everybody else's so he was misunderstood. When he was about 12 and went to the temple in Jerusalem with the multitudes he stayed behind reasoning with the leaders for he understood that he must be about his (heavenly) father's business, while his parents returned, each assuming that he was among the large numbers of relatives and friends travelling.

Then when he was an adult and had just endured 40 days of fasting and would have been at his physical weakest he was especially singled out as the target of the devil himself for some pretty heavy temptations. He used his knowledge of the Word of God to douse the fiery darts of the devil's temptations.

When he was expending his life in teaching the masses via parables, and healing people of illnesses and madness caused by demons, his own mother and brothers thought he was overdoing it. They simply couldn't understand.

And even the 12 men he gathered about him failed to fully comprehend his position or his mission until he had risen from the grave. And remember that one of them betrayed him deliberately for cash.

Of course we know that he was aware all along that he was on a mission, and what a mission. To be the Saviour of the world. And so he appeared a battered and beaten corpse on a cross at the end of his life. Many—even those who had listened to his parables and his teaching and perhaps admired him—would have believed that his life had been a failure in the end. But of course it was all part of God's plan for in 3 days he was to rise again just as he had said he would. He had accomplished the very purpose for his coming. But during the 33 years of his life, he had to swim against the tide of opinion and understanding. So he not only had a tough beginning but a difficult life. But he was victorious over all the circumstances and accomplished the very purpose for his lifetime.

So how about you? Did you have a bad beginning? Are you poverty stricken? Are you suffering a difficult middle part of your life? Are you struggling with temptation? Are you misunderstood? Or betrayed?

Well let me assure you that there is somebody who understands whatever you've had to endure, whatever you are at this very moment enduring. And he didn't come just to save the people of his own time, his sacrifice on the cross is effective for all generations of men and women, boys and girls. And he understands because he himself endured such contradictions. One of his jobs at this present time is to intercede for those who belong to him so if you are one of those then you know that he is on your side. And if you haven't yet given your life over to him, what better time is there than right now? We can always know that we have one who really cares about our welfare, who is on our side and who has the wisdom and the power to make a difference for us.

There is one piece of advice that I sometimes give to those I counsel and it is something I learned especially when I suffered breast cancer in 2010. God whispered into my heart (no I didn't hear him but I just *knew*) that I was not to be a victim. When we face any kind of unsought or unwelcome news or situation we have the choice to become a victim or a victor. And it is all in the power of our spirits and minds to choose.

If we blame our poor behaviour on our bad beginnings or have a 'poor me' attitude, we are playing the victim. And there in the mire and mud we will stay. Unless we decide to become a victor. It's our choice. But of course it's better if we look to the Lord and call on his help. He understands, but not just to sympathise with us - he has the power to make the difference.

Let me share a true story with you. During WW2 a bunch of Aussies were prisoners of war enduring terrible circumstances. But their hearts were touched when they heard that there were children imprisoned further down the road. A number of them decided to make toys for them. One of them had a disabled arm and couldn't make toys so he decided to write a children's book titled The Happiness Box which featured three animals as the characters, while another fellow illustrated it. The original copy is on display in New South Wales today.

Because their Japanese captors were suspicious that the book might be a coded message it wasn't allowed to be given to the children and it was ordered that it be destroyed. But the fellows buried it and dug it up when they were liberated. All these years later a young lady composer heard about the book and decided to compose some music to accompany the telling of the story about happiness which was written under such depressing circumstances. On a recent TV program I saw someone reading the story and acting out the animals' movements while an orchestra played the music especially written for it to the entertainment and enchantment of young children. When one young girl was interviewed after the show she spoke of the lessons that could be learned from the lovely story.

Surely that is a picture of a choice made by those prisoners of war. What could be more debilitating to the soul of a soldier than to be captured by the enemy? The choice was to be a victim or a victor. And in the midst of that situation this delightful book came into being and even the order to destroy it did not snuff it out. It has been printed and after the death of the originators of it, it is still bringing delight and lessons on how to appreciate happiness to little ones.

So which are you going to be in your circumstances? Victim or Victor?

"No temptation has seized you except what is common to man. And God is faithful; he will not let you be tempted beyond what you can bear. But when you are tempted, he will also provide a way out so that you can stand up under it."

1 Corinthians 10:13

If you are confronted with temptation, call out to the Lord to show you his way out...

32

NOT WHAT YOU CAN GET, BUT WHAT YOU CAN GIVE

The title of this chapter sounds a little like those famous words of President John F Kennedy: "Ask not what your country can do for you but rather what you can do for your country". I wasn't actually inspired by his words at this time, but rather I was appalled by what I see occasionally at get-togethers.

Sometimes I have been at wedding receptions and other events where the drinks from the bar are free. Many people imbibe far in excess of what they would under normal circumstances. A similar effect is often seen at 'All you can eat' cafes. People pile their plates so high not another crumb could be fitted on. Why do they do this? Surely it is taking advantage of the suppliers. It is a sign of innate selfishness. Greed is another word for it. Yet people feel no shame at their actions. It is almost a part of our culture. I will only speak for Australia; though I've travelled pretty widely I can't say that I've actually noticed the trend elsewhere. Overseas readers will know whether it applies to them or their culture.

It indicates that those folk are more interested in getting for themselves than in considering the welfare of others. At wedding receptions for instance the father of the bride or whoever is footing the bill for the reception has to pay for every drink. Even at work functions the boss or the company is paying the tab. They are being generous in allowing the bar service to be free for the guests. Is it fair to take advantage of their generosity? By all means enjoy a moderate intake. But keep in mind that their pockets are not bottomless. And even if they are wealthy it is greedy to over-indulge.

But it's not so much their pockets which are my focus in this matter. I am concerned at the attitude of those who over-indulge when it is at somebody else's expense. Jesus' standard was "love your neighbour as yourself". A great way to express that is the Golden Rule which says "Do unto others as you would have them do unto you". Now that is so simple isn't it? When we interact with others on any level surely it is so easy to ask ourselves "how would I like to be treated?" Then treat them similarly. If you have the opportunity to eat or drink freely, ask yourself "If I were footing the bill for this, how would I want people to act?" Then you'll have a good gauge for your actions.

Now we get back to our title. If we are the kind of person who is always looking for what we can get out of a situation, we need to recognize that and shift gears in our brain and heart—from getting to giving. Let's begin to look for what we are able to give in any situation. Say we're at a function or party and we spy someone sitting alone and looking lonely. What would we want if we were in their place? Surely we'd like someone to approach to have a pleasant conversation. There's no more lonely place than feeling alone in a crowd.

If you find it hard to begin a conversation, try asking a few questions. Nothing too personal. Try to find out how they like to spend their time. Are they into music and if so what type? Do they play sport, or watch it? What work do they do? If it sounds like something out of the ordinary, ask more about it. These are just easy, everyday subjects that anybody can begin with. If you find it difficult to keep the conversation going, perhaps you can invite them to join some of your friends where they may find someone they'll have something in common with. You don't have to spend the entire time with them but at least you've saved them from a miserable experience.

The nice bonus in looking for what you can do for or give to others is that you feel good about it too. Sometimes kind words and a little caring have saved lives.

I have heard a story from a well-known Bible teacher who has been a very great blessing to many people. Many years ago, as a young woman, his grandmother, was intending to commit suicide. She went to a beach and was about to leap from the pier into the water to drown when a stranger sensed her troubled heart and approached her. He dissuaded her from her intention and thus not only saved her life but enabled the world to have this great Bible teacher who would never have been born if his grandmother had not been saved.

So whether we may simply save somebody from a lonely evening or actually save their life, a change of attitude on our part—from looking for what we can give rather than what we can get—can make all the difference.

33

DON'T UNDERESTIMATE THE VALUE OF SMALL THINGS

Many of us have a secret desire to be famous. We want to do something which will impress. Perhaps we nurse a dream of our name up in lights. Then again, on a less self-centred note, some would like to do a whole lot of good in the world—running an orphanage in a needy country, researching for a cure for a baffling disease, finding a way to provide food for the hungry or travelling overseas as a missionary.

In the very first chapter of Section One I encouraged readers to 'aim high', to set goals to achieve in their lives. And I haven't changed my mind about those things but, as in many things in life, there is more than one way to view it. There is a place for lofty goals and large dreams. But let's face it, we are not all meant to be Chiefs. Even Chiefs need followers, those who do the lowlier jobs. And here's the best part—the result of the humbler jobs can be just as stupendous as that of the high profile ones.

Let's begin with something we can all do—smile. Sometimes a friendly smile can brighten the day for someone who is struggling in life. It doesn't really cost anything but it can make a difference, even a huge difference. It can make a lonely person feel they have a friend. It can sometimes turn anger away. It may just make someone feel that life isn't so bad after all. And a smile is contagious. A kind word can have similar effects.

There is a story in the Old Testament of the Bible, 1 Samuel chapter 25. It tells of Nabal, a surly, miserly man of wealth.

His actions angered David when he refused to provide food for David and his men though David had guarded his shepherds and sheep. David decided to avenge himself by slaughtering Nabal and his many men. But Nabal had an intelligent wife who hurried to gather provisions and took them to David and his men. She humbly begged David to resist the temptation to take his own vengeance and to accept her offering of meat, drink, grain, cakes and fruit. David was taken with her intervention and repented of his intention to exact vengeance on all these people.

This is an example of a simple act by one woman which saved the lives of many men. What was she doing? Just providing food, but it was done in such a way and at such a time that it was far more than catering. It was a life saver and it also saved David from having blood on his hands needlessly. So it was a small thing with huge results.

I was at a friend's home a few years ago and was having a chat with her sister who was visiting from France where she had resided for many years. She was living with a French man to whom she was not married. She was teaching at a Church school in France and mentioned to me that as she was speaking to one of the priests one day he mentioned her 'husband' to which she said that he was not really her husband. The priest, obviously a broadminded one, said 'Oh! Of course he is your husband'. I was appalled that a priest would so condone immoral living and felt that if I didn't say anything my friend's sister would think that I also was in favour of her lifestyle.

As I never intentionally offend anyone, there was a small struggle within before I very gently said 'what do you think God feels about it?' I thought by putting it that way, I wasn't offering my own opinion. The conversation ended there and she left the room. I learned later from my friend that her sister had been very angry with me, calling me 'intolerant'.

DON'T UNDERESTIMATE THE VALUE OF SMALL THINGS

But the interesting thing is that when she returned to France she soon married her partner. Such a simple question but it obviously threw a challenge in her direction and brought a result. [Actually, John and I have discovered that it is often better if an unbeliever becomes angry when challenged with the gospel rather than to be apathetic. Their anger indicates that they are aware that their life should be different and they are rebelling against that. They are often the ones who eventually surrender to the Lord.]

May I share another couple of examples of very small things which brought *amazing* results? There is a certain church to the north of Brisbane which has one of those sign boards outside on which pithy sayings are displayed. Nothing special about that; it's quite a common thing. But how the Lord used that sign board...

It was approaching the Easter season and a married couple used to drive past the church occasionally. They were sensing the need to get right with God in their lives. They thought the first move would be to attend church but as they looked at the sign board the only words on it were the current saying being displayed. They sent up a prayer something like this 'God, if you are real, get them to put up the times of the services so we know when to go'. The person responsible for the sign had no knowledge of these folk of course but as Easter was approaching and there would be an extra service for Good Friday, he decided to put up the service times on the notice board. Well! The couple had the answer to their prayer and they went along to church at Easter, gave their lives to the Lord and are now walking with Him. Isn't that wonderful?

But God wasn't finished with that hoarding yet...

There was an elderly woman who had recently come to live nearby from overseas where her whole life had been a series of dramas and abuse. She was a very needy lady largely through no fault of her own. She would drive past this church whenever she went to do her shopping. Each time she passed she 'heard' a voice saying 'God can set you free'. But within herself she argued that she had no way of ringing the pastor to make contact.

Round about that time, the person handling the sign board felt that it was time to spruce it up with paint etc. He asked the pastor if he should put his name and 'phone number at the top of the board and it was decided that that would be a good idea.

Isn't God good? He sees the needy heart wanting to reach out to Him and makes a way. The gentle, loving pastor met regularly with this dear lady, winning her confidence. Then, sensing that her need was greater than his experience could fulfil, he called my husband in to help as he's been used over the years to deal with demonic possession in many people. We joined with the pastor and several church people in several sessions until this lady was finally totally free. Instead of pain, anxiety and fear she was filled with joy and love and peace. Soon she was baptised at a Sunday service with her whole family looking on and we all shared in a celebratory lunch after the service.

But remember where it started? With a very small thing, a behind-the-scenes person faithfully attending to a simple sign board outside the church. God was able to direct in this job, and lives and souls were saved. What greater result could anybody desire?

I encourage you, don't despise the small things God gives you to do. He may not have an up-front job for you but sometimes the unseen people are doing every bit as important work as those who receive the kudos here on earth.

As a matter of fact, it's good to remember that God has told us to do our good works privately (when that is possible) and has said that we will be rewarded. But those who display their good works and receive man's applause have received all their reward already.

Cultivate a teachable spirit. If you are humble enough to learn from others you will avoid many pitfalls.

34

ARE YOU A REFLECTION?

Perhaps the question should be 'what are you reflecting?' because virtually all of us are reflections of something or someone.

We each have influences which shape us. We are born as individuals of course with our own personality. But over time there are influences which may alter the course of our life with regard to our attitudes and actions. Then we begin to reflect those people or things which we have taken on board our mind and heart and spirit, perhaps people we admire or want to emulate.

Many people are reflections of Mum or Dad for obvious reasons: they have been our main examples in the formative years of our youth. But as we move about in our world we see and hear other influences and it can be surprising how different from one another siblings can be sometimes. They've had the same parents but have taken their lead from different people or events.

At various stages of our development we may want to be like people on our TV or movie screens — glamorous women, action men, etc. Sadly, some people become clones of what they see and lose their own identity and personality. In some cases, we may be reflecting very superficial attitudes, manners of dress, even accents. Then of course there are those who choose to model the darker characters seen in movies, etc. Thankfully, most of us grow out of our immature first impressions and move on to display more worthy values.

But what is the purpose of our very lives? Well, it actually is just to be a reflection, not of another human being but of the Lord Himself. Does that seem too lofty? How could you go about that? Could you be comfortable in that guise?

Well, it isn't something that we create ourselves. It is the work of Jesus' wonderful Holy Spirit working within us as we give ourselves over to the Lord. God will never force us to do something but His purpose for us is to be like His 'first child' Jesus. Let's look up Romans 8:28 and 29... "And we know that in all things God works for the good of those who love him, who have been called according to his purpose. For those God foreknew he also predestined *to be conformed to the likeness of his Son, that he might be the firstborn among many brothers."* And when the Bible speaks like this about brothers it includes us women as well.

Let's take a look at another vital section of the Bible, Romans chapter 12, the first 3 verses: "Therefore, I urge you, brothers, in view of God's mercy, to offer your bodies as living sacrifices, holy and pleasing to God—this is your spiritual act of worship. *Do not conform any longer to the pattern of this world, but be transformed by the renewing of your mind.* Then you will be able to test and approve what God's will is—his good, pleasing and perfect will."

God always works with males first but as women are faithful they share in the promises. Some women rebel against the fact that the Bible is largely male orientated and doesn't say much about women or 'sisters'. So please consider these few matters...

In the lineage of Jesus several women stand out—Ruth who wasn't even Jewish, Rahab the prostitute who wasn't Jewish either but came to trust in God, and Mary herself who bore him within her body and was pronounced as 'blessed'. As well, there was a sinful woman who came to Jesus and anointed his head with very expensive perfume. Those observing this criticised her as wasteful but Jesus saw the love and faith behind the act and said "wherever the gospel is preached throughout the world, what she has done will also be told, in memory of her."

Cast your mind to the woman 'taken in adultery'. She was brought to Jesus in the temple courts in the hope that he would be trapped into saying or doing something which could be the basis of an accusation against him. Her accusers said that she was caught 'in the act'. We might say if that is the case, how come the man wasn't dragged before Jesus as well? It was the self-righteous Pharisees and teachers of the law who had brought her thus. What was Jesus' response to this sinful woman? He squelched the proud attitude of the accusers by saying that the man without sin should be the first to throw a stone at the adulteress (as stoning to death was the penalty for adultery according to their law). At this the men filed out of the area as they knew themselves to be guilty of sin as well. Then Jesus, left alone with her, turned to the woman and said 'Woman, where are they? Has no one condemned you?' 'No one, sir' was her reply. Then Jesus uttered those transforming words to her 'Then neither do I condemn you. Go now and leave your life of sin'. [Jesus came the first time to earth to provide a way of salvation from sin. When we stand before him at the end of time, he will be our judge and the time for forgiveness will have passed, if we haven't taken advantage of the reconciliation offered.]

Having looked at these women who played a part in God's drama, we need to remember that in the Old Testament, the twelve leaders of the Jewish race were male as were the twelve disciples of the New Testament and all angels mentioned in Scripture are male.

Women who have been influenced by the feminism of this age like to point out that the army of the Jews was at one time led by Deborah, a prophetess but they fail to notice that the Bible points out that it was to the shame of the men that a woman had to take this leading role.

If women need any comforting over this matter, look at the fact that males have to see themselves as part of *the bride of Christ*, as the church is portrayed. And though Eve was the one who fell to temptation in the Garden of Eden and encouraged her husband Adam to also eat of the forbidden fruit, in the New Testament we find that Adam is named as the one at fault. So we see that a husband is expected to be the head over his wife so that he protects her and must take the blame for her wrong actions. That's some kind of responsibility. (It also should remind women to be careful that they don't flout their husband's guidance as he has that heavy responsibility.)

While some of you will need to struggle through the last few paragraphs, let's get back to our subject of reflecting Jesus. Can you see how important this is? It's not a maybe thing. It is the major purpose of our lives. Why? Because God wants others to come to him, to find his redemption, to be saved. And by living as Jesus would in the world, we give others the opportunity of seeing true Christianity being lived out.

Think of what Jesus said in his prayer shortly before being crucified. It is recorded in John chapter 15. In verse 23 his words are "May they (his followers) be brought to complete unity to let the world know that you sent me..." This tells us that to strive to love our Christian brothers and sisters and to pray for them that we may be in unity is a way we reflect Jesus and so draw others to him.

Of course, as I mentioned earlier, it is by having the fruit of the Spirit in our lives that we will be a demonstration of the work and power of God.

35

DOES GOD HEAR EVERY PRAYER?

Some months ago John and I drove past a church with a sign board out the front announcing "God Answers Every Prayer" and we said to each other 'that's not right'. Why did we have that reaction? Simply because the Bible says differently.

One thing we need to be careful of is thinking that everything said in churches or on their sign boards is accurate. Many preachers today are gathering their theology (knowledge of God) from 'Christian' books rather than from THE book, the Bible. And much of our 'Christianity' is humanistic. What do I mean?

God has provided a marvellous manual for life in the Scriptures. Almost every question we may ask has an answer there in black and white. That's why God caused it to be written. People sometimes joke that they wish there was a manual for life as there is provided when you buy a new car. Well, God has provided that very thing. But how many folk truly read it to see what God thinks about all sorts of things? Our aim should be to please God, therefore we need to know what kind of God we belong to and what pleases him and what doesn't. It's all there...

But in this present age there has been a shift and people, Christian and non-Christian, have become centred on human feelings rather than on God's eye view. Thus even some pastors and pew sitters have altered their theology to fit how *they* feel and what makes human beings happy. When they read something in the Bible which doesn't please them they take the view that that must have been 'for *that* time or *that* culture' and it doesn't apply now. This is sometimes referred to as taking scissors to the Bible, cutting out what isn't pleasant and retaining only what is. Thus, our religion has become man-centred—humanistic - instead of God-centred. What a dangerous situation we find ourselves in. So be like the Bereans as recorded in Acts 17:11 **"Now the Bereans were of more noble character than the Thessalonians, for they received the message with great eagerness and examined the Scriptures every day to see if what Paul said was true."** So make sure you become so familiar with the whole of Scripture that you can check up on what people have to say about God and about life

So, to get back to our subject 'Does God Answer Every Prayer?' what does the Bible really say? Let's take a look at Psalm 66:18 **"If I had cherished sin in my heart, the Lord would not have listened."** Jesus quoted from the Psalms so we can have confidence in looking to them for answers.

Then we turn to 1Samuel 8:18. The setting is that the people of Israel were demanding a king such as the nations around them had. Now God wanted to be their king with men such as Samuel to act as his spokesmen. So because they were demanding something which went against the will of the Lord who had led their forefathers out of slavery in Egypt to a land of promise, God warned them **"When that day comes, you will cry out for relief from the king you have chosen, and the Lord will not answer you in that day"**. So sometimes we have to bear the consequences of our wrong choices.

Another Old Testament example happened during a time of rebellion against the ways of the Lord by the Jews. Deuteronomy 1:45 **"You came back and wept before the Lord, but he paid no attention to your weeping and turned a deaf ear to you"**. Wow! We never want the Lord to turn a deaf ear to our prayers do we? You see, God is not a fool. He knows the motives of our hearts and he wants to see genuineness there.

Now please realise that I am not saying that the Lord's ear actually suffers deafness at times. It is a way of saying that he *chooses* not to hear because of the attitudes or actions of the person. To prove this, take a look at Isaiah 59, the first couple of verses: **"Surely the arm of the Lord is not too short to save, nor his ear too dull to hear. But your iniquities have separated you from your God; your sins have hidden his face from you, so that he will not hear."**

Let's move to the New Testament and the words of Jesus himself: This verse in Matthew chapter 5, part of the Beatitudes is not directly referring to prayer but shows one of God's principles—**"Blessed are the merciful for they will be shown mercy."** Thus we see that it is not only prayer which brings us the answers we need but it is the heart attitude we have and the actions which issue forth from that. It is not unreasonable to then deduce from that verse that if we are lacking in mercy toward others we will not readily be shown mercy by the Lord. So if we want to pray for mercy in a situation, we need to look at our own behaviour toward others.

Now the teaching of James from the Bible book of that name, James 4 part of verses 2 and 3: **"You do not have because you do not ask God. When you ask you do not receive, because you ask with wrong motives, that you may spend what you get on your pleasures."** In those few words we see that God wants us to ask Him for what we need but our prayers should not be selfish. There is a difference between our needs and our 'wants'. Further along in James 4 we read **"God opposes the proud but gives grace to the humble"** so again we see a principle of God which we need to understand.

DOES GOD HEAR EVERY PRAYER?

Some folk may say that the Bible doesn't cover everything we face in this modern time but the principles of God remain the same throughout all generations. So when we read the Word of God what we should be looking out for are the principles by which God works. They will usually provide the answer as to how we should live in any situation.

I would like to quote a little more from James 4 as it gives a good overall look at what we need to do to have our prayers answered. (Verses 7-10) **"Submit yourselves, then, to God. Resist the devil, and he will flee from you. Come near to God and he will come near to you. Wash your hands, you sinners, and purify your hearts, you double-minded. Grieve, mourn and wail. Change your laughter to mourning and your joy to gloom. Humble yourselves before the Lord, and he will lift you up."** So there we have the order of things. We need to recognize our own unworthiness and sinfulness (and tendency to sin), humble ourselves before God with sorrow for sin and true repentance then he will lift us to that place of authority in Jesus Christ where we will know the joy that doesn't come from the world but from God himself and we will see the answer to our prayers.

Many Christians today are asking why we don't see the answer to prayers for healing, etc. This is God's prescription. Follow it and expect to see miracles take place in answer to your own prayers.

John and I have seen cancers healed, back problems released, demons sent packing and even several dead people raised over the years. The Lord is still in the business of answering prayer if we align our lives to his ways. Praise his Name!

36

APPRECIATION

This may seem a trivial matter, 'appreciation', but it determines the 'colour' of our lives. We hear of art appreciation and music appreciation for instance. But I want to look at appreciation in its broadest framework. One of the things I've noticed is that modern people want instant gratification because so many things around them are 'instant'. Come on, admit it, today we tap our fingers or feet when waiting for the speedy microwave to do its job. Now, don't we? We have instant potato, instant cameras, speedy elevators, fast trains, jet planes, credit cards and the government is rolling out fast broadband. We don't just want things but we want them NOW. This attitude has come with the computer age and isn't all that surprising. But it has come at a price—the price of *appreciation*.

Years ago all things were slower and because it had always been that way we accepted it without much questioning. There were no such things as credit cards and, though we could use time payment, we tended to wait until we saved up the cost of an item until we went along to purchase it. But here's the secret—while we waited we *anticipated*. And when we finally had the desired object we greatly *appreciated* it.

Don't you find now that, at least in thriving countries, because things are generally obtainable quickly you feel satisfied for a brief time, then you want something else, then something more? This is because we don't readily find *appreciation*. Now for the good news! We can cultivate the habit of appreciation. There's an old song called "Count your Blessings" and this is a good place to begin to learn the art of appreciating. John and I have needed to travel quite a bit in fulfilling the will of the Lord—missionary work in some places, attending or speaking at conferences in others. And this has helped us appreciate all that we have in our homeland.

Actually, it began long before that... When I was 20 I travelled by train from Brisbane to Melbourne with a load of other Christian Endeavourers (for those who remember good old Christian Endeavour) for the annual Convention. While in Melbourne I had my first taste of being a tourist and took in all the sights I could. It opened my eyes to look around at things and places in a new way—with 'tourist eyes'. So when I returned to my home town I decided to look there with these new tourist eyes. Thus I went up to the Town Hall tower to overlook the city, something I'd never thought of doing before though I worked in the CBD. It was the first time I had *appreciated* my home town and from then on I loved Brisbane. Can you see how this simple shift in thinking changed my everyday life? Just a small thing in the great scheme of things but it can be adapted to the whole of our lives.

Did you realise that if you have a roof over your head, food in your stomach and the price of your next meal you are better off than millions of people on our planet? If you look around at what else is available to you, you may begin to know that you are really rich. Our country is rich in education, rich in training, rich in resources, rich in opportunities, in hygiene and health services, in transport, in housing laws which require builders to produce safe residences, rich in weather, etc. We could go on. Start looking for the things (and people) in your life for which you could be thankful. Now there we have it—*thankfulness*—that's the key to appreciation. Not only count your blessings, but begin saying 'thank you' to God and to people for their contributions to the life you live. You will find that you begin to feel much more content, not forever reaching for more and more goods to fill your house and your life.

Appreciation lends colour to our lives, makes it richer. So what else am I suggesting? Well, firstly I would like to say to parents 'don't be in such a hurry to supply something your child asks for'. I feel nowadays that many, not all, Mums and Dads hear a request and automatically see it as something they must do, especially if both are bringing in a wage. We don't have to give in to our children's demands. As a matter of fact, by giving them anything they ask for we are actually depriving them of this 'colour agent', appreciation. The longer we have to wait for something we desire, the longer the period of active anticipation and appreciation. I remember as a child waiting for Christmas or birthday to receive a special gift. My parents didn't rush to give me what I wanted but made sure I received it on one of those special days. And how I cherished it when I received it. How thankful I was. How the enjoyment lingered. But now I can buy myself some new thing virtually any time I want, I have noticed how short is the period of appreciation. So I stop every now and again to count my blessings and to cultivate the art of appreciation.

One thing we see rather regularly on our TV screens is somebody who has been through a flood, tornado, fire or cyclone and lost all their possessions. What do they express? So often, it is that *things* can be replaced but they are thankful that their lives and those of their family have been spared. There's nothing like a major threat to bring perspective to our lives.

So if you want a little piece of advice from somebody who

has seen the advance of immediacy in our lives, it was better when we had to wait. I'm not saying that I would want to go back to the slower life altogether. It is nice to have the speed of computers and the convenience of mobile 'phones, but I don't always buy what I would like immediately because I want to enrich my life by appreciating what I have. I want to have an attitude of thankfulness. And taking time is part of that. Greed can sneak up on us and make us mean.

An allied subject is the overuse of credit cards. We need to be aware of our budget and limit the amount we allow ourselves to spend especially when we are buying on credit. Many people have come to grief by allowing themselves to keep on buying beyond their means just because of that tempting little piece of plastic in their pockets or purses.

A nifty Bible verse says **"Godliness *with contentment* is great gain."** (1Timothy 6:6) And one of the keys to contentment is remembering to be thankful and appreciating what we already have.

37

THE OLD ENHANCES THE NEW

I had better warn you that this chapter is more in-depth than most—for good reason—so maybe you should grab a snack before you begin it.

There are some believers who ignore the Old Testament because they feel that, as we are now under the New Covenant the things of the old are useless. But what they forget is that Jesus came to fulfil the requirements of the Old Covenant. This means that the old can help us understand just what Jesus accomplished. Another vital aspect is that, although we moved into an age of grace rather than the letter of the law once Jesus came to fulfil the old, we can learn much about the principles of God by which he views things. In other words, we can get to know this awesome Lord in a deeper way. And God doesn't change.

When we go to church today, the building can range from a few sheets of iron on 4 posts in the Pacific islands to a rural wooden building holding about 40 people to a lavish cathedral with vaulted ceilings, some with paintings by old masters. But in the Old Testament, 'church' was vastly different. For one thing it wasn't called church at all but rather 'the temple'. And the first thing you'd probably have noticed when approaching it would have been the smell issuing forth. It may have smelled like someone's roast meal, perhaps burnt. Why? Because the priests were presenting burnt offerings of animals to the Lord. The temple was a place of slaughter and butchering and burning.

Quite different from our pleasant church services, wouldn't you say?

What's more, the priests' unique garments were splattered with the blood of these beasts. As a matter of fact, they were instructed by the Lord to have blood purposefully on their right thumbs and right big toes to identify them with the sacrifice of blood. The Bible informs us that there is no forgiveness of sin without the 'payment' of blood as death is the penalty for sin.

Of course, not all offerings were of animals. The people also brought offerings of grain they'd grown or bought and even a kind of cake in some cases, but these were not for the forgiveness of sin.

You may be horrified at the thought of what the temple was like but what did it say to the people? Surely it brought home to them the utter seriousness of sin, the fact that sin alienated them from their God and had to be paid for by the blood of bulls or goats so that they were reconciled to Him once more. I believe that it is partly the fact that we have been largely ignoring the Old Testament with its blood and gore that we have begun preaching such a tame gospel in our pristine churches. You see, sin still has to be paid for. We still need to be reconciled to God by the payment of the penalty for sin. And as I mentioned the penalty for sin is death. The Jews regularly brought animals to be slaughtered and offered to God to pay the penalty for their sin so it was before them at all times.

What is different for us is that a human being who was utterly without sin was willing to die in our place so that we could be reconciled to the Father God. Jesus Christ of course was that human being, actually the Son of God who came into the world as a man. Because he had no sin of his own he was able to die in our place and that is why we no longer need a temple with smoke rising to the sky. His sacrifice was once for all time. But we need to know and understand the absolute filthiness of our sin so that we turn our backs on it. We mustn't play with our sin, making allowances for it. We need to hate it because it is so serious that not only have countless animals had to die because of it but even the precious Son of God.

[I'd like to drop in an example in parenthesis here about seeing sin for what it is. Some years ago we had a dear lady in our congregation who hid the fact that she was a smoker. Now I am not saying it is impossible to reach heaven if you smoke but it is clear that it is not a good habit because of the known health risks and consequences. And as the Bible tells us that our bodies are 'temples of the Holy Spirit', we surely should do what we can to look after them. Well, to get back to our story... This lady, we'll call her Jenny, did all she could to cover any smoker's breath she may have had. A number of times she had tried to quit the habit but she later confessed that each time she did so she would carefully wrap the cigarettes she had in her possession in tissue before placing them in the bin in case she couldn't resist reaching for them again. She sometimes hid a couple of cigarettes here and there around the house for the same reason. Do you think she would have any success under those circumstances? Of course not.

My husband John, her pastor, knew of her habit because she had actually gone forward in a church service asking prayer to help her stop smoking. He visited her at home one day after she had blacked out in the hairdresser's chair because of damage to the carotid arteries in her neck. He knew he had to throw out a challenge to her in the circumstances so he asked her why she didn't just put a gun to her head and pull the trigger. Of course she was shocked at such a suggestion from her pastor. (We would never condone suicide.) But John said that by smoking she was killing herself, only slowly. This put a different complexion on the matter. When Jenny saw that this was exactly what she was doing, she began to hate the habit she had protected up until then. With that, she threw out all of her remaining cigarettes and never touched another one. Sometimes our continuing grovelling in a sin is because we've not recognized how ugly that thing is to God and how it is a shackle around our souls and spirits. From that time Jenny came out of her shell. Instead of the timid, tentative woman we had known she transformed into a radiant victor who enjoyed sharing her faith in Jesus with those she met. If you have what is often termed a 'besetting sin', one that recurs in your life, perhaps you simply need to see it as your enemy instead of loving it. Jenny admitted that she actually loved smoking and that is why she had so much trouble giving it up until its mask was ripped off and it appeared as the ugly thing it truly was.]

Now let's get this clear: I am not saying that we should live sinless lives. We are still in our frail human frames. But we should *seek to and intend to* avoid sin in our lives. We can celebrate Jesus' sacrifice for us, in fact he told us to remember it every time we have Communion—"Do this in remembrance of Me" he said. But while we enjoy our freedom, let us also remember that it came at the awful price of Jesus' suffering and death—and thankfully his resurrection which was the victory over death.

I should mention that God has said that the blood of bulls and goats could not *actually* pay for sin but God viewed the sacrifices as a kind of picture of what Jesus would eventually achieve, and so the old sacrifices were credited to the people as worthy. This is why the sacrifices had to be made on a regular basis. We can see that God stretches himself to provide for man's forgiveness in every way.

A surprising thing is the mercy of God flowing from

the Old Testament to the New. Time and again in the Old Testament the prophets were sent to succeeding generations to offer God's hand of mercy to them as well as to warn them of the consequences of not obeying God. God was not quick to anger but wanted to be reconciled with the people. This attitude of mercy is echoed by Jesus in Matthew 23:37 — 'O Jerusalem, Jerusalem, you who kill the prophets and stone those sent to you, how often I have longed to gather your children together, as a hen gathers her chicks under her wings, but you were not willing.' Don't those words pierce your heart?

I want to speak to you now of the Israelites' slavery in Egypt and their subsequent escape as in the book of the Exodus. I won't go into all the details as it also features in my chat on The Lord's Supper (Chapter 18), but I would like to draw your attention to several things:

At the beginning of the negotiations between Moses and Pharaoh (the Egyptian term for king), Pharaoh said that he didn't know the Hebrews' God. Yet even when he saw the demonstrations of God's reality and power, he kept hardening his heart against God and his people. Then, and this is a warning to all of us, after a time God hardened Pharaoh's heart for him so the full number of 10 plagues came upon the land. Why would he do this? The Bible says that God told Moses to give Pharaoh the following message before the plague of hail: "Let my people go so that they may worship me, or this time I will send the full force of my plagues against you and against your officials and your people, so that you may know that there is no-one like me in all the earth. For by now I could have stretched out my hand and struck you and your people with a plague that would have wiped you off the earth. But I have raised you up for this very purpose, that I might show you my power and that my name might be proclaimed in all the earth..."

It may seem harsh at first reading that God appointed them to be demonstrations of his power (against them). But we need to see that the ten plagues sent on the Egyptians were actually brought upon things which the Egyptians worshipped as gods. I believe that any Egyptian who had chosen to accept the Hebrews' God could have been saved from these plagues. As a matter of fact, the Egyptian officials who took notice of the Word of the Lord hurried to bring their slaves and livestock indoors before the hail struck so they avoided the loss. The Hebrews (Israelites) didn't suffer any harm at all during all this time. God is able to pick and choose, he is able to protect or attack as he knows is right and righteous. And he could see the big picture.

We see over and over again that God lets people act in ungodly ways until 'their cup is full'. It's as though God is counting sins, being merciful to evil people, giving them time to repent. (Check the book of Amos the prophet where the Lord's warning of coming disaster to various nations begins 'for three sins...even for four'. I think this is God's poetic way of saying 'for 7 sins' and 7 is the Lord's number of completion so it's a way of saying their cup was full.) So we see if repentance doesn't come, their cup (of sin) is full and their time has run out. Then judgment from God is forthcoming. And this was precisely the situation in Egypt. The Egyptians were worshipping many creatures and even the River Nile itself. They were holding God's people as slaves in a most unjust way and he hates injustice. God gave them the opportunity to recognize him for who he was—the Creator and ruler over all. When their cup was full, his judgment fell in such a way that the Egyptians should have been able to see that the things they had regarded as gods were no gods at all.

But there was more. Even though the freed Jews wandered in the wilderness for 40 years because of their own disobedience and lack of faith, when the younger generation of them finally reached the Promised Land, the inhabitants of the countries round about could have come against them in war. After all they were a horde of wanderers who had been travelling all those years. But the nations were fearful of them. Why? Because of what God had done for them in Egypt. In 40 years, the rumours of it had reached the ears of all the nations around about and they had no intention of trying to battle the God of the Hebrews. So God's protection of them was complete for all those years.

God accomplished at least 3 things: He brought due judgment on the Egyptians, he freed his people, and his reputation spread throughout the region so that some nations would rather help the Jews than oppose them. Let's also consider that God doesn't play favourites. When his own people disobeyed his expressed will they also suffered. Over the years they were carried off into exile more than once by godless nations. God had warned them that if they obeyed him they would have his blessings on their lives but if they disobeyed him they would experience his curses. As a matter of fact at one point the Jews assembled in a deep valley while a spokesman on the sharply rising mountain on one side of the valley read to them the blessings pronounced by God then a reader on a similar mountain on the other side read the curses to be expected. So God is fair. He gives warnings if people are prepared to hear them. That is mercy.

If you are thinking 'but that was under the Old Covenant', there are a couple of examples of judgment falling under the New Covenant as well. Just think of Ananias and Sapphira.

If you are not familiar with their story, found in Acts 5:1-11, it took place in the early days after Jesus' resurrection and ascension back into heaven. Many poor people were joining the fledgling church and because of the great love between believers those who had property were often selling it to give the proceeds to a fund for the aid of those who were underprivileged. Ananias, with his wife's full knowledge, sold some property and pretended to bring the full proceeds to the apostles. However, he had kept back some of the money secretly for himself and Sapphira. As the apostle Peter said to him, the property had been his to use as he wished. Even when it was sold the money was his to direct as he desired. But as Peter said: 'What made you think of doing such a thing? You have not lied to men but to God.' With that, Ananias fell down dead. When Sapphira came in later and was questioned about the amount received for the sale, she lied about it too. Peter asked her: 'How could you agree to test the Spirit of the Lord?' He informed her of her husband's death and at that, she too fell down dead.

If that happened in your church this week, how would you feel? Would you begin to see your God a little differently? Remember this was under the New Covenant, our current covering with God. Does it say that you need to reconsider the need for integrity and holiness in your life? Remember, although we are under the age of grace (one meaning for this word is unmerited favour, another is an anagram 'God's Riches At Christ's Expense'), God's principles haven't changed; God's standards haven't altered. He is the same God. And the Bible tells us many times that the fear of God is the beginning of wisdom. We can see as we look at this example of Ananias and Sapphira that they would have been much wiser in their dealings had they had a healthy fear of their Lord.

In relation to this I want to quote a rather lengthy passage from Acts 8, verses 9 to 24. I wish I didn't need to stretch this subject out like this as I try to keep each chapter short and snappy so that it is just a small taste which you can follow up yourself. But the sad lack of teaching in today's churches of anything which even smells like fear or negativity makes it needful for a little more depth from me. So please bear with me. It is of the utmost importance.

Acts 8:9-24: *"Now for some time a man named Simon had practised sorcery in the city and amazed all the people of Samaria. He boasted that he was someone great, and all the people, both high and low, gave him their attention and exclaimed, 'This man is the divine power known as the Great Power.' They followed him because he had amazed them for a long time with his magic. But when they believed Philip as he preached the good news of the kingdom of God and the name of Jesus Christ, they were baptised, both men and women. Simon himself believed and was baptised. And he followed Philip everywhere, astonished by the great signs and miracles he saw.*

"When the apostles in Jerusalem heard that Samaria had accepted the word of God, they sent Peter and John to them. When they arrived, they prayed for them that they might receive (the) Holy Spirit, because the Holy Spirit had not yet come upon any of them; they had simply been baptised into the name of the Lord Jesus. Then Peter and John placed their hands on them, and they received (the) Holy Spirit. When Simon saw that the Spirit was given at the laying on of the apostles' hands, he offered them money and said, 'Give me also this ability so that everyone on whom I lay my hands may receive (the) Holy Spirit.'

"Peter answered: 'May your money perish with you, because you thought you could buy the gift of God with money! You have no part or share in this ministry, because your heart is not right before God. Repent of this wickedness and pray to the Lord. Perhaps he will forgive you for having such a thought in your heart. For I see that you are full of bitterness and captive to sin.' Then Simon answered, 'Pray to the Lord for me so that nothing you have said may happen to me.'" [Where you see (the), it is not in the original language

of the New Testament. Therefore the text is referring to the *power* of Holy Spirit.]

You can see how seriously sin was treated in the early days of the New Testament church. How does that stack up against how you or your church views our attitudes today? Do you need to do something about that?

Another point in favour of the Old Testament is that Jesus quoted from the Psalms. The psalms hold quite a bit of prophecy and Jesus showed that his life was fulfilling those prophetic utterances made centuries earlier. And what about the second half of Isaiah 52 and the entire chapter 53? It's all about Jesus. The gospel (good news) of Jesus was threaded through the books of the Old Testament....

Here's just a taste of how we can see this even in the earliest ones: In the first book of the Bible, **Genesis**, meaning beginning or birth, what do we find? Let's check out chapter 3:15b. Here we have the scene in the Garden of Eden after our original parents have fallen for the devil's temptation. God says to the devil that the *offspring* of Adam and Eve (Jesus in the far distance) would crush the devil's head and the devil would strike the offspring's heel. I would see that referring to Satan's part in the suffering of Jesus but the great victory over the devil and his schemes by Jesus in his death and resurrection for the redemption of fallen mankind.

The 2nd book of the Bible, **Exodus**, brings us the story of the Jews in Egypt and the first Passover Meal, still celebrated by Jews today. The Passover was a rushed meal before the Jews fled Egypt and it was a remembrance thereafter every year of the fact that God caused the Angel of Death to *pass over* the homes of the Jews when on his mission of death to every firstborn of the Egyptians. He passed over each home that had the blood of the lamb sacrifice (a picture of the Lamb of God to be offered centuries later). This is a picture of what Jesus' blood has done for every believer who trusts in him for redemption and salvation. As a matter of fact, Jesus died at the hour the Jews of his time were slaughtering their lambs in preparation for the Passover Feast. God is in all the details.

Leviticus, the third book, tells of the laws which the Jews incorporated, at the Lord's instigation, into their everyday lives. As well as blood sacrifices there was a goat chosen each year to be the 'scapegoat'. The priests would lay their hands on the head of the scapegoat, thereby laying on him the sins of the people and then the goat was led outside the city into the wilderness. Jesus likewise had our sins laid upon his head and he too was led outside the city to be crucified.

Next we come to the book of **Numbers** and in chapter 21 we find the incident of snakes biting many of the Jews as they made their way through the wilderness on their way to the Promised Land. The snakes came as a consequence of their complaining about the conditions in the wilderness. God tells their leader, Moses, to nail the image of a serpent (representative of their sinfulness) to a pole which could be seen by all in the camp. If anyone was bitten they could look up at the nailed serpent and they would be healed. We don't even have to wonder if that was representative of Jesus because Jesus himself referred to this Scripture in John 3:14. "Just as Moses lifted up the snake in the desert, so the Son of Man (Jesus himself) must be lifted up, that everyone who believes in him may have eternal life."

For the fifth book, **Deuteronomy**, we think of the verses (chapter 21:23, 24) which say *'...anyone who is hung on a tree is under God's curse...' We look at the New Testament book of Galatians now to find in chapter 3:13 "Christ redeemed us from the curse of the law by becoming a curse for us, for it is written: 'Cursed is everyone who is hung on a tree.' He redeemed us in order that the blessing given to Abraham might come to the Gentiles through Christ Jesus,* *so that by faith we might receive the promise of the Spirit."* So there we find the divine intertwining of the old and the new. The promises from the old have come to fruition in the new. Without the New Covenant, the old is rather a sad litany of events and struggles without a completion, just an endless waiting. And without the old, the New Covenant loses much of its depth and wonder.

As a kind of illustration, let me share with you some of my thoughts. Having worked in the islands of Vanuatu in the South Pacific quite a number of times, I couldn't help but notice that the lifestyle of most of the indigenous people is quite primitive in comparison with ours here in Australia. But I did feel, to be honest, that our forefathers had lived in a pretty primitive state as well. And when John and I have looked back into our genealogy a few generations we find a lot of struggle and even illiteracy. Yes, only about 4 generations back in my Scottish family line, some of them signed certificates with an X. I was blown away.

Then, because I like to delve into matters, I began to challenge myself whether I would have any or many of the benefits of modern living if it had been left up to me. Even though I've used computers, etc. for years they still remain a complete mystery to me. My logic cannot conceive of an ever smaller gadget being able to do such a myriad actions with such speed and what's more, to hold all that data. It still seems like magic to me. So I'm afraid I have to admit that if it was up to me nobody would have a computer, even a basic one. So how are all these inventions developed? Well, I think the secret is in the last word of the last sentence— developed. They usually don't *just happen*, each man or woman *builds* on what was already known. Education plays a part in this, as does need. As they say, necessity is the mother of invention.

So what has this to do with our subject of the old and the

new? Just that, without a knowledge of the old we have no foundation to build onto. So I plead with you don't ignore the Old Covenant. It has much to teach us so that we can go on to understand what God has been doing over all the millennia since creation and how his plans, in the Creator's mind from the very beginning, have been able to be brought to fruition and we are the beneficiaries of those plans and outworkings right now in today's world.

"Because of the Lord's great love we are not consumed, for his compassions (mercies) never fail. They are new every morning; great is your faithfulness." Lamentations 3:22, 23. Aren't you glad there are fresh mercies awaiting you each morning?

38

DO YOU EVER FEEL ASHAMED?

I want to chat to you now about a very important subject which may affect you or someone you know—shame. I have previously dealt with having a working conscience and saying that we should feel guilty if we've done something wrong. That's part of being aware that we need to put wrongs right—for the sake of others and also for our own wellbeing.

Now I want to be specific about this one aspect of guilt: shame. The surprising thing is that people may feel ashamed for the guilt of others, not necessarily their own. *And* it can have a profound effect on those who have it. Sometimes they are not even aware that it is affecting them.

Many people have a less-than-perfect home life—this is obvious. It is possible to leave the situation behind us while still carrying the baggage from it. Perhaps the people who brought us shame have even died yet we may still be living with the effects.

I feel it is necessary to bring this to your attention because, for example, we have found in dealing with many females suffering from Anorexia that the seat of the problem is that they were aware of a family secret and felt deep shame about it. It may have been that they knew that their mother had an affair without their father finding out about it. It could have been that their beloved brother did something shameful. They hadn't been a part of the sin or crime but they were perhaps at a sensitive time of their life or of a sensitive nature and they actually took the shame upon themselves. While this lay deep in their subconscious they could never see themselves as acceptable or satisfactory. What a dreadful consequence of someone else's wrongdoing...

What we are saying is that people can actually develop what is classified as a kind of mental illness from something outside of themselves. *But* it can be remedied, praise the Lord.

Many children and adults these days suffer from abandonment or rejection. Men and women sometimes fall in love with someone other than their spouse and decide to leave their first family to move on with this someone new. For them, it may be possible to bury their shame at being unfaithful to those who are so close to them and so dependent on their love and resources in the flush of a new relationship. But can you imagine the devastation of those who have been abandoned? They suffer greatly from the feeling of rejection. Some children actually deduce that they must have been to blame for Mummy or Daddy leaving the home.

Perhaps you have suffered this very situation? You would then comprehend more than I do the great hole left in the heart. Nevertheless I have seen the effects on many people, young and old. For, unless the feelings of shame or rejection are dealt with they can dog the person for the rest of their days. They can make it difficult for them to form trusting relationships because they are afraid that they really are not worth loving lastingly, or that someone they care about won't be the faithful kind. What an awful dilemma. The problem is that there is the risk that they will therefore be hard to live with in a close loving relationship themselves, because they never feel really secure with their partner, no matter how reliable he/she is.

We've all met people who send out vibes of 'unworthiness'. Some of them can't even look you in the eye. Others act in bold fashion to try to cover up their deep self-doubt or even self-loathing.

I have heard it suggested that shame can even cause a person to suffer a bipolar condition, sinking into depression then struggling to rise above it, only to sink again—and so the pattern develops. John and I believe that this is one possible cause.

Whatever you think about that, it is highly important that we rid ourselves of shame, however it has come upon us—by our own wrongdoing or that of others. How to go about it?

You know that I've said that the answer to every question is to be found in God and in his Word, the Bible. Well, what does the Bible have to say about shame?

Let's take a look at Hebrews chapter 12 verse 2: "Let us fix our eyes on Jesus, the author and perfecter of our faith, who for the joy set before him endured the cross, *scorning its shame*, and sat down at the right hand of the throne of God." What was the shame of the cross? We could say it was the fact that it was a punishment for wrongdoing; it was a brutal, cruel punishment; it was done in public so that all could watch the suffering. But there was one other aspect. The 'criminals' on crosses were stripped of all their clothing. It was the ultimate shame. Do you recall reading how an enemy nation of the Jews generations before shamed them at one time by cutting off half their beards and baring their buttocks then sending them home in that defeated condition? What a way to humiliate people! Well, hanging on a public cross completely naked was much worse, not to mention the anguish and unutterable pain.

Nakedness was a shame to the Jews. We read in Genesis that after the flood Noah drank alcohol and was lying on his bed drunk and naked. One of his sons, Ham, laughed at the sight but when he told his brothers they walked backward toward their father with a blanket to cover him, rather than look on his nakedness. God pronounced a punishment on Ham for his attitude to nakedness which should give us a clue as to our attitude toward it today too. So in a nation which regarded nakedness as shameful, this was aimed at ensuring that the criminal suffered every kind of punishment.

Now let's turn to the Old Testament for that amazing, majestic prophecy by Isaiah telling of Jesus centuries before he arrived on earth, Isaiah chapter 53. Even if you are familiar with this passage, it bears reading again... so here it is from verse 2 to verse 11.

"He grew up before him like a tender shoot, and like a root out of dry ground.

He had no beauty or majesty to attract us to him, nothing in his appearance that we should desire him.

*He was despised and rejected by men, a man of **sorrows** and familiar with **suffering**.*

*Like one from whom men hide their faces he was despised, and **we esteemed him not.***

*"Surely he took up **our infirmities and carried our sorrows**, yet we considered him stricken by God, smitten by him, and afflicted.*

But he was pierced for our transgressions, he was crushed for our iniquities; the punishment that brought us peace was upon him, and by his wounds we are healed.

*We all, like sheep, have gone astray, each of us has turned to his own way; and **the Lord has laid on him the iniquity of us all**.*

"He was oppressed and afflicted, yet he did not open his mouth; he was led like a lamb to the slaughter, and as a sheep before her shearers is silent, so he did not open his mouth.

By oppression and judgment he was taken away. And who can speak of his descendants? For he was cut off from the land of the living; for the transgression of my people he was stricken.

DO YOU EVER FEEL ASHAMED?

He was assigned a grave with the wicked, and with the rich in his death, though he had done no violence, nor was any deceit in his mouth.

*Yet it was the Lord's will to crush him and cause him to suffer, and though **the Lord makes his life a guilt offering**, he will see his offspring and prolong his days, and the will of the Lord will prosper in his hand.*

*After the suffering of his soul, he will see the light of life and be satisfied; by his knowledge **my righteous servant will justify many, and he will bear their iniquities**."*

From that passage we see that he died so that our iniquities (sins), infirmities (sicknesses and diseases) and sorrows (that covers a multitude of problems) could be dealt with. He has carried them so that we don't have to. Isn't that liberating? Have you been liberated from sins, sicknesses and sorrows? Well all it takes is to accept the sacrifice made on your behalf and to allow the Lord to take over the direction of your life. You don't lose your own personality but you can lose all those things which foul up your life and your joy; those things which cripple you physically, mentally and spiritually.

[I will add here that there are times when the Lord has a reason for allowing an illness to remain with us. But he then will give us strength to bear it. This is illustrated in John chapter 9, the story of the healing of the blind man. Yes, this man was eventually healed but Jesus showed that his blindness was for the purpose of displaying the work of God in his life when he was healed. And his healing meant that many, many people including officials heard of the miracle. Some believed in Jesus because of it but those who had their own agenda refused even though the evidence stood before them. Another case is that the apostle Paul advised his young charge Timothy to 'take a little wine' for his stomach's sake. This was practical advice. He didn't say to pray for healing if he got a stomach bug from the untreated water of the time.

I am pointing these instances to you to keep a balance in what we anticipate from the Lord. The main thing is to seek the Lord's will in each situation we are faced with and to trust him for the right outcome.]

We should add a few words from the New Testament: Matthew 8:16 &17 "When evening came, many who were demon-possessed were brought to him, and he drove out the spirits with a word and healed all the sick. This was to fulfil what was spoken through the prophet Isaiah: 'He took up our infirmities and carried our diseases.'"

Why should shame not be included in those things which Jesus came to free us from? If God chose to make an atoning sacrifice via crucifixion which he knew included the shame of nakedness, surely he was taking victory over shame. Why should we be burdened by shame if Jesus has suffered for it already? If we have given our lives over to God to rule over us we need to cast all our cares on him as the Bible tells us to in 1Peter 5:7.

While I have been majoring on shame, everything I say about shame can also be applied to feelings of rejection and abandonment as mentioned above.

I urge you to think about your own situation, your background, your behaviour. Is there something lurking in your subconscious from anything which has occurred in the past (even the recent past); something which has become a ball and chain dragging you down to less than you were meant to be? Then talk it out with the Lord; repent if the sin was something you have done yourself; ask the Lord to take from you the burden of somebody else's sin and 'see' that sin nailed to the cross of Calvary so long ago, yet effective today for you.

The first step to freedom in any matter is firstly to recognize that it is a problem that we have; so a little soul searching may be necessary. You know I don't recommend continual introspection because this is just focussing on self. But every now and again we need to check up that we haven't become a prisoner because something has a degree of power over us. Actually, the Bible tells us that before we take Communion we should examine ourselves to make sure we haven't harboured any ill feeling, resentment, unforgiveness — so that would be a good time to check up on things like shame so that we can get that cleared up as well.

I think of this practice like cleaning a room of cobwebs. You know how sticky those pesky webs are, well that's similar to the emotions and attitudes which plague us if we let them. But we simply need to apply the sacrifice which Jesus made to whatever ails us to gain freedom. Then we can breathe freely and go on our way released. Why not?

39

THE LORD'S SUPPER OR COMMUNION

Communion is celebrated in different ways in various denominations. Even the frequency alters from group to group. In churches which my hubby John pastored we always celebrated Communion weekly. Now that John is no longer a pastor we attend a church which also has weekly Communion. I was asked to give the Communion address at Easter 2012 and the following is what the Lord gave me to say. I hope it is helpful to you:

Everyone relishes hearing and seeing vision of a rescue mission whether it's the rescue of a kidnapped journalist overseas, the helicoptering of a bushwalker who has fallen from a height or the saving of a swimmer swept out to sea.

But this very day we are celebrating a rescue mission of gigantic proportions. As is so often the case, this event was foreshadowed in the Old Testament. As most of you will know, the Jews—the children of Israel—are God's chosen people and in the Old Testament we read how God dealt personally with them. Because of a severe drought in their own land the Israelites moved to live in Egypt and were in favour with the Pharaoh.

However over the years, that Pharaoh died and was succeeded by others. The Israelites continued to grow in number until the Pharaoh of the time began to perceive them as a threat to him and his power. To combat this he made them slaves with slavedrivers over them. They were forced to make bricks for Pharaoh's building projects using straw provided by the slavedrivers. God wanted to free his people from slavery and sent Moses and Aaron to ask Pharaoh to let God's people go into the wilderness for 3 days to make sacrifices to Him.

Pharaoh again felt threatened by the fact that the Israelites were acting as one large group, wanting to worship a God who meant nothing to Pharaoh who had many other (false) gods. Instead of letting them go, he told the slavedrivers to make the burden even heavier for the Jews. No longer would they be provided with straw. They would have to scrounge that for themselves yet the quota of bricks would remain the same. What hardships this placed on the Jews.

God is never taken by surprise and it was part of His plan to make a show of the false gods of Egypt, and over a period of time, each time Moses and Aaron approached Pharaoh to make the same request, they were refused and God sent a plague of the very things that the Egyptians worshipped. This was a dual pronged venture by the Lord. (1) He was bringing judgment upon the Egyptians and (2) He was demonstrating that the things they worshipped were under His control, and not gods at all.

The tenth plague was that the death angel was to visit Egypt in the dead of night and soon every human and animal firstborn were found dead. But before that happened God had warned the Israelites of it and they were told how they were to ensure that they would not become a victim of the angel of death.

This is the origin of the name 'Passover', a feast which is kept by many Jews to this very year and at the same time as we celebrate Easter. The Jewish households were each to take a year old lamb from their flocks on the 10th day of the month of Nisan. As a matter of fact God instructed that this month was to become the first month of their years from then on. The lamb was to be without blemish of any kind.

They were to keep it separate until the 14th of Nisan when they were to slaughter it. They were to take its blood and put some on the sides and tops of the doorframes where they were to eat the lamb. The Lord said 'when I see the blood I will pass over you'. In other words it was the shed blood of a spotless lamb that saved them from judgment. That night they were to eat the roasted lamb in a certain way. They were to tuck their cloaks into their belts, they were to have their sandals on their feet and their staff in their hand. Bitter herbs and bread made without yeast were the accompaniments to the lamb for the meal. They were told to eat in haste. In other words they were ready to leave.

They made their escape but they didn't have to do it stealthily. As even Pharaoh's firstborn had died, he actually ordered them to go to worship the Lord. And the people of Egypt also urged them to go because they were afraid they would <u>all</u> die.

Not only did the Lord miraculously make a way through the sea for His people to cross over but when the Egyptian army followed them—as Pharaoh had had a change of heart—the waters were released in a rush and drowned Pharaoh and his forces, horses and all. God then proceeded to lead His people to the Promised Land where He would be their loving King.

It's a most unusual rescue mission isn't it? And yet it is a picture of the rescue which God later mounted for even more people, for the whole world. All people who have ever lived have found themselves slaves to self and sin. They have an enemy who seeks to lay ever heavier burdens on them. They are alienated from the very God who gave them life—by that sin. But because of His love He, at great cost to Himself, mounted a rescue mission for every single human being.

Sin makes us targets for judgment but God has other plans for us. He wants to free us of the tyrant who goads us. He has another kingdom for us to live freely in, here on earth, an unseen kingdom for the present. And the way to know judgment PASS OVER us is the same as for the Jews of thousands of years ago. It is when we choose the perfect Lamb of God, Jesus Himself, and accept His vicarious death—his shed blood—as the covering for our personal sins. Then, through the power of His Holy Spirit, we gain the means to fight off the powers arrayed against us and to dwell under the kingship of the One who loves us enough to suffer and die for us.

Today (Easter Sunday) we celebrate the resurrection of Jesus from the dead which showed that death was defeated on our behalf. Let us rejoice that we have been one of those rescued. What a glorious thing it is to live with Father God as our King. Now if you are one of those who have repented of your sins, have accepted Jesus as your Saviour you have the right to eat and drink of this very significant and holy food and drink which are symbols of the body and blood of the Lamb of God. If you have not yet accepted God's rescue mission for your life, please don't partake of the bread and juice but just pass them back when the cups are collected.

Let us thank God for the release this communion signifies....

That was my little talk and I will make mention that the reason I asked people who had not become Christians to refrain from taking part in Communion is that we are warned in the Bible that we are in danger of becoming weak and sick or even dying. Let's look at Paul's words to the Corinthian church in 1Corinthians 11: from verse 26 to 32.

"For whenever you eat this bread and drink this cup, you proclaim the Lord's death until he comes. Therefore, whoever eats the bread or drinks the cup of the Lord in an unworthy manner will be guilty of sinning against the body and blood of the Lord. A man ought to examine himself before he eats of the bread and drinks of the cup. For anyone who eats or drinks without recognising the body of the Lord eats and drinks judgment on himself. That is why many among you are weak and sick, and a number of you have fallen asleep (a common first century way of saying 'have died'). But if we judged ourselves, we would not come under judgment. When we are judged by the Lord, we are being disciplined so that we will not be condemned with the world."

Having touched on these serious matters, let me now say that to partake honourably of Communion is to answer a special invitation of Jesus himself. It was he who invited us to 'commune' with him by remembering his death and resurrection whenever we eat and drink. Just think about that: the Lord and Saviour of the world invites his humble followers to commune with him. He *wants* to spend time with us. He wants to *know* us. So let us not cheapen Communion in our hearts and minds because we have it frequently. Let us look upon it as a *feast*. In reality it is the most important food and drink we partake of ever because of what it signifies.

And let us look further about Jesus wanting to know us. On the final Judgment Day when it is decided who will join God in heaven and who will be banished, what does Jesus say to those who are not to find a place with him in heaven? He says "Depart from me, I never knew you." What horrific words, and they were said to people who were claiming to have done marvellous things in his name. So we need to make sure we *know* Jesus, not just *about* him. We need to spend time in his Word and speaking with him, listening for his promptings, obeying what is written in the Bible for all to understand. And sharing in the lovely meal of Communion is just a part of getting to know Jesus. Cherish it in your hearts.

40

HAVE YOU THOUGHT ABOUT RETIREMENT?

Now a word to those who like to plan for the future, or have already arrived at retirement age. Retirement for many people is a dream time when they don't have to rise early each day and go off to work for somebody else. They perhaps daydream of how they will fill all of those wonderful leisure hours; maybe fishing, playing bowls, dancing, sailing, walking along a sandy beach, surfing, skiing or cruising to some exotic place or maybe joining the army of grey nomads caravanning around the country. For some, just being able to put their feet up will be all they want. Yes, the body will enjoy the change.

But I want to draw your attention to another part of the anatomy. What about a retired brain? I have noticed a number of couples whose minds retire when they do. I don't want to be unkind, in fact I want to bestow kindness on all who will listen. I draw the attention to what happens to some folk when they retire so that you might become aware of the dangers of retirement and avoid them. We have noticed some grey heads who used to hold important and influential positions become so different once they bid farewell to their workmates. Of course this doesn't apply to everybody. In fact, many people actually become busier after retirement— travelling to family to help in cases of sickness, looking after grandchildren, taking on part time work, becoming a volunteer for any number of organisations…

But for some they take on a 'retirement mentality'. Whereas they used time well in the past, making the most of it with efficiency, now they appear as though they are just wasting time or filling time. Efficiency goes out of the window. They are almost just amusing themselves, doddering through tasks. Now, please don't get me wrong. As we age, sometimes we do become doddery, our legs aren't as strong as they used to be. That's another matter. What I'm on about is those who are still quite capable but almost take it as a duty to do things in a less than businesslike manner just because they are now age pensioners.

So why should I care about this? Well, I don't believe that there is a retirement plan in God's thinking unless we come to a place where we are no longer capable of even praying. And I'm not thinking only of God's point of view. I believe that we enjoy a much better quality of life while we are still productive in some way. But as usual the arena is the mind. What we think becomes true. And if we feel that we've reached the end of the line when we retire then we'll soon find that our locomotive will chug to a standstill. Come on folks, there's a fabulous life to be lived, especially now that you have all that time to use in pursuit of great achievements.

May I share with you a personal word the Lord gave me in November 2011? I was aged 71 at the time and my hair has been grey for many years. We were in England and early one morning John said to me 'it's the first day of December tomorrow'. I replied 'Oh, the first day of Winter—or Summer', thinking firstly of England then Australia. I immediately began to speak in tongues (a gift given to many people when they are baptised in Holy Spirit). When that finished, I said to John "I believe that God has just said 'Neither Winter nor Summer, but Spring. Look for the new and enjoy it'." What a thrill. At 71 I wasn't to simply wind down but to look forward to a new episode in my life. Actually I believe the 'new' is the writing of this book I've ventured upon, "Why didn't they Tell Me That When I was Young?" But what might it be for you?

Although this was a personal word for John and me, I believe it reflects what God wants for all of us as we age. We're not to surrender to uselessness. We need to check with the Lord just what his plan is for this season of our life. Now let's get this clear: I don't work all day the way I used to. I don't have the same level of energy. But I do what is appropriate for that level.

I think I'll share another personal anecdote with you because it throws light on this matter. Just last week we were having dinner at the home of some friends. As we sat round the table John and I were animatedly sharing some of the experiences we had had on a recent two-month trip in our motor home through 3 Southern States. We had been visiting quite a number of folk and John spoke at several meetings, we had prayer with lots of people and did some counselling and we were enthusiastic because it had been rather an exciting time. One of the people round the table was lovely 21-year-old Brielle and she looked at us and said 'you're really 41 aren't you?'. We laughed at that and went on sharing a number of things, then young Brie looked at me again saying 'you're really 21 aren't you'?

John and I had just come back home after spending several days at the Gold Coast visiting one of our daughters, Anita, after she had had a hip replacement after being involved in more than one accident through no fault of her own. We were preparing meals, etc. to take some pressure off the household. We returned home on Friday, had dinner as mentioned above on the Saturday night, then headed South again on Monday to catch up with John's sister, Leith, for her birthday. Then at 7.30am on Wednesday, the actual day of her birthday, I rang Leith to sing Happy Birthday to her and said that we were actually just driving out of our driveway to deliver more meals to Anita at the Gold Coast. She said 'you're young for your age, aren't you?' So there twice in 4 days someone had remarked about our youthfulness. Why? Because we don't allow ourselves to have 'retirement brain'. We often feel tired, we don't sleep particularly well, our joints aren't as well-oiled as they used to be, but so what? We're not dead, are we? So why act like it?

And for those who really are no longer capable of working in any way through age or illness or disability, you can still pray. And this is not one of those cases of 'well, at least I can pray', as though praying was right at the bottom of the list of worthwhile occupations. No, praying is one of the most important activities anyone of any age can pursue. As Andrew Murray said 'Jesus never taught his disciples how to preach, only how to pray....To know how to speak to God is more than knowing how to speak to man'. Another quotable quote is 'more things are wrought by prayer than this world dreams of'. Sorry I can't remember who said it. There are people all over the world who are suffering for their faith and their cry to carefree Christians is 'pray for us'.

[Today is Saturday, 29th November 2014, and I am doing a final revision of this book before having it printed. Just now, John came to me to tell me a news item he had just heard on TV. Firstly, on Tuesday of this week, John had asked our prayer group which meets each Tuesday morning at the church to pray specifically about the illicit drugs which are plaguing our young people. We prayed that the Lord would continue to expose drugs and drug dealers in our land. (John and I have prayed this way a number of times over the last few years and have rejoiced whenever we hear of a drug bust which has netted drugs and manufacturers and dealers.) Well, imagine our delight at this latest news – police have uncovered the biggest haul of Ecstasy drugs etc. – billions of dollars' worth – and we say Thank you Lord. May your Name be praised!]

So what is your retirement plan? No excuses, now!

We have some friends who run a ministry in Brisbane Australia called Second Wind. It is particularly for retired folk to help out other ministries. They visit churches recruiting retirees to perhaps travel to Asia to relieve a missionary couple so they can return home for furlough or to help out a missionary who has too much to do. What a great idea. Perhaps you had always longed to be a missionary but it wasn't your calling. Could it be that you are being called to it in the latter part of your life on a short term basis? A great Christian couple we know retired early at 55 and they have gone to different countries to help missionaries for 6 or 12 months a number of times. And we can tell you that they don't have retired brains.

You don't have to be young to be youthful. It's all in the mind and spirit. Let's look at some Scriptures to assure ourselves that God doesn't ignore us once we reach retirement age. Psalm 71:17 and 18 "Since my youth, O God, you have taught me, and to this day I declare your marvellous deeds. Even when I am old and gray, do not forsake me O God, till I declare your power to the next generation, your might to all who are to come."

Now there's a clue as to what we should be doing in old age—declaring the marvellous deeds of God to the next generations. Now another couple of verses, addressed to Israel, but still showing the kind of faithfulness we also can expect from our Lord. Isaiah 46: 3, 4. "Listen to me, O house of Jacob, all you who remain of the house of Israel, you whom I have upheld since you were conceived, and have carried since your birth. Even to your old age and gray hairs I am he, I am he who will sustain you. I have made you and

I will carry you; I will sustain you and I will rescue you."

Now keep reading to be truly encouraged. Psalm 92:12-15 "The righteous will flourish like a palm tree, they will grow like a cedar of Lebanon; planted in the house of the Lord, they will flourish in the courts of our God. *They will still bear fruit in old age, they will stay fresh and green,* proclaiming, 'The Lord is upright; he is my Rock, and there is no wickedness in him.'"

What do we see in that passage? Age is no barrier to being fruitful in our lives and the reason is that we have a Rock-like God who doesn't move but is always there to support us. Don't you feel encouraged? I certainly do.

We have had the privilege of knowing many people who have gone on working in the Lord's service into their 70's, 80's and even 90's. They have been a good example for us. John's father George ran a ministry to Jewish people. He travelled by train to his city office right up until the day before his death at 83. We recently lost a friend, Tom Jewett, who was in the process of handing his and wife Anne's ministry over to two couples they had been training when he drew his last breath at 86. Another friend at this present time is dying in her 90's but she has carried on the ministry begun with her late husband. Just in the last few weeks she was counselling and praying with a young woman we know.

So until your toes point upwards keep on looking upward and outward to live a life directed by the Lord and you will hear those wonderful words from the mouth of the Lord 'Well done, good and faithful servant'.

41

THERE SHOULD BE A DIFFERENCE

After John resigned as a pastor, John and I spent years distributing the Bible teaching of David Pawson throughout Australia. We had known of David for many years ever since John was given one of his old audio cassettes in Uganda, Africa of all places in 1971. John was there visiting his sister Ruth and her husband Jon who were medical missionaries. Their friend Don Lloyd, an eye specialist, worked in the area as well and had brought cassettes back from David Pawson's church in England. We were so impressed with the quality of teaching that John met up with the Aussie distributor of the time Peter Bettson who became a dear friend of ours. We helped Peter to computerise his work of distribution in the early days. Peter became an elder in our church and David Pawson was invited to visit Australia and during that trip one of the places he taught was right in our church in Cannon Hill, Brisbane.

Over the years John and Peter communicated with David P. and at one time they travelled to Singapore to follow-up with those who had responded to the teaching. They also worked with David when he toured Australia several times. Thus our friendship with David grew and we respected his teaching all the more the better we got to know him. He is a man of great integrity, fears God rather than man and will not compromise on what the Bible says. As a matter of fact when he is approaching a portion of the Bible to prepare a message he says to the Lord 'Lord, what are you saying here? I will teach it even if I don't like it.' Now that's one for the books isn't it? So many preachers today appear to be trying to be popular with man, trying to make people feel *'comfortable'*. David likes people but God comes first, as it should be.

If you would like to sample some of David Pawson's teaching it is now freely downloadable on www.davidpawson. org or from YouTube.

I want to share with you a true story regarding one of David's most important messages, The Normal Christian Birth. (David laughs about the fact that it has been classified under 'Gynaecology' in one big library but it actually has nothing to do with physical birth—rather spiritual new birth.) About 12 years ago a Romanian man in Victoria accepted Jesus as his Saviour. A lady from his church gave him a set of The Normal Christian Birth videos to help him in his Christian walk. One day he wasn't well enough to go to work so he settled down to watch the video. He was so engaged by the teaching that he continued to watch the entire 4 hours of it.

At the end of the time he went to his tool box and took out any tool which had been 'borrowed' and set it aside to return it to its rightful owner. He went to his computer and deleted any program which he had unlawfully downloaded. He later told us 'I didn't know what it meant to be a Christian' (until he heard truthful teaching). In the intervening years, with our permission, he has spent thousands of hours subtitling David's 'Unlocking the New Testament' DVDs in his native tongue so that they can be a blessing in his homeland.

When we become a Christian there should be a difference in our thinking and our behaviour. If there is none, I would question whether there has been a true born-again experience.

THERE SHOULD BE A DIFFERENCE

Just look at the case of Zacchaeus as reported in the Gospel of Luke chapter 19. Zacchaeus was one of the hated tax collectors. Tax collectors were usually recruited by the ruling Romans from among the Jewish community in Israel. Their pay was the amount they could extract from their own people above the amount of actual tax due. You can imagine the corruption among them: the more they demanded from the citizens the more in their pockets.

Jesus found Zacchaeus up a tree which he'd climbed to have a good look at this speaker who was drawing a good crowd. Jesus looked up into the tree and told Zacchaeus that he was coming to his house. The onlookers were amazed that Jesus wanted to be a guest at a 'sinner's house'. But look what happened in that home. Luke 19:8-10 "Zacchaeus stood up and said to the Lord, 'Look, Lord! Here and now I give half of my possessions to the poor, and if I have cheated anybody out of anything, I will pay back four times the amount.' Jesus said to him, 'Today, salvation has come to this house, because this man too is a son of Abraham. For the Son of Man (Jesus) came to seek and to save what was lost.'"

Do you see the change that salvation brought to Zacchaeus? Before he cheated, now he wanted to give to the poor and to restore what had been wrongfully gained plus more.

Have you become a Christian? Has it changed your thinking and your behaviour? If not, why not? Have you not been given good teaching? Have you not been reading the Word?

Take a look at Matthew chapter 3. Here are relevant words from verses 7 to 10: This section deals with the time the 'religious' Pharisees and Sadducees came to John the Baptist to be baptised in readiness for Jesus' ministry. These religious men were good at doing ritualistic practices but their hearts were far from the ways of God. "But when he

(John the Baptist) saw many of the Pharisees and Sadducees coming to where he was baptising, he said to them: 'You brood of vipers! Who warned you to flee from the coming wrath? ***Produce fruit in keeping with repentance***....The axe is already at the root of the trees, and every tree that does not produce good fruit will be cut down and thrown into the fire."

Repentance is one subject which is seldom taught. To repent of something is more than feeling sorrow. It means that you are sorry enough to stop doing it. And just stopping doing wrong is only half of the story. We then need to fill the void with the good works which God has planned for our lives.

Colossians chapter 3 is a good place to look for guidance on what to take out of your life and also what to put in. Here are a few snatches from it: "***Set your hearts on things above***, where Christ is seated at the right hand of God. Set your minds on things above, not on earthly things. For you died, and your life is now hidden with Christ in God."

"**Put to death**, therefore, whatever belongs to your earthly nature: *sexual immorality, impurity, lust, evil desires and greed, which is idolatry*. Because of these the wrath (great anger) of God is coming. You used to walk in these ways, in the life you once lived. But now you must rid yourselves of all such things as these*: anger, rage, malice, slander, and filthy language from your lips. Do not lie to each other*, since you have **taken off** your old self with its practices and have **put on** the new self, which is being renewed in knowledge in the image of its Creator....

"Therefore, as God's chosen people, holy and dearly loved, *clothe yourselves* with *compassion, kindness, humility, gentleness and patience. Bear with each other and forgive whatever grievances you may have against one another*. Forgive as the Lord forgives you. And over all these virtues *put on love*, which binds them all together in perfect unity.

"Let the *peace of Christ rule in your hearts*, since as members of one body you were called to peace. And *be thankful*. Let the word of Christ dwell in you richly as you teach and admonish one another with all wisdom. And as you sing psalms, hymns and spiritual songs with gratitude in your hearts to God. And whatever you do, whether in word or deed, do it all in the name of the Lord Jesus, giving thanks to God the Father through him."

Now there is a lifetime of attitudes, some to *put off* and others to *grow into*. It was rather a lot of Scripture to quote but I make no apology for it because it gives us an overview of what we need to be aiming for in our lives. It's not all froth and bubble. It's not just a 'bless me' club. It's about growing to be more and more like our heavenly Father. And that is the only way we will bring true change to our world. We will never change the world if we live like the world. We need to live lives which recommend Jesus Christ *to* the world.

I think that's given all of us quite a bit to think about, hasn't it? And I'm not just speaking to you. I need to remind myself every so often of all the words above.

"Give and it will be given to you. A good measure, pressed down, shaken together and running over, will be poured into your lap. For with the measure you use, it will be measured to you" Luke 6:38

"Freely you have received, freely give." Matthew 10:8

42

MORE EVIDENCE OF THE BIBLE'S ACCURACY – THE FLOOD

Now here is a treat for those of you who really care about reality, who like to think, and who like to have a responsible answer for those who think that the Bible is a bunch of fables. The following is the work of two men decades apart. The late Dr. Joseph J. Shelley was a good friend of my father-in-law, George Spall and I met him many years ago. Doc Shelley spent years working as an eye specialist in the Middle East where he investigated various sites which helped him formulate just how the worldwide flood reported in Genesis in the Bible really happened. In 1968 he gave a lecture on the subject to staff at a Brisbane hospital. And John and I have an old leaflet of Doc Shelley's essay on the subject. However, in 2012 Paul Camac, a gifted teacher of Bible subjects living in Nambour in the Queensland Sunshine Coast Hinterland was working on his Ph.D. and chose to build on Dr. Shelley's studies. He not only updated Shelley's facts but researched the subject, thus giving a considerably fuller account than that contained in our leaflet. Paul has kindly given me permission to print his account of the flood here for which I am very grateful for your sake. But he emphasized that we should mention that he had built on Dr. Shelley's work.

In the first Section of this book I presented Exhibits A and B of Evidence of the Bible's Authenticity. Here is Exhibit C. Enjoy...

MORE EVIDENCE OF THE BIBLE'S ACCURACY – THE FLOOD

Was Noah's Flood Worldwide?

What scientific evidence exists for Noah's Ark and the great Flood? Was it world-wide?

Its importance

This is of contemporary importance, because the Lord Jesus said, "As it was in the days of Noah, so shall it be in the days of " The Son of Man". To this is linked the trustworthiness of Jesus Christ. He treats this story as a concrete fact. If it is a myth, He is wrong about the past. If He is wrong about the past, He is wrong about the future, because its much easier to talk about the past than it is to foretell the future. If He is wrong about the future, He is wrong about His Second Coming; His coming is then a mythical coming, if this is a mythical Flood. He even becomes a mythical Christ. However, if there is good concrete evidence of the Flood, there is also good concrete evidence of the reality and the reliability of the return of Christ.

A disaster, which blotted out every human on the earth, every living creature and the land animals that breathed, that tore the earth to pieces, because God said He was going to destroy the earth, is nothing to laugh about. If this story is demonstrated, then the other accounts that follow this in the Bible are demonstrated to be true, because these depend on the Flood. The Tower of Babel, the Dispersion of the Nations and the locality of the nations depend on the Flood.

1. Textual evidence – Hebrew and Greek Scripture.
Luke 17:26-27
As it was in the days of Noah so shall it be in the days of the Son of Man. They did eat, they drank, they married wives; they were given in marriage, until the day that they entered into the ark, and the Flood came and destroyed them all. (2,348, BC.; anno mundi = after creation)

Genesis 7:11 In the six hundredth year of Noah's life, in the second month, in the seventeenth day of the month, the same day were all the fountains of the great deep broken up and the windows of heaven were opened and the rain fell upon the earth forty days and forty nights. In the self-same day entered Noah, Shem and Ham and Japheth, the sons of Noah, and Noah's wife and the three wives of his sons with him into the ark. They and every beast after his kind and all the cattle after their kind, and every creeping thing that creeps upon the earth after his kind, and every fowl after his kind, and every bird of every wing, and they went in unto Noah, into the ark two and two of all flesh, wherein is the breath of life. And they went in went in male and female of all flesh, as God had commanded them and the Lord shut him in. And the flood was forty days upon the earth and the waters increased and bear up the ark and it was lift up above the earth and the waters prevailed and they were increased greatly upon the earth and the ark went upon the face of the waters. And the waters prevailed exceedingly upon the earth, and all the high hills that were under the whole heaven were covered, fifteen cubits upward did the waters prevail. And the mountains were covered and all flesh died that moved upon the earth; of all fowl and of cattle and of beasts and of every creeping thing that creeps upon the face of the earth and every man in whose nostrils was the breath of life, of all that was in the dry land, died. And every standing thing was wiped out which was upon the face of the earth, both man and cattle and the creeping things and the fowl of the heaven; and they were wiped out from the face of the Earth; and Noah only remained alive, and they that were with him in the ark.

(1,656 AM; anno mundi – from the Genesis year of creation)

CAPACITY AND EVIDENCE OF CATASTROPHE

"Is there enough water?" The average depth of the sea is 12,000 feet, (3,657 m) and the average height of the land is only 2,500 feet (762m) above sea level, so that there is $15\frac{1}{2}$ times as much water below sea level as there is land above it; and as twice as much water in area - 139,440,000 miles^2, as there is land – 57,510,000 miles.^{2}

"Could it be distributed on the earths surface?" Halley's theory poses a cometary body passing close to the earth, which would pull the Earth off its axis to the position that it now holds, $23\frac{1}{2}°$ to the ecliptic. Halley postulated it would generate a tsunamic wave at a speed of 1,000 miles an hour (1,609 kph) at the equator and seven miles (11.265 km) high. In comparison, the 20th Century's largest earthquake (1960 Chile) was a 9.5 earthquake which generated a seismic wave 80 feet high (25m) which travelled across the Pacific Ocean at the rate of 530 miles an hour (852 kph). 15 hours later in the Hawaiian Islands – 6,200 miles (10,000 km) away, it crested at nearly 35 feet (11 metres) at landfall. On the Japanese island of Honshu 22 hours after, the waves had subsided to about 18 feet (5.5 metres). Nobody noticed it in the Pacific, because it rose gently so that the ships didn't notice it. The 2011 Chile 7.5 quake wave was 750 kph.

Tectonic flexibility and Lunar tides. Not only does the moon produce the tide in the oceans, but it also pulls on the substance of the earth too. The specific gravity of the earth is only six times more than that of the water. It raise a tide unnoticed by us, in the earth's crust as well as in the sea of about six or nine inches (150 to 230 mm).

Mountain height and wave height. Could a tidal wave cover the Tian-shan Mountains? (Himalayas). In proportion to the Earth's size, these are very low -- 5 miles high (Mount Everest is 29,029 feet (8,848m); the diameter of the earth is 7,900 miles (12,700km) and at the Equator the earth's circumference is 24,901.55 miles (40,075.16 km). English Scientist Charles Babage says that "the highest ranges of mountains we have, relative to the circumference of the earths crust are infinitely smaller than the puckers on an orange skin". The Earth appears perfectly smooth from space. Even the highest mountain (Mt. Everest) is so small compared to the entire size of the Earth that the bump would not be seen from space. In this diagram the bump representing Mt Everest is actually three times too high!

MORE EVIDENCE OF THE BIBLE'S ACCURACY – THE FLOOD

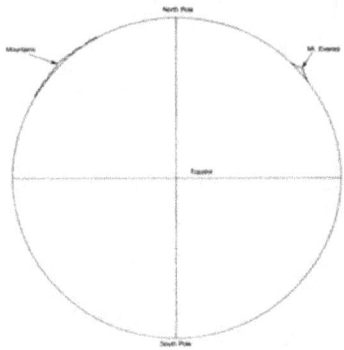

It would take the very smallest tilt in the ocean to send it across those mountains. Does the Earth's axis wobble?" it's called the "Precession of the Equinox" – the weekend's motor traffic which leaves New York city or a great flood on the Mississippi wobbles the pole.

Snap frozen tundra in the Arctic Circle.
Only air compression, and snap cooling explains why the Ice Age followed the Flood. The wave would compress the air in front of it, and rarify the air behind it – the principle of the refrigerator. As each wave tore around the earth, that rapid expansion of cold air and its vortex would allow the intrusion of the cold of outer space (minus 454.8 degrees Fahrenheit (-270 degrees Celsius) at the poles and caused the Ice Ages. That cold would come down in 24 hours all around the North and South Pole. Is there any evidence of that?

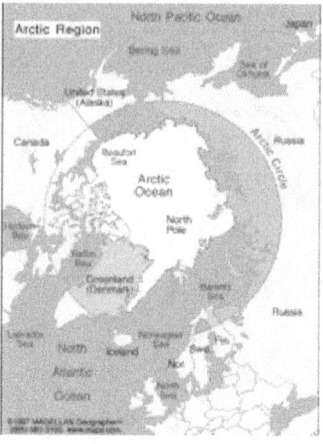

The Siberian *tundra* is frozen solid soil 900 feet deep, (275m) all the year round excepting in the short summer about three or four feet (1m) is unfrozen. In that soil, are the bodies – complete bodies of thousands of mammoths – every possible animal – lions, tigers, camels, oxen, birds, sheep, everything. When the Lena, the Ob and the Yenisei Rivers, which arise in the hot centre of Asia, pass over those frozen plains they sometimes move their course, and unfreeze some of that soil and some mammoths.

South Kensington Museum – Dr. Young – Mammoth Hunting – "as he was coming down the Yenisey River, a piece of the bank broke away and out of it there emerged a huge mammoth – it floated down the river towards them - it's trunk was bobbing up and down and its eyes were open. The natives took flight – they thought it was alive. Of course, it wasn't and they very soon found it wasn't alive because of the smell. Being in cold storage for some 4½ to 5,000 years, when they are unfrozen they go rotten vey quickly, but not so quickly that the dogs and wolves always eat their flesh and on a number of occasions, explorers have saved their lives by eating mammoth flesh. This particular mammoth they towed to the shore and in spite of its odour, they did a post-mortem which showed it had been drowned, buried and frozen so quickly, the food was still in its mouth. In the stomach its green food was undigested – pine, box, hawthorn and fir – because the mammoth does not eat grass – it eats trees. The lungs and blood quality showed it had been suffocated – drowned – the water in its lungs was saltwater."

"One of the chief industries of Siberia is the export of mammoth ivory to the Chinese of the tusks washed up on the shore – on average of 100 pairs of tusks per year for 2,000 years".

The Lena or Yenisei rivers sometimes cut into the riverbanks composed of the bones of hundreds and thousands of animals – lions, tigers, deer, elk, bison, camels – and bone glue is dropping down from the side of it. You can have a mammoth steak for breakfast in Alaska – they mine with hot water. The trawlers called the North Sea "The Boneyard", because with their fish they pulled up so many bones of lions and tigers and mammoths and things out of the sea with the trawlers.

There was a mild uniform climate from Pole to Pole before this disaster. Consider 900 feet deep (275m) of frozen soil – you couldn't hammer the bodies into pre-frozen soil. Therefore, those animals were drowned, and buried while the silt was soft – and frozen in within 24 hours because they are absolutely fresh - never unfrozen. There is every conceivable sort of frozen animal - the more north, the more there are – animals bones, and trees in soil. There is no other explanation but a universal flood. Why? Because nothing buries, nothing kills every conceivable sort of animal including birds, but water. No form of disease attacks more than one species of animal and doesn't bury them.

There is nothing preposterous about the possibility of the water of the seas plus the rain, causing a universal Flood. Courier newspaper: "the sea was Noah's chief enemy".

Forty days and forty nights rain. Where did that water come from? About 20 miles up (30klm) in the upper stratosphere, the temperature of the air begins to rise, to about 175^0 Fahrenheit (80^0 Celsius) - nearly boiling point – higher up, it begins to go down in temperature. In this belt of heated air, all water vapour is steam, not only by the heat but also by the lower pressure. So surrounding the Earth is a vast ocean of superheated steam that cuts off most cosmic rays. Let down, this water canopy could rain for forty days and forty nights.

Preservation of the ark. The rain had another purpose - the ark was constructed near the Euphrates River. Had that tsunamic wave been first before the waters rose, it would have torn the ark to bits. The forty days and forty nights floated the ark – "the ark went on the water" – and made this plain into a lake and gave hundreds of miles (hundreds of klm) of what they call "sea room" before that great wave started, no doubt preserving the ark.

Its dimensions of 30 cubits high, 50 cubits wide, 300 cubits long, at 18 inches to the cubit (45 x 75 x 450 feet; 1m x 23m x 137m) made it the most stable of ship designs and it

MORE EVIDENCE OF THE BIBLE'S ACCURACY – THE FLOOD

would self right at $30°$, $60°$ or even $90°$ under wave impact.[1]

Evidence for a world wide flood in the three classes of Creation: man, animals and the earth.

1 Man Every race has a tradition of a universal Flood. The literary nations are closer to the Bible account. The Chinese – Noah's name – Fo-Hi, his three sons, his wife and his three son's wives built an ark and they alone were preserved. He taught the nations all the science that they now have. The Chinese character for "ship" is eight persons in an ark.

One species Anthropologists agree the present human race is from one species and one species is one family and one family is one pair. Watt Tyler – British Encyclopedia, 1926 – "Anthropology – monyginists – claim mankind is descended from a single stock and generally from a single pair. The other school – polyginists – contended for several primary races being separate species of independent origin. Modern views have tended to restore the doctrine of a single human stock. On the whole, it may be asserted that the doctrine of the unity of mankind stands on a firmer basis that of former ages."

Science Newsletter 1934 – this is Hurdliger, from the Smithsonian Institute in an address to the Anthropological Society of Washington shows that living men are all of one species. You say that does not prove the Flood. No, but supposing science had said that the present human race was not all of one species, wouldn't that have been stressed by opponents of the Flood?

The best division of our race is in the Semitic, Japhetic and Hamitic people – Shem, Ham and Japheth. The history of the nations: (Gen 11) "Javan the son of Japheth, the son of Noah, had four sons and by them were the nations of the

---

[1] John W. Montgomery, *The Quest for Noah's Ark* (Minneapolis: Bethany Books. 1972). p. 48 The Stability of the Ark

islands populated after the Flood. *Yay-wan* – Javan, the son of Japheth, the son of Noah – his name is in the Yahwonian (Ionian) Islands to this day. There is no "J" in Greek and there is no " V" – the Ionian Islands – the Jahvonian islands. He had four sons – Elishar, Rhodanim, Chittim and Tarshish. Elishar (Alasia on the Cicilian Coast) is the ancestor of the Hellenic Greeks. Rhodanim is Rhodes; Chitttim is Cyprus, Tarshish is Tarsus on the mainland.

Population: unless the human race had been decimated a few millennia ago, we should now be standing room only in this world.

2 Animal fossils worldwide If other animals besides mammoths were drowned they would have been torn to pieces in this great rolling flood. You wouldn't expect to find them in tropical countries with their flesh still firm, but you would expect to find their bones. You would and you do. Dr Brune - South African fossilologist, an evolutionist – Illustrated London News,[2] 1947 – Kairu fossil formation near Johannesburg is about 200,000 square miles, (322,000 klm^2). On the surface, or just under the surface – just being under the surface shows that they were simultaneously buried – are the complete skeletons of 800,000 million individuals, mostly amphibians and reptiles. Perhaps the Doctor is wrong – 400,000 million. Perhaps he's wrong again – 100,000 million. What but a universal flood killed and buried them simultaneously?

Animal cemeteries are found in every portion of the world. Scientific American article on Crustal Shift Theory - in America are the fossil bones of four million animals in one

---

[2] ***The Illustrated London News*** was the world's first illustrated weekly newspaper; the first issue appeared on Saturday, 14 May, 1842 and it was published weekly until 1971 when it became a monthly, and then bimonthly from 1989 until 1994. From 1994 until production ceased in 2003, it was published just twice a year.

particular deposit. On every continent are these vast deposits, simultaneously buried all over the world. Nothing buries animals but water. Ice does not bury animals. Glaciers travel at a few feet (metres) per year. The animal would be a very peculiar one who stayed long enough to be overwhelmed and buried by a glacier!

In Cyprus near the top of Buffevento – it's above Nicosia, about 3,000 feet (4,800 m) above sea level. At about 2,000 feet (600m) is a huge deposit of pygmy hippopotamus bones – a riverine animal. What lifted and crushed and mixed with seashells a huge herd of pigmy hippopotami? When Shelley descended from Buffavento, with specimens, saying these things were buried up there by the Flood, a skeptic said, "Prehistoric man took them up there and buried them up there". Pre-historic man had a great many more things to do than to take a vast herd of pygmy hippopotamus up there and bury them. Some dinosaurs were 89 feet long (30 m) and weigh 38 tons (24 tonnes).

In Malta are caves crammed full of bones – giant swans – twice as large as now – with hares, lemurs, tigers, rhinoceros, elephant, every conceivable animal, and birds; bats and tailless hares and horses, lions. Some people say that it wasn't a universal flood. Malta is an island – 170 miles from Sicily – these birds are sea birds - had it been a local flood these giant swans would have taken off for Sicily and been there in half an hour. Seabirds would have never been thought of being drowned – they're seabirds. In New Zealand are vast deposits of moa birds, and amongst these birds which are flightless, are huge geese, half as big again as present living geese – before the Flood all animals were giants in size – the wombats the size of a horse, sheep the size of an ox. The infidel explanation is these birds were bogged and that it was a local flood. Sir Henry Howarth points out that geese don't get bogged. As for those in Malta, he points out birds don't fall out off the sky and fracture their skulls. They flew and flew and flew until they could fly no longer and they died.

If this was a local flood the construction of an ark to preserve the animals was positively foolish. Noah only needed to migrate 200 miles (320 klm) until he was on the top of a huge mountain that no local flood could ever have covered, and he had a hundred years to do it in. If it was a local flood, it's ridiculous to include all birds in the ark. The arctic tern migrates from North Pole to South Pole in the summer – 12,000 miles (20,000 klm) – and back. The hummingbird is the smallest of birds and yet migrates over 800 miles (1,300 klm) of featureless ocean to the West Indies to breed every year. A local flood won't do it. This is why every bird of every wing was taken into the ark. Christians who say they believe in a local flood haven't considered the subject.

Dinosaur fossils are found all over the world, including Queensland and Mongolia. Along the Colorado River they are in their thousands – drowned and buried – big ones, little ones, every age and kin. Fairfield-Osborne, a rank evolutionist says, "The sudden and simultaneous destruction all over the world, of this vast dinosaur dynasty is one of the most inexplicable things which science has to face". Not all - it's the easiest thing in the world – if you accept the evidence that they were overwhelmed by a universal flood and buried.

The dinosaur was on the earth the same time as man even though scientists say that dinosaurs disappeared 70 million years before man appeared. In 1939 they said, "The coelacanth fish disappeared 250 million years before man appeared on the earth." In the same year in the Illustrated London news there appeared a photograph of one – and he was not an orphan. The dinosaur was on earth at the same

MORE EVIDENCE OF THE BIBLE'S ACCURACY – THE FLOOD

time as man. In the painted canyon of Arizona is a coloured drawing on the rock of a dinosaur. In another cave there's a beautiful model of an armoured dinosaur. Prehistoric man was a marvelous modeler as well as a painter. These models, this painting, were done by who – a monkey? No – intelligent man and artistic man. In America and other parts of the world – and in Queensland – you can see within certain strata the strides of a dinosaur. You can tell how big he is by the length of his stride. In one place in America are not only the footprints of this large dinosaur, but also the footprints of a family of bipeds who walked on feet just like ours. What bipeds were on the earth according to these footprints? Monkeys are not bipeds. The only biped in the world with feet like that is man.

3 The Earth – there ought to be in the strata of the earth not only fossils but other signs, if a sea flood tore around the earth. There ought to be in the central parts of the continents, large deposits of seawater left behind by the Flood. Fresh water can be defined as water with less than 500 parts per million (ppm) of dissolved salts.

Water salinity based on dissolved salts			
Fresh water	Brackish water	Saline water	Brine
< 0.05%	0.05% – 3%	3% – 5%	> 5%

We will take Asia. Here for example you see the Caspian Sea.

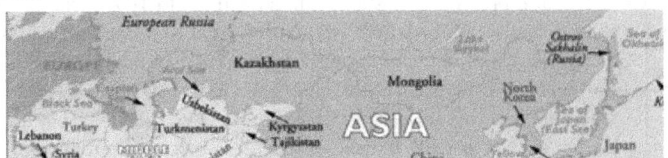

The Don River pours fresh water into this sea from the Hindu Kush Mountains. The Caspian Sea is salt and the fish in it are the same as the oceans – sturgeon, mackerel, seals. Where did the salt water come from? There is no salt in the rocks around it – none at all.

The Sea of Aral is 400 miles (650 klm) away from the Caspian Sea. A few hundred years ago before Christ, the Caspian Sea and the Sea of Aral was united – the Sarmatian Ocean in the centre of Asia. However, it's drying up so quickly, the two seas in 1968 were 400 miles (650 klm) apart.[3] It must have been filled up from the great basin of the seas only a few thousand years ago or they would be dry now.

Aral is salt. So is Lake Balkash in Kazahkstan – the western part is fresh water, the eastern half is saline; salt again. Lake Baykal – not salt. Why not? Lake Bakal is one of those lakes where the water runs in and runs out. Its river goes to the Arctic Ocean and the sea salt has washed out. But in that lake, there are seals exactly the same as in the Pacific only a few hundred miles away.

Ask why the lakes in the centre of the United States aren't salt? Why? – because they broke away over the Niagara Falls and washed the salt out through the Saint Lawrence River. One salt lake in America has never washed out - Lake Utah. In Bolivia – on the west coast – the Bolivian Highlands are 12,500 feet (3,810 m) above sea level. On this Altiplano, 50

---

[3] Formerly one of the four largest lakes in the world with an area of 68,000 square kilometres (26,300 sq mi), the Aral Sea has been steadily shrinking since the 1960s after the rivers that fed it were diverted by Soviet irrigation projects. By 2007, it had declined to 10% of its original size, splitting into four lakes – the **North Aral Sea**, the eastern and western basins of the once far larger **South Aral Sea** and one smaller lake between North and South Aral Seas. The amount of water it had lost is the equivalent of completely draining Lake Erie and Lake Ontario. Over the same time period, its salinity increased from about 10 g/L to about 45 g/L.

miles long by 200 miles broad, (80 klm by 320 klm) there are lakes. These are all salt.

Lake Titicaca is salt, with the same fish as the oceans – e.g. seahorses. Running into these lakes, from the Andes Mountains is nothing but fresh water and there are no saline rocks around. Yet, all around those bitterly saline lakes are salt deserts. It must have been only a few thousand years ago that these were filled up from the main ocean. Only a few thousand years ago, this was the Great Inter-Andean Ocean, 450 miles long by 120 miles broad, (725 klm by 200 klm). All that remains of it are a few saltwater lakes like Titicaca. If we assume the mountains then were as high as now, the tsunamis reached up 12,500 feet (3,810 m) and filled them up.

Consider oil. The bodies of man and the bodies of animals are all built from the same plan in the chemistry of the body. What is called mineral oil is not mineral at all but the same composition as organic vegetable and animal tissue. All oil comes from the bodies of fish, which were thrown on the earth and covered quickly by silt.[4] They turned into oil by pressure – sometimes the oil is 12,000 feet (3,650m) below the earth – and the action of a marine bacillus *di-sulpho vibrio* – a bacillus which very quickly turns them into oil - if they hadn't been covered they would have been oxidized, decomposed and gone up into smell.

Geologists will never bore where there are no marine fossils. The great bugbear of all oil drillers is water and that water is always salt. They pump up shark's teeth and fish scales from most of the deposits all over the world.

Was there enough fish? In 1991 the biomass of the world's fish was estimated at 1,000 million tons.[5] What would it have been in a pristine pre-flood world? There is a shoal of bluefish which passes up the gulf stream past New York every year. There are about a 1,000 million in this shoal – a small shoal compared to herrings – each eats ten large fish every day – so to feed that one shoal of fish takes 10,000 million fish every day.

Coal. Text books once taught Lyle's uniformitarian theory, that coal was formed by tropical swamps which once probably covered the earth – one fern leaf fell and another fern leaf fell – in the end they built up vast seams of coal one above the other. Then that lake disappeared and the soil came over the top and another lake formed on the top - sometimes there were fifty seams of coal one on top of one another. However, coal is formed from the same foliages as are now on the earth. The great Carboniferous Period as it

---

[4] *The Science of Geology,* Oxford Publications

[5] **The world's biomass**: In 1991 was estimated at 75,000 million imperial tons. This was made up of: trees, plants and seaweeds 73,000 million tons; fish 1000 million tons; land animals 700 million tons; insects and bacteria 15 million tons; and 5 billion humans weighing 250 million tons. A History of Knowledge. Charles Van Doren. Ballantine Books. NY Random House 1992) p 392.

was called was not tropical because in that era there was a mild uniform climate from pole to pole.[6]

When that wave rushed around the earth, it ripped up forests, churned the pieces, mixed them with marine fossils and with animals. It laid them out and another wave came and laid silt over the top; that's how the coal stratum were formed, and in these coal formations there is always marine fossils, not lake fossils. Most coal has pyrites in the overburden with it - a sulphur compound. There is no bacillus in the world but a marine bacillus, which generates sulphur. Therefore what deposited these stratum was sea-water – the pyrites proves it.

Archeological evidence Pre-Flood. In Ur of the Chaldees, in the pit which Woolley dug – is a layer 11 feet thick (3m) of water-laid clay – below that was a civilization superior to the one above it. He came to the conclusion that was the Great Flood. All over Mesopotamia this layer of silt is found, right into India. In 1939 in Bohemia (now the western half of the Czech Republic) Absolem found the prehistoric confines of a mammoth hunting village covered in sixteen feet (5m) of silt. He found these people that lived by mammoth hunting had fled that quickly, they had left their spoons and their instruments and everything behind them. They and their village were inundated by this sudden disaster of water-born silt and was buried. If had been a local flood mammoths would have come back above that. After that flood, there were no mammoths. It is known by any competent scholar that a great disaster wiped out the whole fauna of Europe. It is a recognized fact that it was replaced by a completely different fauna – not the same animals.

Underneath that layer, Absolem found implements and ornaments and knives of the blade bones of horses. They had a decimal system. They played on pipes. They were brilliant

---

[6] Pierre Esckrew – *Illustrated London News*

artists and made plastics out of bone and blood, in which they excelled in representing animals. They did not live in caves, but they used caves as storehouses and factories. Before the Flood there was a mild uniform climate from pole to pole and man was not a cave dweller – he didn't need to live in them – but with the cold after the Flood, man had to take to the caves. He found two needle factories[7] – the needles were made of bone, 1 1/3 inches long, (35mm) equal to the finest product in Europe. Man was not a fool in burying animals or making needles for nothing. He had something to sew.

He found cosmetic factories and lipstick and face paint. He found the ornaments that these people used to wear around their necks and the statues of the men and women. Out of modesty, he didn't publish the statues of the men and he published only some of the women. His article ends, "Pre-flood (antediluvian) man thought of only two things - eating and sex." Jesus said, "As it was in the days of Noah so shall it be in the days of the son of man - eating and drinking, marrying and giving in marriage". What are the people of your city thinking? If cinema and media are any indication, they are pre-occupied with eating, drinking and sex. Our days are like the days of Noah, no question. Jesus Christ said that there is a time coming before which even the days of Noah would pale.

Consider the ark. This is the one question many think will nullify the Flood. It can't do so of course, because once you have demonstrated a universal Flood, you have demonstrated the necessity of an ark, and once a proposition has been definitely demonstrated by unequivocal evidence, no other doubts can force it away. (Butler's principle).

The late Dr. Rimmer was lecturing in Canada. A skeptic said, "The ark was not big enough to contain two of every species in the world". Rimmer asked how big was the ark.

[7] *Illustrated London News*

The man said, "450 feet long, 75 feet wide and 45 feet high." Rimmer replied, "We will take that; that's the small cubit – it was probably much bigger". The ark could therefore contain the cubic equivalent of 569 railway stock cars.[8]

He asked, "How many species are in the world?" The man said, "About a million." Rimmer replied, "We will take that. I would point out that of that million species, sixty percent live in the water and were not candidates for the ark. Of the remaining 40%, 60% are insects, and you can park a lot of fleas on an elephant."

However, even that is not the full answer. Notice that the Hebrew text says, Noah took into the ark all animals that breathed. That's land animals, mammals and marsupials and possibly amphibians, if you include these even though they live in the water. However, of species, not varieties, there are only 240 above the size of a sheep – the elephant, rhinoceros, hippopotamus, camel, horse and zebra - by the time most count 25, they stop. It wouldn't take a big ship to take 500 animals. In World War II, 600 horses were easily loaded in a small transport ship plus men and equipment.

Below that, between a sheep and a rat, there are 750 species, not varieties. There was only one dog, one pair because a wolf is a dog; the jackal is a dog; these are only varieties of dogs. I don't mean that every single variety was there, like St. Bernards and the King Charles spaniel, no, every species. Below that, only 750 between a sheep and a rat. You could put those in the ark in the dining saloon.

Below that, from the size of a rat down to the tiny little mole and vole – 1,250. You can put those in the bathroom. So it's not so difficult as you think. I am quite prepared to admit

---

[8] 450 x 75 x 45 = 1,518,750 cubic feet or 56,361 cubic yards. (43,000 m³) A standard railway stock freight car holds 2,760 cubic feet. Dr John Montgomery. The Quest for Noah's Ark. Pyramid-Bethany Publications, Minneappolis, 1974, p 47.

that this was a miracle, but it was by no means unnatural. All God's miracles are supernatural, but they are not unnatural, so there is nothing unnatural about this.

This is then is the indisputable evidence for a universal Flood of only a few thousand years ago. It would be a bold person who said there was no Flood and that would be speaking out of ignorance, not out of knowledge.

Editor's Note:
Dr. Shelley delivered this same lecture to the 57th General Hospital, with forty specialists and doctors listening. When he was finished he said, "Any questions?" There was not one.

The lecture was delivered by Dr. Joseph Shelly in Brisbane, Queensland Australia in 1968 and transcribed from the original reel-to-reel recording. Some minor edits were made to allow for the necessary transition from speech to clarity in writing. Every effort has been made to substantiate the proposals made by Dr. Shelley. Also, as some words were unable to be transcribed due to lack of clarity in the original audio or the resource material is not known to the editor, these are in red typeface, and may be amended in future versions of these notes. Dr. Shelley encouraged his hearers to feel free to research, copy and distribute this material so it is done posthumously with his kind permission. Please contact the editor for any errors in transcription or typing and likewise copy and distribute it as "freely received, freely given".

In summary of the scientific evidence for a world-wide great Flood and Noah's Ark:

CAPACITY AND EVIDENCE OF CATASTROPHE WORLD-WIDE
- **Enough water** above, under and on the earth and in the sea
- **Sufficient tectonic forces** if activated could distribute it on the earth's surface
- **Snapfrozen arctic tundra** – sedimentary layers with a churned sea, land and air bio-mass
- **Sudden destruction of mammoths** and animals by sea water and sediment in the Arctic

MANKIND WORLD-WIDE
- **World-wide Flood traditions** – written and oral
- **Mankind is of one species** despite racial variations
- **The three divisions of anthropology** of the races are Semitic, Hamitic, Japhetic
- **The ancient names of lands** are the same as mentioned in the Bible record
- **Present population size** argues for mass annihilation some 4 to 5,000 years ago

FOSSIL RECORD WORLD-WIDE
- **World-wide fossil cemeteries** were made by a sudden flood that smashed and mixed the bones of all living species with marine fossils and saltwater
- **Worldwide destruction of dinosaur species** by sea-flood sedimentary layers
- **Long-distance sea birds** mixed with other land fossils

GEOLOGY WORLD-WIDE
- **Seawater salt lakes** – closed saline systems in non-saline areas of Asia and Americas
- **Oil deposits** are organic vegetable or animal
- **Oil deposits** are sedimentary, with marine fossils and saltwater
- **Coal strata** are suddenly formed sedimentary layers with marine fossils
- **Coal beds** have a marine-sulphur-formed pyrites component

ARCHAEOLOGY WORLD-WIDE
- **Pre-flood advanced mammoth hunting civilizations** in Asia and Europe – under the sediments exist mammoth art and implements but above the silt no mammoths
- **World-wide sediment strata are** laid down by a simultaneous catastrophic event

THE ARK
- **Perfectly designed specific dimensions** for its flotation task – stable & self-righting
- **Adequate size of the ark** for the task of preserving all breathing land species
- **Histories of the ark resting in Armenia** and its consequent traditions

We must put on the armour of God ready for battle but we must remember that the power to do battle comes from God, not from our own strength.

**People may not believe what you say, but they will note what you do*

PART THREE

Introduction

I have lovely memories of times after I married of occasionally sitting round the Spall family table to eat a tasty meal. But it was a feast in more ways than one. My husband John's father, George, was a good Bible teacher who had delved into the Old Testament as well as the New, and had a thorough understanding of Jewish ways and the prophecies of Scripture. On top of this, he kept his ear to the ground listening for fulfilment of those Scriptures. Because the Bible centres on the Middle East he had a Jewish newspaper delivered – the English edition, though he was pretty familiar with Hebrew – so that he could hear what was really happening in the region, rather than rely on our local news which is often filtered or skewed according to the opinions of the reporters or their bosses.

So as we feasted on the food we would be treated to some of George Spall's wisdom. I absolutely loved these times where holes in my knowledge could be shrunk and my faith could be stretched. A double feast... Actually, when John and I had our engagement party George made it a 'Conversation Evening' where topics he suggested were discussed back and forth. He said that such Conversation evenings had been popular in London early in the 20th Century and we found it fascinating ourselves. If you have some thinking friends, you may like to begin having some Conversation Parties too. Why not start a trend? (Thinking parties rather than drinking parties.) The next morning you wake up recharged with ideas rather than with a headache.

Thinking back further, I have realised over the years how much understanding of everyday things my mother passed on to me as we did the washing together or as I watched her prepare the evening meal. Things like 'never wash a stain in hot water or you will set the stain'; 'don't put too much blue in the water, you want white clothes, not blue'; (this was in the far off days when we washed by hand, almost all linen was white and we gave a few shakes of the good old 'blue bag' in the rinse water to help keep the fabric snowy. She taught me honesty as well. When I began my working life as a teen, she warned me 'don't bring home as much as a pin from the office'. I followed her lead but I know that some others thought nothing of taking home pens or other supplies.

In more recent years, John and I have had the pleasure of being the ones to whom our children or grandchildren come for help of some sort. On the 'phone: 'Papa, I have an assignment from school and I need to know…' or 'Dad, I was reading the book of Ezekiel… what do you think about…' Because I love gardening, the questions addressed to me may be along the lines of how to look after a particular kind of plant, etc. And, perhaps the times I love the best, when we sit around our dining table with family when they visit and their questions begin. I have such a warm glow as I see the intent expressions on the faces of young ones and listen to John answer their queries. Our lives have come full circle – the enquirers have become the answerers.

As you read this Section – or the other Sections of this book – I would like you to feel as though you are sitting around our dining table as we chat about things we've picked up along our journey through life. And I hope one day you will have the privilege of passing on the wisdom you have gleaned on *your* journey…

43

THE POOR

Let's stop for a short while to think about how we should look at people who are poor in this world's goods. But first, to keep things in perspective, let's peep into a very intriguing episode in Jesus' life. It was during a visit to someone's house for dinner, and Mary Magdalene went to Jesus and opened a jar of very expensive perfume and anointed him with it. It was a touching scene where a woman who had lived a sinful life wanted to show her love for the Son of God and actually washed his dusty feet with her tears and dried them with her hair.

There are times when we feel so much love and thankfulness that we cannot express them in words. We search for a way to show how we feel to the one who has blessed us so much. Of course, often it is God who makes us feel this way. We are carried aloft by his love and joy. We have known our sins forgiven. Perhaps we have been healed of a disease that threatened our very lives. We can hardly believe that we have been so visited by God when we know that we don't deserve it. How do we express the gratitude that is flooding our being? Well, that was Mary's position. She had not been a godly woman in her lifestyle yet she had recognized that God had not sent his Son into the world to condemn. Jesus had sometimes criticised the religious people because of their hypocrisy and yet he was able to accept sinners who repented of their way of life.

Her response was so complete that she poured out her

gratitude by giving of herself. If a household had a slave, it was usually the slave's job to wash the feet of the visitors because in those days most people travelled by foot in sandals and the streets were dusty or muddy. Women would not usually make such a demonstration in public as this woman was doing. And those who witnessed it neither understood nor appreciated it. The thieving disciple Judas pretended that he was so concerned about the poor in the community that he decried the extravagant 'waste' of the perfume, saying that the money could have been used on the poor. As usual, Jesus saw through the deceit and showed the better perspective: 'The poor you will always have with you.' Jesus was pointing out that the poor could be helped at any time. And here's the heart of the matter – Mary Magdalene, whether she actually realised it or not, had anointed Jesus in preparation for his death on the cross and his burial.

Now Jesus was not saying that we should not give to the poor but he was showing that there are times for doing one thing and times for doing another. Before we choose how to spend our money it is good to check with God how it will be best used.

Having said that, there is ample evidence in Scripture that we certainly should look after those in need when we are able to do so. So important is it that this very issue is presented in Matthew's gospel in a most sombre scene. Matthew is foreshadowing the Day of Judgment when all of us will stand before Jesus as our judge. There will be a sharp division between those who will enjoy Heaven with God and those who will be consigned to the same fate as Satan and his host. And yet, in summing up their cases, very similar words will be said to each group. And it concerns their attitudes and actions toward those – and particularly believers - who were in need on earth. The vital message is that when we reach out with aid to those who are hungry, thirsty, without accommodation or suffering persecution, God sees it as though we are doing those very things to him. Conversely, if we ignore the needs and suffering of people, particularly believers, it is as though we are turning our backs on God himself.

There are at least two things to note here. Firstly, that God's earthly family is so important to him that he demands that those with goods share with those who are in need. Secondly, our ultimate destination for eternity is not judged simply on whether we believed in Jesus as Saviour but also on whether we made him Lord of our lives and thus fulfilled his will here on earth. Now that's a sombre thought, isn't it?

My heartache is that so many modern churches are so keen to tell people that all is right with them if they have accepted Jesus as Saviour that they don't emphasize that there are attitudes and thoughts and deeds to be done to complete God's work here on earth. This is not 'working *for* our salvation' but it is 'working *out* our salvation' as mentioned in Philippians 2:12: Paul, in writing to the believers in Philippi said "Therefore, my dear friends, as you have always obeyed…..continue to work out your salvation with fear and trembling, for it is God who works in you to will and to act according to his good purpose." When we first believe in Jesus to be our Saviour from sins, we have taken the first step on the road of salvation. Many, many times we are told that it is the person who continues on that road who finds full salvation at the end of this life.

1Corinthians 3:13 warns that every man's work will be 'tried by fire'. This indicates that what we do now is noticed by God. He has a plan for our lives and expects that we will, to the best of our ability, seek to fulfil that plan. If we have simply done foolish things, they will be swallowed by the fire. Only those things which please God will remain.

We don't need to do mighty things or noticeable deeds but they need to be those things which please our Maker. In fact we are told not to make a show of our good deeds just to be noticed. If we do them quietly God sees them in secret and is pleased and will in fact reward us when we meet him.

So, who would have thought that being mindful of the poor would have such serious consequences? This doesn't mean that giving to the poor is all you need to concentrate on but it does show that it should be part of our understanding of what life is all about. God doesn't want our thoughts to be so lofty that we are not practical. It is good to read the Bible but it doesn't do much good unless it directs our lives. It is good to pray but it needs to be balanced by practical help to those in need. That's pretty simple really isn't it? And it makes a lot of sense.

God has always shown himself to be practical. Let's look at that in the next chapter…

44

GOD IS A PRACTICAL GOD

I have a feeling that many people think of God as an old fellow with a flowing grey beard who kindly pats people on the head as if to say 'There, there, it will all be okay.' Sweet, but totally useless and irrelevant – that's the picture. But the picture of God we have in his Book is quite the opposite. Yes, he is kind to those who seek him but he is also immensely practical.

Let's look at some of the aspects revealed about this God. Firstly, he is the only God there is. We can't just add him to other gods because he is shown to be the only living God and his son Jesus and the Holy Spirit are aspects of this solo God. This is sticky territory for some minds of course. How can we comprehend a God who is three in one, a Triune Godhead? It has never worried me I must say because he is God. And if everything about God was really easy for me to understand then he probably wouldn't be much different from me. But in fact I am just part of what he has created. And his tools of creation were the very words from his mouth 'Let there be…..and there was'.

That aspect of God – being the Creator of everything there is – gives us a picture of his greatness and power. The multitude of differing things he made reveals his vast creativity. After all, if he wanted to have trees on the earth he could have made just one kind of nice tree all over. But instead, because he knew it would bless us he made hundreds of different kinds of trees, shrubs and flowering plants, not to mention the grass which not only is pleasant to look at but is good to walk on and feeds animals. And as if that was not enough, he saw to it that the trees and grass absorb the carbon dioxide we breathe out, thus purifying the air. Practical! Practical, yes, but also kind because it is good for our emotions to have such picturesque landscapes to look out upon. And let's not forget that the Bible let us know that 'every herb of the field is for the service of man'. Again, practical and helpful. We often hear about herbs which the Chinese have used for centuries but it was, after all, God's intention all along and we Westerners let that knowledge slip as we came up with man-made drugs (which sometimes risk side effects).

We won't go into detail about the infinite variety of animal life which makes this earth an interesting and exciting place to live and which is part of this great creation. Just a couple of points – some animals provide us with protein food, meat and eggs, and some are wonderful companions or workers (sheep and cattle dogs, donkeys, horses, camels and elephants for the latter).

Let me share with you a most practical piece of advice God gave the Israelites when he led them to the land of Canaan which was to be their home. He told them that they were to battle against those who dwelt in the land because their ways were evil but he said that they were not to accomplish that in a single year or the land would become overgrown and the wild animals would become too numerous for them to manage. Now, how practical is that!

So what can we learn from God's dealings with man as recorded in his book? For one thing, God is reliable; he sticks with his word. He is also longsuffering, slow to anger and abounding in mercy. But the other side of the coin is that God is also a just God. There's another word for God which doesn't really apply to anyone else (except in the way it is given to us when we align ourselves with Jesus) and that word is Holy. To be holy means to be sinless, incorruptible, pure, with good thoughts, intentions, words and deeds.

Now because God is holy and just, he must punish sin. And the penalty for sin is death. As we were born in sin because our first parents sinned in the Garden of Eden, we are automatically sinners. So how does a holy God deal with this dilemma? Especially as he is merciful as well as holy and just... If he were to be the old fellow with flowing beard patting us on the head he could turn a blind eye to our sin but then he wouldn't be just or holy. He would be merciful only. And would it really be merciful to allow sin to go unpunished? The world would spiral downward into total chaos extremely quickly. We only have to look around us and at the news in newspapers and on TV to see that all kinds of sin and crime are abounding more and more as God is cut out of homes, schools, universities, workplaces and even in some cases, churches. People from the very young to the elderly and frail are being abused physically and mentally now that God has almost been excluded from our societies.

But God had a plan. As a matter of fact, because he is such an all-seeing Being, this plan was hatched before time began. God would enter our world in the form of a man who would be born as we are – tiny and helpless. This man would experience life just as we do. He would not be spared the difficult issues. To the outside world it appeared that he was illegitimate because his mother had become pregnant before she and Joseph married. This was because her pregnancy was not the result of a sexual encounter but because of the power of the Holy Spirit causing the baby to be formed in her pure womb. We see from Scripture that the religious leaders of the time threw that issue in his face when they said to him 'WE have Abraham to OUR father' insinuating that he was ill born. His very birth was in an animal enclosure because Mary and Joseph had travelled to the town of their birth to comply with a census being taken and the influx of people had resulted in no rooms being available for them. Could there have been a more humble beginning for Jesus? On top of that, his parents were poor people as we've discussed before.

Jesus spent his youth being obedient to his earthly parents but even they did not fully comprehend that his mission in coming to the earth was to become a sacrifice for the sin of the world. They misunderstood why he lingered at the temple as a 12-year-old boy debating with the learned priests. (Luke 2:41-52)

As he grew older he submitted to John the Baptist's baptism in the Jordan River. John was calling people to repentance so it was a baptism of repentance which Jesus did not actually need. But in relating to the sinners all around him, he too went down into the water as an act of obedience. John recognized that Jesus did not need this baptism because God revealed to him that Jesus was the one whom God had sent into the world but he baptised him because Jesus insisted on it. At that time, the Father God visited Jesus by speaking from heaven words of being pleased with his Son, and the Holy Spirit came upon him in the form of a dove.

This would have been a wonderful sign to Jesus but it was the prelude to a terrible 40 days when Jesus fasted in the wilderness. At the end of the fast when he would have been hungry and weary Satan confronted him with temptations. One thing we learn about Satan is that he is no gentleman and he sidles up to us at times when we are at our weakest, perhaps when our guard is down. But Jesus was up to it. He met each of Satan's tempting words with answers from the Word of God. So he was able to resist the devil's traps.

Then for 3 years Jesus had a public ministry, calling a dozen men to follow him as his disciples. He didn't choose learned or clever men but ordinary fishermen and even a tax collector. They gave up their jobs to walk the territory with him and to witness his teachings and miracles – miracles of healing and forgiveness and miracles of multiplication of food to feed hungry hordes. But even the disciples were a trial to Jesus because their thoughts were often centred on the things of the earth rather than on the spiritual truths he was trying to plant into them so that they could carry on his work after he left.

So life wasn't easy for Jesus in many ways but that was just the beginning. What he was to endure in suffering and dying for the sins he did not commit was horrendous. Thus the Creator of the world – for the Bible tells us that nothing was made which was not made by him – entered the world limited to the boundaries of our lives as human beings. There was a grand purpose for this of course. Jesus is to be our judge at the end of time and he will be a just judge because he understands what it is to be a man – to endure difficulties, poverty, being reviled and misunderstood and to suffer humiliation and pain. He has the right to judge us.

But the good news is that before that Day of Judgment arrives his job is to be at the right hand of God interceding on our behalf. This means that we have a high priest of the highest order who understands our struggles and difficulties because he has endured them himself. He is able to help us, strengthen us, and to ask forgiveness for us. As we align ourselves with Jesus – our sacrifice for sin – God sees us 'through' his Son so we are seen as right with God as long as we stay within the kindness of God. No-one can take us out of this privileged place. The only way out is for us to turn our backs on God, to slip away. How foolish would that be when we have such a God who is even willing to suffer to reconcile us to himself?

Thinking further on the practicality of God, when Jesus

walked the earth he taught the common people about the values of God by the use of parables. These were stories about situations they would understand. Most of these folk were unschooled so he used simple situations to help them comprehend God's ways and values.

When he came upon sick people he healed them unless there was such unbelief that it negated the good Jesus would do. God works in an atmosphere of faith.

Thinking of healing, down through the ages God has gone on healing people miraculously. We must also acknowledge the work of medical people who have continued to improve treatments, many of whom have been depending on God to lead them. For instance, when our daughter Nicole needed an operation to close a hole in her heart which she'd been born with, one of the top heart surgeons in Australia was to perform the operation and he was a keen follower of Jesus. We, of course, were praying earnestly. My aged mother, who was not given to visions, stayed at home while we were at the hospital. When we arrived home later, Mum told us that she had had a vision of Jesus standing at the doctor's side and directing him. We were able to tell her that when we spoke to the doctor after the op., he told us that he had done things during the surgery which he had never done before. So, whether by direct miracle or via medically trained men and women, God is still in the healing business.

However, even when there is no healing, God is still being practical. As an example, the Apostle Paul revealed that when he sought healing for himself God let him understand that the 'thorn in the flesh' he had to endure was there for the express purpose of keeping him from becoming proud of his many achievements. Now, to some of us, that may seem harsh. But it is really a mercy. Paul must be one of the most outstanding Christians of all time. He accomplished the evangelising of the then known Gentile world. He had been responsible, under God, for healings. He had been unhurt when bitten by a poisonous snake. He endured many hardships – lashings, imprisonment, shipwreck, abuse both verbal and physical – and had continued with his work. He surely would have been a prime candidate for pride and God was leaving him with a constant reminder that pride 'comes before a fall'. Now that is both practical and kind.

One thing we haven't mentioned is that God – right at the beginning of time – provided us with everything we need for life. We have the ability to use wood, thatch, bricks and even mud and straw to build ourselves shelter from the elements. There are yarns of many differing kinds – wool, cotton, flax, even bamboo these days - to clothe ourselves. Crops of myriad varieties can cover all the nutritional needs we have for health. Now how much more practical could God have been?

So why should we not think of prayer and Bible study as practical as well? If we get to know the whole Bible, we can understand so much about our Creator and how to live the life he has given us. And to pray is simply to communicate with him in an intimate and loving way. We can find guidance for specific circumstances and we can express our gratitude for all he has done for us.

I want to add one more aspect of God's practicality. He gave us love – different kinds of love to help and comfort us. Brotherly love, Family love, Romantic love.

So let's just list the ways we've looked at which illustrate God's immense practicality:

He was willing to suffer to reconcile us to himself

He provided plants to be used as medicine and lotions and balms

He spoke in parables when addressing the uneducated folk he wanted to share God's love with

He provides miraculous healing when there is faith to

receive it and it won't cause people to slip away from him

He withholds healing from those it wouldn't serve

He has put at our disposal food, building materials, clothing fibres and animals to be our helpers or our special companions

He gave us love and the ability to give and receive it. *What a wonderful, bountiful, practical God!*

45

TREASURE THE MOMENTS

As children, it seems an eternity until the next big event in our lives – a party, our birthday, the holidays or Christmas. But it's as if the older we get the speedier the years become. And if the years fly by, how much more the days, the hours and the minutes? We sometimes feel as though we are on a treadmill without a stop button; there are so many things to do, so many people to catch up with, our job takes a third of our day, hopefully sleep takes another third, there are jobs around the home, we need to keep track of friends' and family's birthdays to choose gifts and cards, and if we are parents of young children they claim our attention most of their waking moments. And so it goes on.

If we're not watchful we can develop a 'negative radar' mentality. What's that? Well it simply means that we are so pushed and prodded by life that we are subconsciously on the lookout for all the negative aspects to complain about them or to try to shield ourselves from them. One result of negative radar is that it misses out on all the positives. Radio receivers are tuned to pick up certain signals whilst resisting others. And human negative radar does a similar thing. It is tuned in to the negatives and can completely miss out on the benefit of the lovely positive events of our lives.

Have you ever met a married couple like this? He is a friendly outgoing fellow but she never sees him as anything but a nuisance. His every light comment is met with a complaining response as though he had just criticised her.

What is wrong? Well, it may be that in some way he has disappointed her, so – without realising it – she has activated negative radar and now she sees only the negative side of every single thing he says or does. If he compliments her, he's trying to hide something he's done wrong. If he says nothing, he doesn't appreciate all the work she does for him. And so it goes on... What a tragedy! And even more so because I have met quite a few couples just like that, and sometimes it is the husband who has his negative radar switched on. Of course it can happen in all sorts of relationships, not just marriage. Harassed parents can develop the same attitudes toward their offspring. Instead of forming a warm cherishing of them, they can see them as demanding too much of them and find it difficult to nurture them fondly, giving them the security they need.

If I could offer advice to such people, I would say something like this: Please switch off that negative radar. Look for the lovely moments, the kind word, the moment you shared some laughter, the warmth you felt when some earlier event was recalled, the hug around the knees from a tiny child. Treasure the moments.

Now, what about us? Even if we don't have strong negative radar, perhaps we've forgotten how to treasure the moments. Things are busy and it seems to take all our energy to keep up with demands. Well, here's a secret for us: treasuring the precious moments actually generates more energy than feeling stressed does. It does require that we develop the habit of thinking differently. Firstly, acknowledge to ourselves that we have become caught up in an unhelpful way of thinking. Then take some time to realign our 'radar dish'. We are going to begin being more thoughtful toward those around us. We are going to try to incorporate small kindnesses toward them into our day. It may be just a friendly smile as we see them for the first time each day and a genuine enquiry as to how they are going instead of a clipped 'Hi'. It may be that we will offer to make someone a cuppa when we are making our own. It really doesn't take much more time to make two. And when those small nice moments happen we decide to hold on to the memory of them for some time.

There are a few words in Psalm 23 which I treasure. Right at the beginning it speaks of God as our Shepherd providing good pasture and refreshing water. Then those special words 'He restores my soul'. For myself, I had years when I felt stressed by my circumstances and then, as I read the 23rd psalm for the umpteenth time the impact of those words struck home. I cried with relief and I realised that the one who understands me better than I know myself wanted to bring refreshment and restoration to my inner being. Nothing and no-one can do that so thoroughly as God can, and we need to let down the walls of protection we have built around ourselves so he can achieve it. But I believe that God has made us so that we can also determine to help ourselves. This is not to say that we don't need God to work in us but it means that the responsibility for our wellbeing is not entirely with him. We can develop ways to counteract the negative effect of life's buffeting.

God does not treat us as children all of our lives. When we are new believers we are like babes in spiritual understanding so he treats us accordingly. There are parts of Scripture that are like spiritual milk – easy to digest, easy to understand, bringing comfort. But as we mature, God expects that we will adapt and adopt principles which will enable us to wrestle with life and win. When we look at Jesus' relationship with his disciples, sometimes he was frustrated with their lack of understanding. He had invested his life in them so that they could be the leaders of the believers when he returned to his heavenly father. But they were still so often like children – so earthly - in their views. We hear echoes of Jesus' frustration in Paul's writings too when he has to go over the basic spiritual principles with those to whom he wrote long letters. They should have been able to discern things from a better perspective by now but they were still making the same old mistakes from their past.

You know that I went to Sunday School where I learnt about God and his Word from the age of 4. For quite a number of years I was literally conscious of the presence of the Lord at any given moment and I sought to live a life that would please him. Then into adulthood I found that I no longer was aware of God's presence although I trusted that he was still with me. For a long time I felt rather bad that I had 'lost' something precious. Then one day a woman was relating to me how her husband had come to the Lord. She had become a believer so he told the Lord that he would believe in him for three months and at the end of that time he would reassess whether he could go on believing. For those three months he was aware of the presence of the Lord and at the end of that time he felt God tell him that he would now have to live by faith. The man was satisfied with that, knowing that he really was dealing with a living God.

When I heard my friend's words it finally dawned on me that I had not really lost something which I should have kept, but rather God had withdrawn the feelings so that I would mature in my faith by walking with him without being able to feel his presence at all times. Of course I still had the awareness of his presence during particular times – when I was seeking guidance from him or when I was going through very difficult events.

So, as I've emphasized in the previous Sections in this book, we need to think for ourselves. God has provided all we need to base our way of life on. He has shown his character through the Bible and we can see what things please him in his people – things like justice and mercy, faith and faithfulness. We are told that the fruits of God's Spirit living in us are these: love, joy, peace, patience, kindness, goodness, faithfulness, gentleness and self-control. (Galatians 5:22, 23a) If we do not find any of these fruits increasing in us, we need to yield to the quiet work of the Holy Spirit daily. God never forces himself on us but he is ready to work in us and on our behalf as we allow him to do so. Some folk are egotistical and even narcissistic (it's all about them) and they have the job of humbling themselves and turning their attention onto God instead of themselves so they can develop as godly people.

We have spoken about relational moments to treasure so far. There are many others. What if you are in a situation where there isn't much opportunity to relate to others? The extreme would be to be a castaway on an island, but there are other situations where people cannot readily reach out for companionship. What about those who are bedridden at home or in a hospital, or wheelchair bound? How about missionaries who venture into territory where they are not yet fluent in the local language? Consider a young school teacher who has been sent to a far-flung area where she knows no-one. And what about refugees who have had to flee their homeland because of persecution or war? These folk have to find special moments in other things. But what?

Well, God has provided many things to help in such times. He writes his spectacular signature across the skies every morning and evening. I know how much this beauty fills my heart with joy, even if I am a lone spectator. Treasure the moment. Have you noticed how much better the landscape looks after rain when it has been preceded by a dry time? It does you good just looking at how fresh and green it all appears. We feel refreshed as the land is refreshed. And how much greener still the grass is some time after a fire has gone through an area. It is a promise of life after death. Treasure these moments. And don't you feel your heart leap a little when a bush springs into flower for the first time this year? If you are a gardener you relish the wide variety of shades and textures in leaves and petals, the exciting colours of exotic flowers, the tactile patterns of tree bark and the joy of eating something you've just taken from your vegetable patch or orchard. Treasure the moments.

There are countless little encouragements most days if we have the eyes to see them. The gurgle of a happy baby, the courtesy of a kind stranger, ringing a friend and finding them immediately available, waking up and finding that that headache has gone, finishing that assignment you had been dodging for too long, playing an instrument for your own pleasure or to worship the Lord, trying something new (whether you succeed at it or not). There are hundreds of lovely small innocent pleasures to hold in your heart.

Some of these are done without seeking our own pleasure. We reach out to help or comfort someone else and we find that we are blessed when we sense that we have been of real value to a person in need of our aid. It is in disregarding our own needs and looking after another person's needs that we often find the greatest fulfilment. Treasure the moments…

Isaiah 33:6 –
"He will be the sure foundation for your times,
a rich store of salvation and wisdom and knowledge;
the fear of the Lord is the key to this treasure."

46

FEARING THE LORD?

Did you notice the quote on the previous page? In case you missed it, it's worth repeating here:

Isaiah 33:6 "*He will be the sure foundation for your times, a rich store of salvation and wisdom and knowledge; the fear of the Lord is the key to this treasure.*"

If there's one thing which stirs our interest it is the idea of a treasure, especially a hidden one. How many novels and movies have been written and made about just such a theme! And the theme excites us from childhood to old age. Most of us have ideas about what we would do if we ever had a windfall, all the more exciting if it was a hidden treasure…

The quote above mentions a '*key to this treasure*' which tips us off to the fact that this treasure is elusive. It requires a key… I was watching a detective story on TV recently where one couple knew about some gems which had been hidden many years earlier. In their search they found a key in a secret drawer. Now they had the key, they had access to the treasure.

Well in the quote above, the prophet Isaiah revealed not only the key but also the treasure. What is the treasure, and is it valuable to us in this present age? After all, Isaiah wrote this millennia ago…

Well, let's look at what the treasure is… Isaiah says it will be a ***sure foundation.*** Now who doesn't want a sure foundation? We all know what happens to anything we build on a faulty foundation, it sinks or goes awry. What does he say next? *For your times*. So Isaiah wasn't writing just for his period of time, this treasure is a lasting one. It applies to us and our lives. So far so good. Next we see that this store of treasure which could open up to us contains *salvation, wisdom and knowledge*. Wow! You can't buy any of those things in a store. If you are clever and you study you may gain some knowledge but that knowledge pertains only to those things which can be seen, touched and measured. It still leaves us empty of the knowledge of the larger things – God himself, his ways, how to operate in a way to be eternally successful and safe from our enemy, the Devil.

We have established that the treasure is desirable. It's not something that you would take or leave. You would want to secure it for yourself. Well, Isaiah wasn't devious, he gave us the key. What was it? *The fear of the Lord* is the key to this treasure.

I feel that not only is the fear of the Lord absent from most lives these days but also, even for those who think about it, it is a little tricky to comprehend. We hear that God is a God of love. And that's true, but it's only part of the story. God is a God of wrath when it comes to rebellion and sin. His love overrode his wrath by the sacrifice of his son, Jesus, to bring salvation from sin to us. So sin is obviously a really big deal. It's not something to be winked at, as though it really doesn't matter whether we sin or not once we are on the way of salvation.

Once we are aware of sin and Jesus' suffering on our behalf, sin should be something we hate, not something we are careless about. What did Jesus say on this subject? In Matthew 10:28, we read: '*Do not be afraid of those who kill the body but cannot kill the soul. Rather, be afraid of the One who can destroy both soul and body in hell.*' These are Jesus' words so we should pay very close attention to them. He is saying that our concern should be about our eternal safety rather than our earthly security. And there is only one who can send us to hell and that is God Almighty. It's not the Devil because hell is for his punishment as well as for those who refuse God's offer of salvation. I know that human beings tend to think of hell as the home of the Devil where he is enjoying a party, but that's false information. The Devil will be dreading hell because he knows that that is his final destination and he's trying to take as many men, women and children with him as he can.

Why is fearing God so important? One reason is that it gives us the correct foundation on which to build our lifestyle, our value system, our thoughts, words and deeds. God told Moses in the Old Testament that the fear of the Lord would keep the people from sinning.

So, somehow, we have to see a rounded picture of God in our minds and hearts. We have to combine a God of love with the Judge of all the earth. It may seem tricky to some, but if you have had a good father in your childhood, he would have loved you but disciplined you. He would have punished you to teach you right from wrong. God does that with us. He disciplines us by the things we suffer in life. But the danger is that if we become careless about sin we can be chopping away at the foundations of our salvation, our wisdom and our knowledge.

Because I know that it is difficult for some folk to see love and fear together, I want to look at another Scripture. Here's the setting: The people of Israel were afraid that if they heard personally from God himself they would die, so they asked Moses to listen to God and report back to them. In Deuteronomy 5:27-29, we read: '*Go near and listen to all that the Lord our God says. Then tell us whatever the Lord our God tells you. **We will listen and obey.**'* Then Moses said, '*The Lord heard you when you spoke to me and the Lord said to me, "I have heard what this people said to you.*

Everything they said was good. Oh, that their hearts would be inclined to fear me and keep all my commands always, ***so that it might go well with them and their children forever****."*

Now, there you have the rounded picture of our Heavenly Father – fear and love. He knows that fear will keep them walking his way and then he can bless them rather than punish them. If he delighted in punishment he would not have made a way for us to be saved, especially at his own pain. But, as I've said before, because he is just he must punish sin. Many believers today think that because their sin was laid on Jesus on the cross it really doesn't matter if they sin now. But surely this is thinking cheaply about the sacrifice and suffering of our dear Saviour, our Lord Jesus! Rather, we should realise that God views sin so seriously that he was willing to suffer to save us, therefore the last thing we want to do is sin. And if we do slip into a sin, we must turn quickly to the Lord to ask his forgiveness which he will give us if we are sincere.

So are you getting the picture more clearly now? Fearing God doesn't mean we can never relax in case God comes down on us with some punishment. It means that we revere him so much that sin is horrendous to us and we don't want anything to do with it because we want to please the Father who loved us enough to suffer for our sakes.

Can I think of something which may illustrate this situation more clearly? Well, how about an oven... An oven is a good thing because it enables us to cook food, both nutritious and scrumptious. But we have to teach our little ones to have a healthy fear of the oven because it can burn us because of its great heat. Perhaps we can liken fearing the Lord to that. God is good but if we abuse his goodness we may be burned so a healthy fear will keep us safe.

The great thing is that if we fear God, we don't need to fear anything or anybody else because God sees everything that happens to us and there will come a day when he takes revenge on our behalf. Remember that the words "fear not" appear in the Bible 366 times so God does not want us to live in fear and anxiety about what may happen to us from other sources.

You may like to pray this simple prayer: "Our loving heavenly Father, we thank you so much that you are holy, just and fair. You tell it like it is. You call sin, sin. And because of your love and mercy you save us from sins past by the sacrifice of Jesus on the cross, and you save us from committing more sins by giving us your Holy Spirit to live within us. Lord, help us to have a healthy fear of you so that we will not want to sin, but if we do sin, we know that we have Jesus to intercede for us so that forgiveness is still available as we repent and confess. You are a good God. We pray in the Name of our Saviour Jesus Christ. Amen."

Make sure you read chapter 17 of Section 4 because I have two examples of how reverencing the Lord works out in everyday life. It can have truly amazing results in the way of knowledge beyond everyone else's...

47

HOW SECURE IS OUR SALVATION?

I very much want to chat with you about that mystery – 'salvation'. Because I owned and read a Bible from an early age, it has helped me recognize some skewed theology. I noticed as a young person that there were quite a number of verses that told me this about salvation: "He who continues to the end will be saved." So, without any fuss or bother, I was careful to follow the Lord at all times because I knew there was danger in falling away from him. I could lose my salvation.

Why was this piece of information so important? Because in later life I discovered that there are many, many people who have been taught that it is impossible to lose your salvation once you have believed in Jesus Christ as your Saviour. Does it really matter which way you believe about salvation? I certainly think it does. Just think for a moment, if you believe that you have a guarantee of eternal life in heaven, there is the risk that you could undervalue your salvation. You may feel, even subconsciously, that it doesn't really matter how you live because you have your ticket to heaven. And what if you missed out on eternal joy with God because of faulty theology? Could anything be more terrible?

Firstly, let me say that when we put our trust in Jesus, we are told in the Bible that no-one can pluck us out of God's hand. Now that is a wonderful security. But that is the only verse I can think of that gives such a sense of security. And what it is saying is that there is no power that can force us to lose our salvation. But what it is not saying is that there is no way we can lose our salvation. Can you see the very real difference?

Now, as I've said before, it doesn't really matter what my opinion is. But it does matter what God has said via his chosen spokesmen in the Bible. So, I am giving you here what the Bible says on the matter:

<u>In the second letter of Peter chapter 1</u>, Peter says that God's power has given us everything we need for life and godliness through our knowledge of him. He goes on to warn the recipients of his letter to see that they escape the corruption in the world. They should see that they add to their faith, goodness; and to goodness, knowledge; and to knowledge, self-control; and to self-control, perseverance; and to perseverance, godliness; and to godliness, brotherly kindness; and to brotherly kindness, love. Peter says that possessing these qualities in <u>increasing</u> measure will keep them from being ineffective and unproductive. A significant verse says "Therefore, my brothers, be all the more <u>eager to make your calling and election sure</u>. For <u>if</u> you do these things you will never fall, and you will receive a rich welcome into the eternal kingdom of our Lord and Saviour Jesus Christ."

There is so much talk these days about the ***unconditional*** love of God. But we see from the verse above that there is a condition to making our calling and election sure. And it is in continuing to follow after the spirit life and the fruits that come from that.

This next section of Scripture brings a delightful balance to the matter. Again from the <u>second letter of Peter, this time chapter 3:17 & 18</u> "Therefore, dear friends, ... be on your guard so that you will not be carried away by the error of lawless men *<u>and fall from your secure position</u>*. But grow in the grace and knowledge of our Lord and Saviour Jesus Christ..."

So there we have the two aspects of our salvation – *security and risk*. Perhaps we could put it this way: I am as secure in my salvation as I determine to be. No-one can rob me of it, but I can choose to turn away or drift away. Let's look at more Scriptures. I want you to see that there are many verses saying similar things

Now let's turn to the letter to the Hebrews chapter 3:6 & 7. "But Christ is faithful as a son over God's house. And we are his house, *if* we hold on to our courage and the hope of which we boast."

From the same chapter, Hebrews 3:14: "We have come to share in Christ *if* we hold firmly till the end the confidence we had at first."

Now we turn to the book of Romans 11:22. Here, Paul is speaking about the fact that as the Jews have in general rejected Jesus as their Messiah, God has rejected them (for a time) and sent the message of salvation and grace to the Gentiles. "Consider therefore the kindness and sternness of God: sternness to those who fell, but kindness to you, provided that you continue in his kindness. Otherwise, you also will be cut off." (Verse 23 continues with a note of hope for the Jews "And if they do not persist in unbelief, they will be grafted in (as branches into a tree) for God is able to graft them in again.")

Hebrews 3:14 "We have come to share in Christ, *if indeed* we hold our original conviction *firmly* to the *very end*."

There are more verses along those lines but I think by the half dozen quoted you can see that this is a very serious point of belief. Our salvation is assured as long as we continue in trust and developing our spiritual life with the indwelling Spirit of God himself. Perhaps it is better if we think of our spiritual life as being "on the way of salvation". If we have begun to trust in Jesus as our Saviour, we are now on the way of salvation and if we continue in that way, we will eventually find ourselves in heaven with a welcoming heavenly Father.

Be sure to read Chapter 6 as we look at many of the resources and encouragement "on the way of Salvation".

48

OUR RESOURCES AND ENCOURAGEMENT AS BELIEVERS

If the Way of Salvation was strewn with rose petals as the warming sun shone down upon us, perhaps there wouldn't need to be this conversation. But the fact is that every person on Planet Earth is in a war zone whether or not they are aware of it. What am I talking about? Well, have you noticed that right from the start of our lives the stories we are fed involve good and evil, goodies and baddies? Have you noticed how sinister our nursery rhymes are? You haven't noticed? Well here is a sample, right from the cradle...

"Rock-a-bye baby on a treetop
When the wind blows the cradle will rock
When the bough breaks the cradle will fall
Down will come baby, cradle and all."

Now isn't that a charming introduction to song and rhyme? Then how about...

"Ring-a-ring-o' roses, a pocket full of posies
A-tishoo! A-tishoo! We all fall down."

It is believed that this last line referred to the sneezing symptoms which heralded the dreaded plague which killed thousands. And we innocently sang that as young school children. But, there's more. What about 'Sing a Song of Sixpence'...

> "The king was in his counting house,
> counting out his money;
> The queen was in the parlour, eating bread and honey.
> The maid was in the garden, hanging out the clothes
> When down came a blackbird and pecked off her nose."

How sweet!

Well, as you can imagine if that is what we are fed as tiny children, it can only get worse as we develop. We 'graduate' to cops and robbers and cowboys and Indians, as I said the goodies and the baddies. It's hardly necessary to discuss the horror shows that are on the menu for adults. But we have to acknowledge that it all follows the pattern of good and evil or dreadful events befalling ordinary people.

Why is this so? Probably because that is the scenario in the whole universe and beyond. Right from the first Bible book, Genesis, we are introduced to the enemy, Satan, also called Lucifer or The Devil. Satan is the Hebrew name and Lucifer a Latin version for The Devil. God is thoroughly good and originally Satan was one of his beautiful angels and in charge of worship in the heavenly realms. However, Satan became dissatisfied with his position and desired worship for himself. He wanted God's place and as a result he was cast out of heaven and has jealously drawn human beings to himself ever since, still desirous of their worship. This of course makes him God's adversary, God's enemy, and consequently our enemy as well. God is seeking to save his creation, Satan is working to corrupt us and enslave us. So the war continues to rage to this very day. If you haven't been aware of it, you really need to be. One of the dangers is that our enemy is quite clever and devious. The Bible tells us that he comes to people as an Angel of Light so that he tricks them into following his ways. After all, if he came in leotards with horns and a trident we'd recognize him right away.

Wasn't this supposed to be a chapter of encouragement? Yes, it is – well, it will be. But first, if we don't understand how things really are we won't see that we need to take hold of God's encouragement with both hands to carry us through this war zone in victory. Haven't you ever seen how quite nice people feel secure in their way of life – maybe following the New Age concepts with crystals, having people read their palms, etc. etc.? Why have they been so fooled when the living God is being preached in our churches regularly? Because the Devil has come to them as an Angel of Light. He speaks about healing and especially likes to convince them that they are basically good and have all the power within themselves to accomplish anything they desire. He doesn't reveal his true colours. He hasn't told them to murder or rape. He tells half-truths – he says it's fine to put the baby and cradle into that tree where the breeze will rock the cradle, but he doesn't mention that the bough will break and there will be no saving the baby. He lures the maid out into the garden without warning her that he has prepared a large black bird there... You get the idea?

In fact, the Bible says that the Devil roams the earth *like a roaring lion* seeking whom he may devour. So there we have the double trouble that the Devil brings. He *appears* to be an Angel of Light but in reality he is a *roaring ravenous lion*. It reminds me of the recent war in Afghanistan where the enemy was impossible to recognize because they didn't wear a uniform to tell our soldiers which side they were on but looked just like the friendly citizens who were thankful that we were helping them.

By the way, the devil has a horde of underling devils in his army.

This all means that we need to be armed and protected.

Well, that is where the encouraging news begins. Let's turn to the book of Ephesians chapter 6 verses 10 to 18. Here we find the Armour of God. I've heard that some believers find it helpful to act out putting on each piece of this armour each morning so that they know they are prepared for whatever comes their way that day. Here are the verses…

"…Be strong in the Lord and in his mighty power. Put on the *full armour of God* so that you can take your stand against the devil's schemes. For our struggle is not against flesh and blood, but against the rulers, against the authorities, against the powers of this dark world and against the spiritual forces of evil in the heavenly realms. Therefore put on the full armour of God, so that when the day of evil comes, you may be able to stand your ground, and after you have done everything, to stand. Stand firm then, with the <u>belt of truth</u> buckled around your waist, with the <u>breastplate of righteousness</u> in place, and with your feet fitted with the <u>readiness that comes from the gospel of peace</u>. In addition to all this, take up the <u>shield of faith</u> with which you can extinguish all the flaming arrows of the evil one. Take the <u>helmet of salvation</u> and the <u>sword of the Spirit, which is the word of God</u>. And <u>pray in the Spirit on all occasions</u> with all kinds of prayers and requests. With this in mind, <u>be alert and always keep on praying for all the saints</u>."

You may need to read those verses several times to get the feeling of this armour prepared for you. And it is good to remind ourselves of our armour and weapons every so often. Some of us are not naturally bold and we feel vulnerable. The idea of a 'roaring lion' of an enemy is scary. Whether we are naturally outgoing and confident or not, we need to know that we can be prepared for any eventuality. If we are walking with God, we have access to every protection he gives. This doesn't mean that we will always be saved from trouble – sometimes, yes – but it does mean that we will be able to have victory. Victory doesn't necessarily mean that we vanquish the enemy. It does mean that we know that Jesus has already defeated them in our lives. It means that we are able to go through the war zone without giving in. We maintain our assurance, our confidence in the Lord. We don't drop our godly standards. We are not ashamed that we belong to the Lord Jesus Christ. That's victory in any circumstances. And we will eventually see the final vanquishment of the enemy at the Judgment Seat of God.

You will notice that the armour and weapons alluded to are not our modern ones as this was written 2000 years ago. But the needs are the same today as they were then and the recommended armour and weaponry are just as effective today as when this was written *because they are spiritual in power.*

Now what other treasures has God provided for his people to keep them from becoming the Devil's slaves?

Jesus is our most important ally, and he has said "I am with you to the end of the age." Bearing in mind that the words of Jesus spoke creation into being, we can be most encouraged in knowing that his power is available on our behalf. Another Scripture adds to this assurance. God has said "I will never leave you nor forsake you." As mentioned in an earlier chapter, we may not be always aware of God's presence, but we can always trust that he is with us if we are 'with him'.

Next, something that we may not usually think about – *hope.* Colossians 1:5 speaks about the fact that the hope which is stored up for us in heaven causes faith and love to be evidenced in our lives. So when you are thinking of treasuring the moments, think about that hope which keeps you steadfast in following the Lord and which brings out powerful evidences in your life.

I'd like to mention a verse which I have printed out in

lovely script and have displayed in my bedroom to remind me: "*Be still and know that I am God*". This is from Psalm 46:10. There are times when we need to stand up for a godly principle, even at the risk of a friendship or our job. But there are also times when God wants to fight on our behalf and we simply need to stand still – calmly with assurance – and God will bring the victory in answer to our prayers. Ask the Lord to reveal to you in each situation whether you are to stand and 'fight' or simply stand and watch the Lord accomplish his will. When I speak of fighting, I am not implying physical fighting but rather living the truth and speaking the truth whether others are with us or against us.

The 2nd book of Chronicles in the Old Testament tells of a physical battle where God fought the war on behalf of his people. When they were in right relationship with him he always helped them in their battles. But on this occasion they were told to be still and they would see the Lord win their battle for them. By the time the Hebrews arrived at the battle scene, their enemies – large in number – were already corpses on the ground. The Lord had brought confusion upon them and they had turned and fought each other. And though our battles under the New Covenant are not the physical kind, our problems can be slaughtered by the Lord.

As we are speaking about physical battles in the Old Testament, I'd like to mention that God sent his armies out to kill their enemies as these peoples were ripe for judgment. God usually allows some time for people to repent but if they refuse his mercy and grace, judgment will come – either in this life or the next. The neighbouring people groups were idol worshippers and they provided plenty of temptation to God's people. God was sometimes protecting his people from their ungodly influences.

When we dig into the book of Hebrews in the New Testament we find more encouragement. Before Jesus' death on the cross God dealt with his people the Jews with a series of laws which governed their lives. Because God is holy and natural men are not, there had to be continual sacrifices of animals to pay for the sins of the people which allowed them to have a distant relationship with the Lord. God had set in place a system of priests who were the mediators between God and people. They were the ones who offered the sacrifices and prayers on the people's behalf as well as for themselves. As the priests were human themselves they could relate to the weaknesses of their people, but what about God? How does he relate to our weaknesses? Well here's the wonderful news.

Hebrews 4:14-16: "Therefore, since we have a great high priest who has gone through the heavens, Jesus the Son of God, let us hold firmly to the faith we profess. For we do not have a high priest who is unable to sympathize with our weaknesses, but we have one who has been tempted in every way, just as we are – yet was without sin. *Let us then approach the throne of grace with confidence, so that we may receive mercy and find grace to help us in our time of need.*"

So there you have another treasure. Our mediator with God is the very Son of God himself. Of course, by walking closely with God, we should be growing in wisdom, strength and godliness the longer we live. And that leads us on to another aspect – putting off and putting on.

I've noticed that some folk emphasize 'putting on' without seeing that they also need to 'put off'. Sounds mysterious? Well, it's quite simple. Ephesians 4:22-24 has this to say: "You were taught, with regard to your former way of life, to *put off your old self*, which is being corrupted by its deceitful desires; *to be made new in the attitude of your minds; and to put on the new self*, created to be like God in true righteousness and holiness."

We have already touched on 'putting off and putting on'

but let's explore a little more: Ephesians goes on to speak about the kinds of things which need to be _put off_ – falsehood, anger which continues to smoulder, stealing, unwholesome talk, bitterness, rage, brawling, slander, sexual immorality, impurity, greed, obscenity, foolish talk or coarse joking. And in their place we need to _put on_ truthfulness; useful work so that we will have funds to help the needy (as well as support ourselves); words that build people up; kindness; compassion; forgiveness; love and thanksgiving.

I think it is really helpful that the Bible spells out clearly those things which please the Lord and those which do not.

Now let's leave this subject with an enormous dose of encouragement from Hebrews chapter 11. The writer is referring to the heroes of the Old Testament and this is how he sees things, from verse 32: "And what more shall I say? I do not have time to tell about Gideon, Barak, Samson, Jephthah, David, Samuel and the prophets, who *through faith* conquered kingdoms, administered justice, and gained what was promised; who shut the mouths of lions, quenched the fury of the flames, and escaped the edge of the sword; _whose weakness was turned to strength_; and who became powerful in battle and routed foreign armies."

Are you oh so aware of your weakness? Then be glad, because you will rely on God to strengthen you in the times you will need great heroism. When trials come in your daily life don't complain but *know* that God is giving you training in becoming his hero or heroine.

Are you suffering opposition as a Christian? Here's what the disciple Peter had to say:

"Dear friends, do not be surprised at the fiery trial you are suffering, as though something strange were happening to you. But rejoice that you participate in the sufferings of Christ, so that you may be overjoyed when his glory is revealed. If you are insulted because of the name of Christ, you are blessed, for the Spirit of glory and of God rests on you. If you suffer, it should not be as a murderer or thief or any other kind of criminal, or even as a meddler. However, if you suffer as a Christian, do not be ashamed, but praise God that you bear that name."

1 Peter 4:12-16

49

GOING THROUGH A TRIAL?

Sometimes life becomes a series of difficulties, doesn't it? What is your reaction? Do you grumble at the first sign of a hitch in your day? Do you want to blame someone? Here's a different take on trials which may help you to think differently in future...

James was one of Jesus' brothers in his earthly family. His advice is "Consider it pure joy ... whenever you face trials of many kinds, because you know that the testing of your faith develops perseverance. Perseverance must finish its work so that you may be mature and complete, not lacking anything." (James 1:2-4)

There are various kinds of trials. We may suffer directly because we are Christians. This is persecution. But there can be other trials in life – a long illness, loss of a job, a car accident, destructive weather, having a harsh boss, living with someone who is hard to get on with etc. Though these are not related to our faith, they challenge our faith. We believe in a good God. Why is he allowing these trials to come our way? We *could* say that's just life. It has its ups and downs. Well, here James gives us one answer to that perplexing query – God is giving us scope to develop our character.

Don't we want to be mature and complete personalities? It would be pathetic to remain like children as we grow older, wouldn't it? Good parents seek to help their children to develop not only physically but emotionally and spiritually as well. They want to see their offspring able to take their responsible places in the world, to be useful citizens. And God is a good parent. We are his children and he wants to make sure that we have the benefit of difficult life situations so that we will develop a well-rounded character, able to deal with whatever comes our way. The next life – with him in heaven if we walk with him in this life – will be trouble-free. It is guaranteed. The Bible actually says that God will wipe tears away. In other words, there won't be anything to be sad about. Our joy will be complete.

And, as I've said before, as we walk with the Lord here on earth he gives us his joy to cheer us but also to strengthen us for this earthly journey. "The joy of the Lord is your strength" says Nehemiah chapter 8 verse 10.

I have experienced this joy through a time of trial and it is amazing how it literally carries us through the experience. I also heard about a pastor in an Asian country who was strung up to a tree by his thumbs (Ugh!) to punish him for being a Christian. When his followers rescued him he was able to tell them that he had not even felt any pain because the Lord had filled him with such total joy. Isn't that amazing, and encouraging? (I am not saying that this is always the case when we go through trials but it was for him.)

We read a few verses from the first chapter of James at the beginning of this chapter. Let's look at the following words: James 1:5-8 "If any of you lacks wisdom, he should ask God, who gives generously to all *without finding fault,* and it will be given to him. But when he asks, he must believe and not doubt, because he who doubts is like a wave of the sea, blown and tossed by the wind. That man should not think he will receive anything from the Lord; he is a double-minded man, unstable in all he does."

It's always good to read the verses before and after any section so that we have the full import of what is being said.

Firstly James was telling his readers that their different kinds of trials would develop their character. Now he is reinforcing that truth with two things – firstly, that wisdom is available from God and secondly, that if we doubt God we are not becoming a person of mature and complete character but we are proving that we are actually unstable. When we put it all together it rounds out our understanding of how life with God really works.

I need to add another patch from this first chapter of James in case I have left you with the feeling that God is actually *tempting us* in order to try our character: James says (verses 13-15) "When tempted, no one should say, 'God is tempting me.' For God cannot be tempted by evil, nor does he tempt anyone; but each one is tempted when, by his own evil desire, he is dragged away and enticed. Then, after desire has conceived, it gives birth to sin; and sin, when it is full-grown, gives birth to death." Don't you love the word pictures in Scripture? It brings truth to life for us.

So, going back to the start of this subject, what do you intend to have as your response to any trials you come up against? Grumbling? Blaming? No, let's remind ourselves that this is to cause us to become persevering which in turn will develop a solid character in us so we will not be tossed around in our thinking and emotions and we will be people who can be a blessing to others. Now that's a cause for celebration surely…

We need darkness to see the stars.

From Isaiah 29 verse 13 –

> *"The Lord says*
> *'These people come near to me with their mouth*
> *and honour me with their lips,*
> *but their hearts are far from me.*
> *Their worship of me is made up only of rules taught by men.'"*

The Lord is looking for genuine honouring, not just lip service.

50

WHAT DOES GOD WANT?

Sometimes we long for simplicity. And if we are to pass on understanding of the Gospel to others, how do we put it in simple terms?

My husband John and I have chosen Micah chapter 6 verse 8 as our personal motto: *"He has showed you, O man, what is good. And what does the Lord require of you? To act justly and to love mercy and to walk humbly with your God."* Now that's simple, isn't it? Of course, there's much more to the Gospel but that is a good start and something to refer back to when life becomes a little overwhelming.

So what is another simple element to life with God? James puts it like this in chapter 1 verse 27: *"Religion that God our Father accepts as pure and faultless is this: to look after orphans and widows in their distress and to keep oneself from being polluted by the world."*

Jesus travelled about Israel on foot and via boat teaching groups of people. Wherever he went in public, people followed to hear his words. In Matthew chapter 5 we have a series of things he taught to show who would be blessed. Some versions of the Bible translate the word to 'happy' but it is much more than happiness. Happiness tends to happen haphazardly, according to circumstances. But Jesus was showing a way of life which would attract the favour of God upon us. Let's look at just what he said.

"Blessed are the poor in spirit, for theirs is the kingdom of heaven. Blessed are those who mourn, for they will

be comforted. Blessed are the meek for they will inherit the earth. Blessed are those who hunger and thirst for righteousness, for they will be filled. Blessed are the merciful, for they will be shown mercy. Blessed are the pure in heart, for they will see God. Blessed are the peacemakers, for they will be called sons of God. Blessed are those who are persecuted because of righteousness, for theirs is the kingdom of heaven."

We notice that this portion of Jesus' talk on the hillside in Galilee gives us tips on attitudes which please God. What are they?

To be *'poor in spirit'*; what does that mean? It is humility. There are those who become spiritually proud but God is looking for those who remember that without him we are of little value.

To *mourn*. This seems a little strange, doesn't it? John and I believe that it is not so much the mourning that comes with a great loss, but rather mourning over sin – either our own or the sin in the world. I know that sometimes John and I are so sad over the attitudes of the world that we apologise to God for what he has to suffer in watching over the world which goes on its way without considering him at all. We see God's hand in some circumstances when he has saved people from a great disaster in answer to Christians' prayers and we hear the people say that they have just been 'lucky'. They don't even consider that God was involved. Another attitude that makes us sad is when people refer to 'mother nature' rather than 'Father God'. Of course, we are also sad when we think of ways we could have done a better job ourselves...

To be *meek*. Meekness, to me, is somewhat similar to humility but it also refers to a quietness and gentleness. A meek person isn't seeking the limelight. Some see meekness as weakness but it is possible that a meek person is actually much stronger than the one who is a motor mouth. After all, the meek person has control over his/her tongue which is the most difficult thing in the world to train. I should say that someone who works in the limelight can, nevertheless, be meek if they are not doing that particular line of work just for the light to be shone on them. 1Peter 3:4 is speaking of the true beauty of a woman and says "...*the unfading beauty of a gentle and quiet spirit, which is of great worth in God's sight.*"

To *hunger and thirst for righteousness*. This speaks of a continual looking to be right with God every day, not just when it suits the circumstances. We will probably always have 'Sunday Christians', those who attend church and put on a good show but live differently from Monday to Saturday. That is really hypocrisy, certainly not yearning for righteousness.

To be *merciful*. English Bible teacher David Pawson says that justice and mercy travel down the same road but mercy goes further. Mercy reaches out to the weak who struggle, and lifts them so they try again. Mercy is not blind to the fact that someone deserves punishment, but it wants to give them a second chance. And what a consequence! Did you notice that those who are merciful will receive mercy themselves?

To be *pure in heart*. I think this is readily understood. No double-mindedness here. What they say is what they mean. They look for the noble thoughts and actions.

To be a *peacemaker*. Have you noticed that some folk stir up trouble wherever they go? They broadcast gossip, mention people's weaknesses, side with angry people. But to be a peacemaker, we look for ways to pour oil on troubled waters, to placate an angry person, to show them a side of an argument that perhaps they haven't considered. One thing to watch out for is the person who comes to you with negative comments about another person. If you take up the conversation you quickly find that you are condemning too. When this happens, try to find a way of saying (gently) that you don't wish to discuss that subject as you don't want to be found criticising a friend/relative/ colleague/Christian brother or sister.

To *live such a pure life that it would be possible to be persecuted*. Nobody wants to attract persecution – unless they have a mental bent – but as somebody once said "If you were arrested for being a Christian, would there be enough evidence to convict you?" There should be evidence of a Christian life in your ways and words. And under some circumstances that may bring persecution. You might be surprised to know how very many believers are suffering persecution in parts of the world right now. There are as many Christians being martyred every four days as people who died in the attack on the World Trade Centre on 9/11. Jesus' words make it clear that if we suffer for living a righteous life we have citizenship rights in the kingdom of heaven.

From the Old Testament, we have a helpful chapter in Isaiah 58 where God peels back the cover-ups and reveals just what sort of lifestyle he wants from his people. God was saying that his people seek for him day after day (sounds good), they seem eager to know his ways (really good), they ask him for just decisions, and say '*Why have we fasted, and you have not seen it? Why have we humbled ourselves, and you have not noticed?*' Now listen to God's answer: "*Yet on the day of your fasting, you do as you please and exploit all your workers. Your fasting ends in quarrelling and strife, and in striking each other with wicked fists. You cannot fast as you do today and expect your voice to be heard on high.*" Then God uses some strong words to grab their attention: "*Is this the kind of fast I have chosen, only a day for a man to humble himself? Is it only for bowing one's head like a reed and for lying on sackcloth and ashes? Is that what you call a fast, a day acceptable to the Lord?"* Then he gives the example of what he wants in his people: *"Is not this the kind of fasting I have chosen: to loose the chains of injustice and untie the cords of the yoke, to set the oppressed free and break every yoke? Is it not to share your food with the hungry and to provide the poor wanderer with shelter – when you see the naked to clothe him, and not to turn away from your own flesh and blood?"*

Now listen to the answers from heaven they will receive if they become genuine seekers after God and live his way: *"Then your light will break forth like the dawn, and your healing will quickly appear; then your righteousness will go before you, and the glory of the Lord will be your rear guard. Then you will call and the Lord will answer; you will cry for help and he will say: Here am I. If you do away with the yoke of oppression, with the pointing finger and malicious talk, and if you spend yourselves in behalf of the hungry and satisfy the needs of the oppressed, then your light will rise in the darkness, and your night will become like the noonday. The Lord will guide you always; he will satisfy your needs in a sun-scorched land and will strengthen your frame. You will be like a well-watered garden, like a spring whose waters will never fail."*

Now, when we look through that passage it is clear what kind of life God wants; it shows that going the wrong way will bar us from receiving God's attention and blessings; and that if we repent and align our lives with his loving ways we can know marvellous blessing and answers from the Lord. That really is simple enough, isn't it?

I hope you will find these passages will give you somewhere to begin when you want to share the heart of the Lord God with your family and friends. Again, he is a practical God, a holy God, a just God and though he is a merciful God our lifestyle can result in either his anger or his favour. And we will bring that upon ourselves. The choice is ours...

From Isaiah 33: 15,16:

> *"He who walks righteously*
> *and speaks what is right,*
> *who rejects gain from extortion*
> *and keeps his hand from accepting bribes,*
> *who stops his ears against plots of murder*
> *and shuts his eyes against contemplating evil –*
> *this is the man who will dwell on the heights,*
> *whose refuge will be the mountain fortress.*
> *His bread will be supplied and water will not fail him."*

51

SMALL-MINDEDNESS

Have you noticed that a lot of what is thought, said and done is based on dwarfed thinking? For some of us, virtually everything in our days is small stuff – the weather, what to wear, what she said, what he did, etc. etc. Small stuff can be a way of relating to others and good as a beginning but if that is all we ever talk about – and horrors! *all we ever think about* – we are small-minded. Don't think I'm saying that I always have high and noble thoughts and conversation. I enjoy some small talk at times. But I want to challenge all of us, myself included, to stretch ourselves. We are part of a great big world and we need to have big thoughts and large visions.

Let me share some instances which illustrate this small-mindedness. Take the way we speak about the weather. How often do we moan and groan that it's too hot, too wet, too dry, too cold? How often could we say how wonderful it is that the hot dry weather will dry up people's mould problems? Do we say how thankful we are for the rain which will revive the farmers' hopes and refresh the gardens? Do we ever think that the dry spell will ease the aches and pains of those suffering from arthritis and rheumatism? Do we realise that the cold kills off some kinds of harmful bugs? Now, I'm not saying that we have to be always mentioning these things, but if we extend our thinking we can have a positive attitude to changes in the weather instead of always complaining. And remember, it is God who brings the

Seasons and he has good reasons for doing so, so if we are murmuring about them, we are actually complaining about how God is doing things with his world.

A different and more serious situation – I know a man whose mother went guarantor for him in the purchase of a house. As a result, as he was unable to keep up the payments, she lost her home and now lives downstairs from him and his family. That man used to be a keen churchgoer. But he no longer goes to church and has become rather cynical. Now I know how very important it is to people to have a home of their own, but we really need to be careful what conditions we put on our relationship with God. It's as though some of us say to God that as long as he plays the game by our rules, it's all good. But if he doesn't answer our prayers for the things we desire, it's all over.

I think many of us – if we are honest – would have to acknowledge at least to ourselves – that we are like that. We are merry as long as God grants us our wishes but if he dares to let us go through a tough time, well he can just watch our backs as we walk away...

When we boil it down, that's small-mindedness! God has a whole universe to maintain. He has millions of people outside his family. He loves them and wants them to have the opportunity to join his 'mob', as the Aborigines would say. So he has strategies in mind. He will place this person here and that family there where they can be the most useful with the gifts he has equipped them with. And in the meantime, he will allow some storms into their lives so they learn to persevere (as discussed in chapter 6), so they develop strong character which they will need in dealing with the jobs he has for them.

Meanwhile, back in our minds and hearts, we are sulking because life hasn't turned out the way *we* wanted. We had a perfectly good plan and God spoiled it! We wanted a home in a good suburb to raise our children. Isn't that a good plan? We wanted to take our family on an overseas holiday which they would have loved but an accident meant that there was so much time off work the savings were swallowed up. We feel quite justified in weeping and wailing and accusing our Heavenly Father. That is small-minded!

Until we recognize this kind of thinking for what it is, we will feel no pang of conscience about it. But it is *small* thinking.

When we consider the weather we have to bear, let us also consider that there are many people in the world who live without decent shelter through no fault of their own. When storms blow up, they are easily unhoused... Are we thinking about them? Well, good. What are we *doing* about it? Now, that is where we need to be stretched...

There are thousands upon thousands of people who are in severe suffering – they've lost loved ones in a plane crash or a ferry sinking and they don't even know about a Heavenly Father. To see their faces on the TV screens is to see utter hopelessness and anguish. Are we thinking about them? Good. What are we doing about it? Do we need stretching?

There are men, women and children in various countries who are refugees wandering without a job, a status or a country to call their own. Are you considering them? Good, but what are you doing about it? Please invite that stretching.

We can't be personally involved in aiding all these people but the very least we can do is to pray for them. When you hear a news item involving suffering, stop to pray for those involved. When I hear an ambulance or police siren I pray for those who are in trouble of any kind – an accident, illness, etc. And I sometimes include the paramedics and police officers in my prayers. It's a small thing but God is listening and he is powerful. So prayer is the first thing to stretch ourselves around. And we don't need to pray only for their physical wellbeing but also that their circumstances may corral them into calling out to God.

Then, we may need to devise plans to help in a practical way. Can we be of use by going to those in need because we have the necessary skills? Can we donate money so that others can take aid on our behalf? Now we are beginning to have larger thoughts. Can we support missionaries who go to take the great message of the Gospel of Jesus Christ to those who are still living in darkness? Now our vision is growing...

To put it all in a nutshell, all we need to do for this stretching to take place is to take our attention from ourselves and all that is ours, and to put ourselves in the shoes of someone else. And maybe the person who needs help doesn't even have shoes. Perhaps he could do with a pair of yours, or one of your coats, or even one of your T-shirts...

I'll leave it to you to decide how and where you fit into the scene, but no more dwarfed thinking, okay?

52

DO YOU HAVE A HERO COMPLEX?

I've never heard of a Hero Complex from anyone but I've coined the term for what I've seen. We know that men in general have a desire to be admired, respected. Of course, women like to be admired as well, but it is usually more for their beauty, style or elegance; whereas, men like to be looked up to. Even if only secretly, men would like to be seen as heroes. Now that doesn't mean they have a Hero Complex. It is simply a part of their innate nature.

As in so many things, an attitude can be quite normal but if it is taken to an extreme it becomes a complex or a problem. So in this regard, if it is overly important to a man to be seen as a rescuer or hero he can become a victim of his own desire.

We need to understand that whatever we desire has the power to ensnare us. If we desire money or possessions it can turn to downright greed. Yet, to want some money and some possessions is quite normal. If we like playing football it can be a great outlet for energy, a way of improving our fine motor skills, a chance to form great friendships and a lot of fun. But if we spend all of our spare time playing football, perhaps it has too great a hold on us. The same can be said for any other sport or for dancing, singing, playing an instrument, playing computer games or cards and even work. When something becomes the centre and focus of our lives to the exclusion of other normal activities, it has enslaved us. The fact that we may enjoy it does not change this situation.

What could possibly be the trap in wanting to be a hero? Well, a man can begin to think of himself as the answer to everybody's need. We have all heard the tales of a handsome young man who rescues a damsel in distress who thinks he is the greatest hero, and the two marry and live happily ever after. But if the man is married and he still wants to rescue any damsel in distress he may be carried away by the admiration that the damsel naturally feels for her Superman. Then we have the recipe for a tragedy instead of a sweet story.

If you are a Christian man, recognize that God is the real hero in every situation. You may be able to rescue someone, but be careful to give God the glory for it. If you begin to take the accolades for yourself, your toes are already dangling over the trap.

And may I say to every Christian man, if there is a woman – married or single – who needs rescuing, engage someone else to share the rescuing so that you are not tempted. Many good men have been ensnared in a sexual encounter they didn't set out looking for because they simply wanted to help. When a woman looks up to a man because he has played the hero in her life, she may, intentionally or not, draw him to herself to be her regular hero. It is very seductive. Beware men, young or not-so-young. And all the more if you or the woman in need are married. Marriages have been broken by this very thing.

I would suggest that if you really want to be a helper – and let's face it, 'helping' is one of the gifts of the Spirit of God – look for some others who can accompany you whenever you go on one of your missions to bless someone. (The Bible reference is this: 1 Corinthians 12:28 – "And in the church God has appointed first of all apostles, second prophets, third teachers, then workers of miracles, also those having gifts of healing, *those able to help others*, those with gifts of administration, and those speaking in different kinds of tongues.")

One of our daughters and her husband have a 'ministry of helping'. This is nothing official but they both have felt that God has put it on their hearts to help people in various kinds of need. One woman had a very sick husband and a garage which badly needed cleaning and tidying so off they went to spend an afternoon at this chore with the woman. When our State's capital, Brisbane, was badly flooded, they, along with their teenagers, went as part of the army of volunteers to clean the mud out of people's houses and dispose of things which had become ruined. When John and I have needed help with jobs which are a bit heavy for us, there they are – chopping, clearing and lifting beside us. What a blessing they are. So, by all means be a helper – rather than a hero.

It is sad that some Christian churches
Still revolve around Ritual.
Ritual was needed in the Old Covenant
because it was a shadow of the Reality which was to come.
Now that Reality has arrived
In the Person and Power of the Lord Jesus Christ
and the gift of the Holy Spirit.
So Reality should have replaced Ritual.

I have been in ancient churches overseas
where there is still a dividing wall between
priest and people.
Don't they realise that when Jesus died,
The curtain in the temple which divided priest (and God)
from people was torn from top to bottom
because it was God who did the tearing?

53

RITUAL OR REALITY?

Some of us are drawn to ritual. We feel good when we have things to do, things to touch, special words to say, etc. And attached to rituals there are artefacts – crosses on the wall or round the neck, special clothing worn by priests or choir, rosary beads to help with ritual prayer, furniture which mustn't be moved, set sermons which are read so that everyone in that denomination round the country hears the same words spoken that day. We can also see this tendency in non-Christian groups who love prayer flags strung across their verandas, their back yards, even the back window of their cars; prayer beads round their wrists; burning incense at a temple then fanning the smoke with their hands to have it waft 'blessings' over them; chanting; sitting in lotus position; meditating. They may feel good, they may feel 'spiritual', but have they touched God?

Those who study us genetically say there are genes to govern many things about our natures, even our tendency to be religious or not. But our believing must be more than just a genetic tendency. Religious feelings make some folk think they are *spiritual* and we hear that word 'spiritual' bandied around in many differing groups of people these days, and some are certainly not Christian nor would they claim to be. But if we are to be wise we will take God's perspective on life and to be spiritual according to God is not just to be *religious*. In fact, in the Bible, James 1:27 reminds us "Religion that God our Father accepts as pure and faultless is this: to look after orphans and widows in their distress and to keep oneself from being polluted by the world." So we see that Christianity is more than ritual, it is a lifestyle.

As Christians we often say that Christianity is not a *religion* but a *relationship*. And this is so true. We must look within ourselves and ask are we just religious or do we actually have a relationship with God.

Before we go any further let me say that ritual isn't *necessarily* wrong. But we need to take a step back and look at what is going on in the church. Does it match the words of the New Testament – or New Covenant - which is the current Covenant that links us to God? And then a deep question we must ask ourselves – is there life in this service, in this worship or is it *just ritual*? God is looking for reality, for life, for genuineness. Does he find that in you or in your church? You see, I believe that a ritual may have been introduced to be helpful but as time advances, the ritual becomes an end in itself. People begin worshipping the *thing* instead of what it represents, what it is pointing to. A couple of examples: Churches had spires built into them so that their very shape pointed people to look upward, toward God. But when travelling through America today we can see small white spires attached to all kinds and shapes of churches. They look as though most have derived from the same factory and some don't even suit the church to which they've been attached. Are they really pointing people to God or have they simply become a *tradition?* I must admit that on the right style of building they are charming and picture perfect but I think their original purpose has been forgotten...

Then we have *relics*. These are articles venerated because of their origin. For instance some churches claim to have pieces of wood from the very cross on which Christ died, but it is said that if we were to put all the pieces from around the globe together there would be enough to make much more than one cross. Now whether or not some of those pieces really came from the cross, what effect do they have on worshippers? Is there not the danger that the *relic* becomes what is worshipped?

Under the Old Covenant there was plenty of ritual to guide and guard the lives of God's people the Jews. There were priests appointed and they had to wear very specific clothing, they must offer regular sacrifices for their own sins as well as those of all their people, they had to sometimes dip their thumbs and big toes in the blood of sacrifice, they had to wave grain offerings before the Lord. There were several solemn feasts which had to be kept each year by everyone. And they were in fear of their lives if they dared break the weekly Sabbath by doing any kind of work on that day. The temple was constructed of very specific timbers, fabrics, skins, minerals. Measurements had to be exact. Designated colours were vital. Even what was embroidered was specified. And the temple was divided into the Holy Place and the Holy of Holies. This latter was to be entered only by the High Priest and only once a year. Inside was the Mercy Seat watched over by sculpted angels.

Yes, almost all of their life was governed by rituals. But if we realize that the ritualistic elements were all a shadow of Jesus Christ and what he would accomplish, we then know that the ritual is no longer needed. Before, every item was a foreshadowing of what was to come - the shedding of blood was a picture of Christ's death on the cross. Even the laver – a bowl in front of the altar where the priests washed their hands – was a picture of the cleansing work of the Word of God. The people didn't understand why there was need for all of this ritual but by obeying they were looked upon as righteous *because Christ would bring God's righteousness in time*. But now, we have that righteousness. Let me show you the incredibly beautiful passage in Romans 3:21-28:

"But now a righteousness from God, apart from law, has been made known, to which the Law and the Prophets testify. *This righteousness from God comes through faith in Jesus Christ to all who believe.* There is no difference, for all have sinned and fall short of the glory of God, and *are justified freely by his grace through the redemption that came by Christ Jesus.* God presented him as a sacrifice of atonement, through faith in his blood. He did this to demonstrate his justice, because *in his forbearance he had left the sins committed beforehand unpunished* – he did it to demonstrate his justice at the present time, so as to be just and the one *who justifies those who have faith in Jesus.*

"Where, then is boasting? It is excluded. On what principle? On that of observing the law? No, but *on that of faith. For we maintain that a man is justified by faith apart from observing the law.*"

Can you sense the breaking of the chains of obedience to a large set of laws and rituals? For the time being, God had counted people as justified if they kept his law but now, because the penalty for our sins has been paid by a sinless Jesus, we are free to be all that God wants man to be – by exercising faith in Jesus. It doesn't mean that we live any way we want, but we have the power of God's Spirit to live within us if we have faith in Jesus. Things have changed! The order of life is different! Or it should be. Jesus summed up what was required of us in these words: Matthew 22:37-40: "*'Love the Lord your God with all your heart and with all your soul and with all your mind.' This is the first and greatest commandment. And the second is like it: 'Love your neighbour as yourself.' All the Law and the Prophets hang on these two commandments.*" So it is the law of love! After all, if we love God and love our fellow man, we will keep nine of the ten Commandments. We will not lie, steal, be sexually impure or murder etc. if we live a life of true love.

The other commandment is the one referring to keeping the Sabbath work-free. It was to be a day of rest. It was a day to be kept sacred for God rather than their own pursuits. But now the Bible tells us that we have the opportunity to enter into God's rest, in other words that we can have his Spirit empowering our lives every day of the week. We no longer need to *strive* to please God. His Spirit working within us provides the impetus and the strength for that – *if* we rely on God as he wants us to.

There is another intriguing aspect to this. Because God has made us different from each other in our temperaments, he has given us permission to do some things differently from other believers. His Word says that some folk will want to keep one day as special and others won't – that's okay! Some will want to refrain from eating meat and others won't – that's fine! So for some there will be a little ritual in their lives which is meaningful to them. But it is important that we watch ourselves that we don't let the ritual be the end result. It should be just a small part of how we live for God. For instance, some folk like to refrain from having certain food during the period of Lent – the 40 days before Easter – as a way of calling to their minds the suffering of our Lord Jesus. If that helps them express their appreciation for what he did for them, that is perfectly in order. But they must realise that it doesn't earn their salvation.

And that's where we come to the crux of the matter about religion and relationship. Our belief system – whether Christian or not – and whether this denomination or that – has come to be defined by the word *religion*. So on census forms etc. we are required to state what religion we adhere to. So we write down Anglican, Baptist, Catholic, Uniting etc. (Placed in alphabetical order so that I am not preferring one over another.) And that is the recognized way of saying which church we attend or in some way adhere to. But when we look at the worldwide religions, we see that non-Christian religions are often lived out in fear of reprisal from their gods, and are systems of *doing something to earn a right standing with those gods*.

The very reason we say that Christianity is not a religion is that there is *nothing we can do* to earn our salvation. We can't recite magic words, we can't punish ourselves because the punishment for sin is death and we haven't been given the right to take our own lives or anyone else's. But the amazing and unique truth in Christianity is that God Himself, through his son, has paid the price for our sin by dying in our place. *He* was the sacrifice so we don't have to sacrifice any more. The only way we sacrifice is to offer our lives to God to live them the way he desires, to offer praise to him as an offering of thanksgiving.

God's whole purpose in providing the sacrifice for our sins was so that we could be reconciled to him. He wants us in his family as his sons and daughters. When our first parents sinned in the Garden of Eden there was a separation of man from God. He had made man to have fellowship with him but man had blown it. In this present age, the separation has been done away with. We have the opportunity to be right with the Creator of the Universe. And he has done what was necessary so there is no need for us to buy our way to him. There is no need for all that ritual of the past – in fact, that ritual can be an offence to God because he tore the curtain between the Holy Place and the Most Holy Place in the temple in Jerusalem at the hour of Christ's death. Could he have been more clear in his meaning? Man is now able to have a relationship and fellowship with their Father God.

It isn't cheeky or bold of us to go straight to God with our thanks, our repentance or our requests. We have been told that we have a high priest and that high priest is Jesus himself who is at the right hand of God the Father and he's interceding for us. So we can approach the very throne of God in prayer, using the Name of Jesus as our seal of approval.

God's mercies are new every morning.
If you failed yesterday, sincerely ask for forgiveness in Jesus' Name
and begin today with a clean slate.
How cool is that?

54

DO WE REALLY NEED RULES?

When we are young we sometimes think it's normal and fun to ignore rules. We know Mum or Dad said not to do something but we do it anyway. And if we're not found out by them we maybe smirk and feel smart. And perhaps it becomes a way of life – laughing at rules and breaking them.

That may be part of the learning path for children but, have you noticed, some folk never grow up? They follow that same pathway – cheat the taxman, break the speed limit on the road, cheat on girlfriends/boyfriends/wives/husbands, lie to colleagues or the boss, steal, and so the list goes on.

So let's ask the question – Do we really need rules? Well, the short answer is 'Would you want to live in a world where everybody did the above? Who would you trust? Who could you feel comfortable with?'

John and I were in Cairo round 1988 and were amazed at the traffic. I guess they did have road rules because there were lanes marked on the wide roads but nobody took any notice of them. Instead of 3 lanes of traffic it varied between 4 and 5 as everybody zigged and zagged around anything in their way, constantly blowing their horns to let the others know they were squeezing through. It was utter chaos. Our taxi driver said they were just blowing their horns 'to let their brothers know they were coming through'. And I thought 'yeah, right! And they have plenty of prangs with their brothers too.' We saw evidence of this every so often.

Years later we were in China and we wondered whether

there were any road rules there as well. The roads were packed with cars, motorbikes and many bicycles unreasonably laden with all manner of loads. There were traffic lights but most of the traffic ignored red lights and even the occasional policeman trying to direct it. As pedestrians, we learned to be very bold. Where there was the slightest break in the stream we would begin to cross and the vehicles would weave around us as we made our way across. I reckoned a timid person would have to live on the same side of the road all their lives, never venturing to the other side. (By the way, let me go on record as saying that I don't blame the Chinese for loading ridiculous amounts of goods onto their bicycles. If you have no other way, you do what you have to. And they are quite inventive. You have to see it to believe it.)

Of course, discovering the alternate ways of other countries and cultures is part of the adventure and education of travel, and it gives you great stories to tell when you return home. But we have to acknowledge that these are dangerous practices and people die because rules have been broken. Back home we have plenty of rule-breakers and lives are lost here as well.

How many times have we heard that road accidents are often caused by alcohol, drugs, excessive speed or 'phone texting? And people have lost their lives because of it, often innocent lives. The loss of one life through breaking rules is tantamount to murder in my book, though the intention may not have been there. And for each life lost there are many, many people who suffer. Family and friends miss out on the benefits that person brought to their lives, even if it was just someone to love. Communities have lost perhaps a doctor, dentist, pastor, fire fighter, volunteer, or a darling child who might have grown up to be a great benefactor. So rule breaking is an extremely serious matter. That's why I'm addressing it here. The sooner we see that there is a good reason for rules, the sooner we will become mature people who don't cause unnecessary suffering to others. It is *not* smart or funny to break rules. They are there to protect us.

Something missing from our society these days is respect. Recently a young man was convicted of bashing and kicking – with CCTV proof – two elderly men who were having a quiet drink at a hotel. He told them they were too old to be there. They were down in the city because one of them was being treated for cancer. It was claimed that the young man had taken illicit drugs. Is there a day go by when the morning news doesn't contain an item of a shooting or stabbing in Sydney, most often ending in death? And of course New South Wales doesn't have it on its own, it just has a larger population. In the other States we have constant TV vision of road rage and violence outside nightclubs, etc.

Flowing from the disregard for God in our nation there is disrespect for rules, laws and regulations. Doctors and nurses witness the awful results of illicit drug use. One of our daughters is a nurse and she has said that some people end up with schizophrenia after just one use of marijuana; other users are always angry which is hardly a happy result for themselves or those who have to live with them. The results of using the drug Ice are frightening yet people go ahead in their droves using these mind altering drugs. Why is it that the very term 'mind altering' doesn't warn them that they are playing with fire (and sometimes death)? I am afraid that our largest hospitals in the future will be psyche institutions filled with those who have bucked the rules to get high from drugs.

I would say to young people if you want a high, look for something which is fulfilling and do that and you will have a high which will benefit others and be safe for you. How simple is that? You say 'what will be fulfilling?' Well usually it is something which fills a need. It can be your job or you can be a volunteer in your spare time. You will usually find that the happiest people are those who are making someone else happy...

Excessive alcohol is just another form of drug taking by the way... And what horrible messes people make of their lives with this form too.

People often think of Christians as goody goodies who never have any fun. They don't realise that joy is one of the benefits of following Jesus and joy stays around even when circumstances take a downturn. In fact when we are facing the most difficult times God sometimes gives an extra injection of joy to carry us through. And this injection has no nasty side effects. We don't need to get high by artificial means.

And some of the most adventurous people are believers. Have you noticed that for centuries single women have ventured across oceans alone to take the good news of the Gospel of Jesus to primitive people who have sometimes been hostile? And many times they have remained there for the rest of their lives. Of course there have been some single men who have done so as well but many more single women than men. And let's not forget the young families who have done similar things, braving diseases like malaria. So being a goody goody doesn't mean you are a 'weakie'. But taking drugs and getting drunk say that you are...

So, let me recommend God's way. Every rule he gave the Israelites in the Old Testament was for their protection and their good. Now, under the New Covenant, we don't have so many rules but we do have the high standard of loving God and loving our neighbour. And 'our neighbour' is anybody, not just the man next door. And God has thought of everything. He makes His very own Spirit available to believers so they can live by his standards and provide light to the communities in which they live.

Don't be swayed by mates who think they're *cool* taking drugs or getting drunk. Remember that *cool* rhymes with *fool*.

"No-one can make you feel inferior without your consent."
Eleanor Roosevelt

"The Devil can't make you feel unworthy to worship God without your consent."
John Spall

55

IS IT WRONG TO FEEL GOOD ABOUT YOURSELF?

When we are young it is not unusual to feel some confusion about right and wrong, good and bad, when it comes to personal things. Take for instance the way we feel about ourselves. I remember that my mother didn't heap praise on me because she didn't want me to become proud. And I can understand that. But it left me without much confidence in facing the world. Being an only child, and with a father who had been injured during the war and was consequently far from well and in pain, I had limited socialising with people outside the family. I was a shy child naturally so these circumstances found me without great social skills.

I certainly wasn't a proud person but I didn't have what I would now consider a really healthy self-image either. Of course, the world has changed a lot in the meantime and young people have been encouraged to think much of themselves in more recent years. I probably wasn't so unusual in my youth because it tended to be an adult's world then. Young people weren't expected to have strong opinions until they were becoming adults.

When I was growing up in Australia, the voting age and the age at which people were legally able to drink alcohol were both 21. So you can imagine when laws were passed allowing both of these activities at age 18, it caused young people to feel they were mature much earlier. Now to be honest, I believe that it was much safer and more sensible for people to be 21 before stepping into these privileges and responsibilities. Though young people feel they are mature in their teens the truth is that we do much more maturing after we emerge from those years. I can remember when I was 18 or 19 chatting with a fellow I worked with. He was in his mid-twenties and he said 'Jean, you grow up a lot between 18 and 21'. I was surprised to hear him say this as I felt I was pretty grown up already but as time went on I realised that he had been absolutely correct.

Allowing for this development in mind and body, in perception and understanding, I'd like to give a pointer or two about how we can view ourselves in the large scheme of things. I have touched on this in one of the earlier Sections in the series but let's look at it again.

Life is a balancing act. We want to be good but not a goodie-two-shoes who turns everybody off. We want to have fun but not waste the whole of our lives. We want to accomplish something but not neglect relating to people in the process. We want to feel good about ourselves but not to be 'stuck up'. We want to express our opinions so we can make a difference, but not be rude in doing so. How do we work it all out?

As I've said before, we are important to God therefore we *are* important. But so is every other person important. So that helps to balance how we think about ourselves. God has a plan for each life so we can be sure that we can accomplish whatever it is that he wants of our life. That should bring a measure of confidence, but that confidence should be based on our relationship with God as it is in his strength that we will accomplish all that he wants and expects of us. We know that God loves us so much that he gave his own Son to pay for our sins so we should feel secure and snug in that knowledge, but not smug as though we had earned that love. Can you see the balancing of our opinion of ourselves when we reason it all out like that?

IS IT WRONG TO FEEL GOOD ABOUT YOURSELF?

So, if you have decided to walk with God, there is no reason why you should not feel good about yourself – you are loved, you have value – but it is kept in balance as you respect others as also loved and valuable, even if they have not yet realised it. You may be the one to unlock *their* good self-image by encouraging them....

> *"I thank my God every time I remember you.*
> *In all my prayers for all of you, I always pray with joy*
> *because of your partnership in the gospel from the first*
> *day*
> *until now, being confident of this,*
> *that he who began a good work in you*
> *will carry it on to completion*
> *until the day of Christ Jesus."*

The Apostle Paul to the believers at Philippi.

56

WATCH OUT FOR THE MEDIA

I have often said that the media rules the world. Why would I say that? Because our concept of what is happening in the world, both here at home as well as in the most far-flung corners of the globe, is very largely shaped by what news is delivered to us via newspapers, TV broadcasts, radio reporting, magazines or social media.

Is this a bad thing? Not necessarily. It is difficult to hear about what's occurring without this constant reporting and journalism. However, we need to realise that the way an event is presented depends on the opinions of those doing the reporting or their superiors. Sometimes it is outrageously obvious that certain reporters have a political agenda of their own. They attack the 'messenger' because they don't like the message. They pull down anyone on the opposite side of politics from their own bias. Others simply like to pull down anyone who is prominent whether they are doing a good job or not. This means that what we are hearing/seeing is not always the truth. So always be just a little sceptical when listening to the news. Try to vary the avenue via which you receive news so that you may escape someone's bias.

Let's look at an example of twisted reporting. Recently we have noticed that the media are always bringing up polls on the popularity of leaders. Let's be wise in judging a politician – is his popularity really the important issue? Surely it is his policies which impact the people. But by constantly harping on a man's popularity or lack thereof, these reporters are assuming a power that should not belong to them. If they were really interested in what is best for the country they would look beyond popularity to the policies he espouses as to whether they will bring good or ill to the country and its people. If they really cared they would focus on the benefits or liabilities policies would result in. And after all, popularity often depends on whether or not the politician is throwing money at popular projects. He may be drawing in the purse strings because he doesn't want the country to end up like some of our European brothers and sisters with drowning debt.

What are news bureaus and media corporations in general interested in? Could it be their bottom line? By that, I mean the money they engender for themselves by deliberately reporting in a way which curries favour for themselves from the viewers/readers/listeners. Could it be that they want something controversial to keep excitement in their presentations? Is it their ratings they are most concerned with? I have often noticed headlines on the cover of popular women's magazines but when you read the article inside you very much doubt that the person concerned actually said the words that had been put in their mouth on the cover.

In other instances, I have heard TV newsreaders 'quote' someone they had interviewed earlier, making it sound as though the interviewee had said something quite inflammatory. But as I had heard the live interview earlier, I knew that they had simply been answering a question put to them and they had not actually said what was later quoted at all. It's like the 'reality shows' which have obviously been staged, it's all smoke and mirrors.

Let me say right here that I respect those reporters who put their lives on the line to bring us accurate news from dangerous arenas of wars or rescues. Reporters are sometimes required to suffer discomfort as well as danger – relaying their news from areas experiencing cyclones or bushfires. And I take my hat off to them. But I am angered when I know the news delivered at times is not accurate. I have taken the time to write to television channels on occasion to complain about attitudes or words used in programs and I would urge you to do the same. If they receive enough feedback that people are not appreciating what they are presenting they won't want to lose their following. Don't let them do all the 'exerting of power'. We need to exert a little of our own by speaking up. If we remain silent, they will assume that their popularity is total.

Someone once said 'the pen is mightier than the sword' and that still holds true, though today it may be the computer keyboard in place of the pen. Armies don't need to go out to war armed to the teeth to control people. Reporters just need to report things from their own perspective. So be wary. Put the shoe on the other foot – take up your 'pen' (or computer) and give them a piece of your mind when they deserve it...

Well, that's one aspect of the media. But there are other traps. What about advertising? Remember that when someone advertises a product or service, it is to their advantage if you take up whatever they are offering. So one of the ways they seek to lure you into parting with your money is to butter you up. Have you noticed how many advertisements speak about doing it '*your way*', telling you that '*you are number one*', or that '*you are worth it*'? There may be a few genuine people who really do want to offer you a service or a product because it will change your life for the better, but remember that the bottom line is that you will part with your cash and it will end up in their pockets.

Don't be charmed into buying things you don't need. You will regret it later, you will end up poorer than you need to be, or you will end up with the clutter of things you bought that you didn't use. I would suggest that when you see something that looks good you question yourself: Do I really need that or will it just sit in a corner after the first week? Is this a good deal or should I look around further? Can I afford this now or would it be better to save until I can pay cash for it?

I hope I have just given you a little warning so that you won't be gullible but will see the events taking place in the world from the Father's point of view. If you get to know your Bible well, you will quite often see that current world events have already been predicted there...

As an example, did you realise that the Bible said that earthquakes would increase? Did you know that it said knowledge would increase and travel would too? These things were written thousands of years ago when no-one could humanly imagine motorised vehicles let alone computers and mobile 'phones and 'planes... And Bible readers have known all along that we would eventually hit a period when the whole world would suffer recession and would hail an identity who would appear to have the answer the whole world is wanting. However, he will be anti-Christ and against those who follow Christ. He will be empowered by Satan, be able to do supernatural things and will – *for a time* – defeat Christians, killing many. But then Jesus Christ will return and the tables will be turned – totally. When you read your Bible thoroughly you will see world events in a new light...

The Bible speaks about the world and its values (that is, the humanistic world system, not creation) and warns us not to be a part of it: 1 John 2:15-17:

*"Do not love the world or anything in the world. If anyone loves the world, the love of the Father is not in him. For everything in the world – the cravings of sinful man, **the lust of his eyes** and the boasting of what he has and does – comes not from the Father but from the world. The world and its desires pass away, but the man who does the will of God lives forever."*

57

ARE YOU SOARING WITH THE EAGLES? OR PECKING WITH THE TURKEYS?

Most of us would like to be more successful at life itself, wouldn't we? Well, there are keys throughout the Bible to help with all sorts of situations, and life in general. There is a rather well-known section of the writings of Isaiah the prophet in the Old Testament that I would like to print here. It's a little lengthy but it is so encouraging and holds one of those special keys. Here it is: Isaiah 40:28-31 –

"Do you not know? Have you not heard?
The Lord is the everlasting God,
the Creator of the ends of the earth.
He will not grow tired or weary, and his understanding no one can fathom.
He gives strength to the weary and increases the power of the weak.
Even youths grow tired and weary, and young men stumble and fall;
but those who hope in the Lord will renew their strength.
They will soar on wings like eagles;
they will run and not grow weary,
they will walk and not be faint."

Did you notice that there are two important facets for us to profit by in that reading? Firstly, we are told what God is like – He is everlasting, he is the Creator of everything, he hasn't grown old and tired and he has more understanding than any human being. Spend a little time – or a lot of time – digesting those things about God. This is a great God. Why do people fashion gods of their own when there is an amazing Father God to turn to, to learn from and to serve? One can only wonder... and pray.

The second facet is what this wonderful Creator will do for people – He will give strength to those who feel weary, he will increase power to those who are weak, he will do this to such an extent that it will be as though they are soaring over the circumstances of life, and there will be a continuing renewing of their strength as it is used up.

BUT...did you pick up on the key? All these wonderful resources are available to those who HOPE IN THE LORD! An earlier translation of the Bible put it this way – 'those who wait upon the Lord'. These wonderful treasures and promises are for those who look to the Lord for their supply, who spend time in his presence, who try to understand God and his ways.

John and I often say out loud to the Lord 'Our eyes are on you, Lord'. We are seeking to understand every circumstance of our lives in the light of his wisdom. So if we catch a cold or stub our toe or have bad news from the doctor, our first response is 'our eyes are on you Lord, what are you saying in this situation, are you trying to get our attention, to tell us something?' You see, our hope is in the Lord, our trust is in the Lord, we belong to him and we have the right and privilege to hear our guidance from him. When we feel off-colour, we don't rush to the 'phone to ring the doctor as our first defence, we talk to the Lord about it. If we feel that we should claim healing, then that's what we do. If we think that we should take a natural remedy, then that's what we do. If we feel that we should see the doctor, then that's what we do. He has given skills to the medical profession so there's no sin in seeking medical help – at the right time. But they are not our first port of call. God is. It's so simple.

There is a confidence that comes to us as we see God as our source and our goal. What a high calling we have. It doesn't matter whether we have a University degree or just basic schooling. As a matter of fact if we go back just a few generations many of us find that our ancestors had no schooling at all. They couldn't even write their own name. But if they trusted in Jesus as their Saviour, they had a high calling; they were children of the King of Kings and the Lord of Lords. They had the right to expect God to guide them and to bless their lives.

One of the things I love about God is that he is mindful of the most humble of people. Do you recall the time Jesus was at the temple watching as the people put their offerings into the treasury? He drew his disciples' attention to the fact that a poor widow had dropped in two tiny coins – with very little value – and he observed that from God's point of view she had given more than the large amounts given by the rich people. Why? Because what is given is judged by what is kept back, rather than the value of the offering. He said: *"I tell you the truth, this poor widow has put more into the treasury than all the others. They all gave out of their wealth; but she, out of her poverty, put in everything – all she had to live on."*

Doesn't that give you hope in the Lord? You don't have to be clever because you can ask for wisdom from God; and you don't have to be rich or important because God sees the intention of the heart. He sees the humble, poor person. He saw the love this widow had for God. And she obviously was trusting God to provide for her or she wouldn't have given all she had to him. So she had the key to God's treasures – her 'hope was in the Lord'.

God is not wanting to keep his resources a secret so he has revealed so many of them in his Word. But we need to be on the lookout for the keys to his treasures because they are included as well. It is surprising how many times promises from Scripture are quoted by people without the accompanying keys. The promise is not for you unless you qualify for it. But to qualify, you don't need super intelligence, you just need to have a humble heart and a determination to walk the Lord's way.

William Wilberforce is credited with causing legislation to be enacted in Britain which ended slavery. This was a marvellous work but this man was a small man, a frail man, not a handsome man according to one friend, and though he was a Member of Parliament, never held a Ministry but he steadily chipped away at the attitudes of the people current in his time and over several decades he brought about a change for the better in the morals of the English and the ending of the terrible slave trade. He was not tied to his physical limitations and he not only soared above his circumstances during his lifetime but he is remembered with admiration more than 180 years after his death.

So, the only question you need to consider is: Are you going to soar with the eagles, or peck with the turkeys?

"Samuel saw Eliab and thought, 'Surely the Lord's anointed stands here before the Lord.' But the Lord said to Samuel, 'Do not consider his appearance or his height, for I have rejected him. The Lord does not look at the things man looks at. Man looks at the outward appearance, but the Lord looks at the heart.'"

1 Samuel 16:6 & 7

58

COULD GOD LOVE YOU?

We speak about God being a God of Love, but there are some folk trekking through life feeling as though they are disqualified from God's love. Why do they feel this way? Well, it could be for a number of reasons – perhaps they have done something terrible earlier in their life and feel it is too bad to be forgiven; they have spent a large part of their life ignoring God or speaking against him and feel it wouldn't be fair to expect him to accept them so late in time; maybe they came from a family situation where their father left much to be desired and it has given them a distaste for fatherhood; or they have never achieved anything in their own eyes and feel they are below the radar of God's love; perhaps they are of a nationality where Christianity is not the major religion and they feel that God wouldn't be interested in them. And there could be many other reasons...

Let's look at some of the folk in the pages of the Bible whom God had his eyes on. We know that the Israelites were God's Chosen People in the Old Testament. God had called their ancestor Abraham and led him from his own country of Ur of the Chaldees to the land of Canaan, later called Israel, and gave him that land for himself and his descendants. But there is a lovely story of someone in the New Testament who was certainly not an Israelite. He was a coloured man from Ethiopia in Africa. More than that, he was a eunuch. As obnoxious as it may seem to us, in some countries, men were chosen to be guards of the royal family or to occupy other positions of trust; and to be sure they would be reliable men around the females of the family, they were castrated, thus becoming eunuchs. This man could have felt that God would not be interested in him but he was a convert to Judaism and had actually travelled to Jerusalem to worship at the temple. Now he was on his way back to his homeland in a horse drawn carriage. Have you read what God did on this man's behalf?

God's angel visited one of the early Jewish Christians, Philip, and instructed him to go to the desert road between Jerusalem and Gaza. When Philip obeyed, he came upon this Ethiopian eunuch who was sitting in his carriage reading the book of the prophet Isaiah. The Holy Spirit told Philip to go to the chariot and when he did he heard the man – whose name we are not even told – reading, so he asked him if he understood what he was reading. The African man said he needed someone to explain it to him and invited Philip to join him. I have a very special reason to now print the passage he was reading:

"He was led like a sheep to the slaughter,
and as a lamb before the shearer is silent,
so he did not open his mouth.
In his humiliation he was deprived of justice.
Who can speak of his descendants?
For his life was taken from the earth."

(He was reading Isaiah 53. It is recorded in Acts 8:32/33)

Before we go on with the rest of his story, can you see why I wanted to give you the reading he was looking at? This man was a eunuch which meant that he would never have descendants of his own. He had been deprived of the right and privilege that many of us take for granted. This passage of the Bible, as Philip explained to him, though it was written centuries earlier, referred to Jesus himself. It was a prophecy. Jesus was put to death as the sacrificial Lamb of

God, he did not try to defend himself because he had come to earth for this very purpose. He was deprived of justice because he was not guilty of the charges laid against him. Then that question which must have pierced the Ethiopian's heart – 'Who can speak of his descendants?' Eunuchs must have felt that they had been robbed, not only of their manhood but also of the opportunity to know cuddles from their own children, the joy of nurturing their own offspring, and perhaps even to see the next one or two generations of their descendants.

Philip began at that very quotation to show him that the Old Testament of the Jews was in reality pointing to the coming of the Saviour, Jesus Christ, who gave up the opportunity of having his own descendants as well.

Can you see how very personal God is, that he should send his servant Philip to minister to one man, a man from another country, from another nationality, a man who was a eunuch; and that he should arrange for Philip to arrive at the carriage at the precise time that he was reading a passage that he would have related to in a most personal way?

Having heard the good news of the Gospel, as the carriage came to an area of water, the eunuch asked to be baptised and Philip was only too pleased to oblige. God had other work for Philip so he transported him by the Spirit away from the Ethiopian who went on his way rejoicing in his new-found understanding.

So God is not just interested in the hundreds and thousands. He is vitally interested in the individual who is seeking him, whatever their circumstances or their background.

Can I share a little personal story with you? It's not about me, but about my hubby John. He was ministering in South Africa a few years ago. As well as speaking to congregations in churches, as is always his custom, he would go out of his way to speak to those who are doing rather menial jobs, serving him food, or taking cash at cash registers anywhere he is purchasing something, regardless of their colour or appearance. One woman was around the area where he was staying and she noticed what he was like. Before he left for home she went to him and presented him with a beautiful lamb. It was shaped from wire and beaded all over, white with black ears and tail. It is a delightful thing. She said to John that some people are after the hundreds and thousands, but she could see that he was interested in the one lost lamb here and there. It reminded me of the story Jesus told of how a good shepherd will wander over all sorts of terrain seeking for the one lamb which has gone astray, though he has many who are safe in the sheepfold. So if you think you are the black sheep of the family, be assured that Jesus is the Good Shepherd seeking for you...

Who else can we look at who was noticed by God?

How about Hannah? In ancient times, men had more than one wife and Hannah was in just such a position. Maybe that wouldn't have been so bad except that the other wife, Peninnah, had children while Hannah produced none. To make it worse, as Peninnah saw that her husband loved Hannah, she provoked Hannah about her failure to give their husband a child. Hannah was greatly distressed by her situation and on one occasion when the family was at the temple Hannah wept and prayed to the Lord for a son. Now here was a woman living in an unhappy family situation and the Lord heard her prayer and granted her the son she craved. An interesting and important note in this story is that when Hannah prayed for a son she also promised to give him back to the Lord to serve him. Isn't that an indication of Hannah's heart? She didn't want this son so much for herself or her husband or even to pay back the meanness of her rival wife. When she had weaned the baby (and that may have been when the child was 3 or 4 years of age) she honoured her promise and took him to the priest to be brought up as a servant in the temple. The extra blessing in this story is that that very baby was Samuel who became a mighty prophet of the Lord who ministered to the king. But the story began with a humble woman crying out to the Lord. (This story is found in 1Samuel 1.)

Let's look at another widow. This time we are in the town of Nain in Israel and Jesus came upon a funeral procession. This widow's only son had died and Jesus saw her and "his heart went out to her and he said, 'Don't cry.' Then he went up and touched the coffin, and those carrying it stood still. He said, 'Young man, I say to you, get up!' The dead man sat up and began to talk, and Jesus gave him back to his mother." So don't ever think that it is the great people in the eyes of the world who have a monopoly on God's attention.

Who next? How about some more widows? The story focuses in on Tabitha (also called Dorcas) who had lived near the modern city of Tel Aviv. She was a believer in Jesus and when she died, disciples sent for the Apostle Peter to come, Jesus having already ascended to heaven. Tabitha had been a woman of good works and the widows around had all been blessed by her. They showed Peter the clothes she had made for them. Peter went to where Tabitha's body was laid out and he called for her to get up. With that, she opened her eyes and was restored to life and to the needy widows she loved to help.

So far we have looked at a foreigner - the eunuch - at a wife Hannah, and a number of widows. Let's refocus – this time at a baddie. Can you see, in your mind's eye, a man nailed to a cross? Crucifixions were fairly common at this time so it wasn't strange to see that there were two other crosses nearby. On one of them was Jesus, the Son of God, who chose to die in this horrific way, suffering on our behalf. On the other, there was an unrepentant thief who hurled insults on Christ. The man we are looking at was also a thief but at this late hour in his life he could see beyond what his fellow criminal was focussing on. He rebuked the other robber saying that they were enduring what their crimes deserved but Jesus had done nothing wrong. Then he said the words which were the most vital he ever uttered: *'Jesus, remember me when you come into your kingdom.'* Had he been in the crowd at some time when Jesus was talking with the people out on the lake or on a hillside? Had he heard about him while in jail? We don't know, but what we do know is that, even at that late stage in his life, when his life was already ebbing away, God was listening, God was watching...

"Jesus answered him, 'I tell you the truth, today you will be with me in paradise.'"

So, can you still believe that you are not qualified to be one whom God has his eyes on? Your background won't disqualify you, your gender won't either, your poverty certainly won't, and neither will your sin, or your age.

I want to again share with you a wonderful verse; wonderful doesn't seem a good enough word to describe it, perhaps amazing, maybe stupendous! Here it is:

"For the eyes of the Lord range throughout the earth
to strengthen those whose hearts are fully committed
to him."

You can find those words in 2 Chronicles 16:9. What is that verse telling us? Firstly, it doesn't matter what little hole in the earth we are hiding in, the Lord's eyes are searching. What is his purpose? He wants to strengthen people. Isn't that great (stupendous)? But who qualifies for this individual attention? Those whose hearts are fully committed to him. Not the beautiful, not the rich, not the powerful, not those who have never sinned, but those who have decided to commit their way to him fully.

So, now – are you qualified for the love and care and

guidance of the Creator of the Universe? Only you can make the decision that will qualify you. I hope you have done so already, or that you will do so right now...

There's an old saying "the proof is in the pudding" which, I suppose, really means the proof is in tasting the pudding. Then, and only then, will you know whether the dish is a success. There's something in the Bible which says something similar. Psalm 34:8 begins *"Taste and see that the Lord is good..."* It's not enough to stand back and think about following the Lord. You must step forward and 'taste' of him. You will never know the love of God in your life until you risk yourself to his care. You will not know the power of God in your circumstances until you abandon yourself to him. He is looking for you to come to him, or to come closer to him. You take a step toward him, and you will find that he was there waiting all the time. So, now is the time to 'prove the pudding'.

59

WHAT KIND OF GOD DO YOU HAVE?

Does the title of this chapter seem a little strange? Well, to clarify it, I'm not thinking of foreign idols. Rather, there are people who would call themselves Christians but they may have many and varied ideas of what the Christian God is like.

We are told in the Bible that we were made 'in the image of God' which is great news. But when it comes to the kind of God we have in our minds, many of us make God in *our* image instead. For instance, if they are careless people, they think of God as winking at sin as though it didn't really matter. If they are kind, they may think of God as being all kindness with no wrath at all. If they are strict people, they may expect God to strike them down if they don't measure up. Do you see now what I'm getting at?

When we first become followers of Jesus, we may have a pretty stunted concept of God. Then again, if we have been exposed to really good teaching, we may have a very good idea of the greatness of the Lord. But whatever way we begin, as we grow closer to the Lord it is to be hoped that we are flexible enough to perceive more and more of what our God really is like.

I don't pretend to understand God fully but as the years have spun round, I believe that I have a sense of God that is more accurate than it was when I was young.

In the Old Testament we sometimes are presented with a wrathful, punishing God when his people are rebellious and refuse to walk his way. It's no wonder because God says that 'rebellion is as the sin of witchcraft'. You see, we often classify sins to our own way of thinking, large or small. But if we study God's Word, we find just what he sees as serious. We might think that a little bit of rebellion is fun but we need to remember that it's no laughing matter to Him.

I wanted to mention his wrath first because it doesn't get much of a mention these days. There were earlier times when preachers dwelt on 'fire and brimstone' in their sermons. This may have been laboured too often then. But the pendulum has swung to the extreme on the other side and it's as though God is now incapable of wrath. But there are plenty of New Testament Scriptures which speak about hell and the danger of going there. And when Jesus spoke of hell, it was always to believers. So we need to keep God's wrath as a 'small' part of our picture of our Lord.

But what I want to emphasize now is what I believe the main aim of God is. He wants everyone to be safe in his care. He wants them to achieve his plan for their lives and it will be something which will bring them joy as they accomplish his will. Now, I don't know about you, but to me this is a delightful state of affairs.

Many other religions have no assurance of going to a happy place when they die. They spend their lives making sacrifices in the *vague* hope of appeasing their idols. Some even whip their bodies, again in the *wish* that good things *might* happen in their lives, whereas we can have the assurance that our God *intends* good upon us if we are committed to him.

There is a rather well known portion of the Bible in the book of the prophet Jeremiah in the O.T. Chapter 29:11-13 – (God speaking) *"For I know the plans I have for you," declares the Lord, "plans to prosper you and not to harm you, plans to give you hope and a future. Then you will call upon me and come and pray to me, and I will listen to you.*

You will seek me and find me when you seek me with all your heart." Having read that, do you need to realign your focus on God? Is that the picture you have of God?

When we read the Old Testament, we see that every generation had to hear the same things. The Lord had to keep raising up prophets to carry his invitations and warnings to each succeeding generation. If human beings were ideal, each generation would have taught their offspring the ways of the Lord and they would have obeyed and passed on the same teachings to their children. But because we are not perfect or ideal, we need to be reminded ourselves to keep on 'the straight and narrow' way of following the Lord as well as seeking to teach our children.

Thus we find again and again the Word of the Lord to the people of Israel was to call them back to himself and his ways. Though they suffered because of their wickedness and rebellion, God was always ready to call them back because of his mercy and his desire to bless them.

Can you imagine how much sadness we must heap upon the Lord when we turn away from him? His desire is to give us a hope (i.e. a firm hope, not something vague) and a future. He wants to give us peace and love and joy. How wonderful is that? But, as we have been warned, 'what we sow is what we reap'. So *we* actually decide what will be ours. Will we have hope, joy, love and peace in our lives and in our hearts? We will - if this is the crop we have sown in our hearts and lives. If we plant lettuce seeds in our gardens we should have lettuce to eat. But if we plant weeds our plates will be bare. It's the same on the spiritual plane. If we are argumentative, we won't have peace. If we are rebellious, we will lack joy. And so it goes on. God is so fair that he has allowed us to choose what kind of an existence we enjoy or endure.

Of course, there are outside pressures in our lives

sometimes and we have to endure some suffering which we haven't caused. But inwardly at least we can still know peace of mind which is priceless. And we need to keep in mind that if we give generously to those in need God will be able to give generously to us as we have need. As I have said previously, this doesn't mean a 'give to get' mentality. But as we make it our habit to give, we attract God's generosity and favour into our lives.

So I would recommend a couple of things – talk to the Lord often to get to know him better, and read his word for he has made himself known within his word. Then put into practice what has been revealed.

If we had tried to dream up the greatest God, we wouldn't have come up with one who is better than the real, living God who invites us to walk hand in hand with him and to know his grace and blessings.

"Come, all you who are thirsty, come to the waters;
And you who have no money, come, buy and eat!
Come, buy wine and milk without money and without cost.
Why spend money on what is not bread, and your labour
on what does not satisfy?
Listen, listen to me, and eat what is good, and your soul
will delight in the richest of fare.
Give ear and come to me; hear me,
that your soul may live."

Isaiah 55:1-3a

60

YOUR POWER OF CENSORSHIP

Whenever there is something raised about preventing the population from doing dangerous things, there is a group which raises its voice in opposition, claiming that people's civil rights are being violated. Some of them probably think they are on the side of right, but I strongly suspect that others of their number know exactly what they are doing and it is far from right.

Let me say that people do have freewill and they can choose how they live their lives but we need to remember that some things which people choose to do affect not only themselves but others, and then they are trampling others' civil rights.

I have spoken previously about pornography and the trap that it is. John has young – and not-so-young – men come to him seeking to be free of their addiction to this plague. Not only has it spoiled their view of women and sex, it causes their wives to lose respect for them and sometimes breaks up marriages.

I remember a time in our State of Queensland where our former Premier, Joh. Bjelke-Petersen was strong on censorship of films. He was a living example to the people because I heard that on one occasion he had the duty of opening a new drive-in movie venue. After completing the official opening he and his wife began to watch the movie showing but when it took a turn for the worse, he and his wife left.

Because he stood up for righteousness, Joh as he was known was attacked on every side. I don't wish to go into claims and counter-claims about what he may have done or not done, but this I know: he was vilified because he tried to protect his people from crude and rude material. Many of us Queenslanders loved having someone who honoured God and protected his people as our leader but in other States of the country there were jokes about having to turn the clock back ten years when you reached our border. Southern newspapers were merciless. But Joh didn't back down. Of course, his time came to an end and we now look back on the loosening of the reins over ensuing years – brothels have been legalised, witchcraft is no longer an offence, censorship of films is almost non-existent, but strangely enough the restrictions are now upon people such as school religion teachers who are not allowed to teach children the whole Gospel. Parents are not allowed to hit their children to discipline them. Isn't it notable that there are more restrictions but they are against the things of God?

Just a note: The Bible says "*Spare the rod and spoil the child*". This means that children need to be punished for disobeying or they will never see that it is important to live within certain parameters. The Bible is **not** saying that a child should be beaten severely, but there is a powerful message in a smart slap to the rear end. (Some parents used to keep a ruler or a wooden spoon handy and after using it once or twice at appropriate times, they found that they only had to threaten to use it to bring the child to order.) The Bible also cautions fathers not to be harsh with their children so when we put the two messages together we see that it is wise and loving.

If you have grown up more recently, you may think that the modern laws are normal and good, but if you had been alive in former times and able to see the difference these laws have made you may think otherwise.

Yes, people have been given the choice to live their lives in wickedness, but has it improved the society that we live in? I have mentioned that the age of being lawfully able to vote and drink alcohol was lowered from 21 to 18. They are two more things where laws have been loosened. When you put all these things together – the strengthening of evil and the weakening of Godliness – we have a great recipe for anarchy, law breaking, theft, violence, blasphemy, drunkenness, gang warfare, drug addiction, rape, paedophilia, witchcraft.

And these are the very things which have grown out of all proportion over the period since the brakes have been taken off our society. We now see governments and police running around the edges of society trying to mop up the damage, trying to put in boundaries to stop the torrent of violence and wickedness. I actually wish people had to turn their clocks back 30 years when they reach the Queensland border. Then I can guarantee that we would have an influx of decent people who would want to live within our borders and flee the problems of their regions.

Now, what am I leading up to? I could suggest that we speak more loudly when new laws are mooted which will further weaken our society. But as well as that, I want to draw your attention to your civil rights. You have the right to deny yourself these freedoms which have been foisted upon us. Deny them to yourself. You are free to read filthy literature, to listen to or tell dirty jokes, to binge drink, to watch questionable shows on TV, etc. etc. But you are also free to refuse to do any of these things, to have true freedom.

One modern phenomenon which troubles me greatly is the music video as well as modern stage dancing in general. The natural inclination for human beings is to go downhill, to push the boundaries – push, push, push. We gain a freedom but it is never enough, we must push it further. As part of the absence of reasonable censorship we are seeing dancers with very little clothing or skin-tight clothes gyrating in a most sexual and sensual manner and the audience clap and cheer.

Firstly I would challenge the singers and dancers and secondly I would challenge the audience. Firstly, why would you make yourself an object of lust? Is that all you are looking for? Is that healthy for society? Is it helpful for women to obtain respect? Secondly, to the audience – why would you welcome this kind of display? Is this really the kind of woman you would value? Is this the standard of womanhood or motherhood a country needs? Please think it through...

If you have already given yourself over to a lustful attitude, you need release. God loves you and he can give you a new heart, a fresh attitude. It is difficult in this modern age to have pure thoughts because sensual pictures, in print, on film or in life, are constantly before your eyes in advertising and entertainment. Turn to God for a fresh focus. He made us sexual beings but he wanted us to have sex within love and the covenant of marriage, rather than raw lust ...

Now here's the awkward part. Perhaps you have friends who have laughed with you at all sorts of sordid material. If you want to walk God's way, you need to make some decisions. Either you don't join your friends when they are taking part in unsavoury activities and risk their wrath or at least their mocking, or you find new friends. Exercise your rights to make those decisions...

61

ANCIENT WONDERS

Let me tell you a story – a true story from my own life. When I was just 13 a friend and I decided that we wanted to travel together when we were a little older. Our idea was to begin by visiting Italy and work there while we looked around the country. Lots of young people do that now of course, but not so many in 1953. However when we had left high school and been working and saving for a while my friend was in a steady relationship with a young fellow and her travel dreams had evaporated. My goal was still the same so I went on working and saving.

My father died when I was 20 and several months later my mother suggested that we go to Scotland – the land of my father's birth – to visit his relatives. I was eager to do that so I began making plans. When I was preparing to book our passage on a ship – for that's the way most people made such a journey then – the Lord spoke to me. No, I didn't hear an audible voice, though some folk do, but I knew by a very strong impression within that the Lord was saying that he wanted me to go to Bible College.

I had no resistance to the idea of Bible College as I had been a believer from childhood, but *not now! My mother had been recently widowed. I'd said that I would accompany her. How could I let her down!* These were my sincere arguments with God. And I literally wrestled with God for 3 days. This was not only what my mother wanted but of course I had been working toward this goal for 7 years...

Because I knew God – in a much more limited way than I do now – I knew that there was nothing for it but to be obedient to the Voice within. I agreed to go to Bible College but then I went in trepidation to tell my mother. As an only child I hated to disappoint her at such a time as this.

Amazingly, she took the news quite well and never once made mention of the matter again, except that when I met my future husband soon afterwards and became engaged to him while I was in College, she said quite sweetly 'It looks as though it was meant to be'.

John and I married as soon as I completed my course and I became the wife of a very busy man. My savings had all been used to pay my college fees with just a few pounds (before dollars in Australia) left to pay for the material for my wedding gown. Children followed and though John travelled overseas quite a bit on business in succeeding years, I was always at home looking after our Darlings. It wasn't until I was 33 – 20 years after my travel goal was set – that I was able to join him on a trip to America. And because wives were included on this business trip there was a sightseeing itinerary for us so that we travelled by train across the fabulous Rocky Mountains to Banff in Canada and drove through the desert of Arizona fascinated by the huge cacti on our way to the Grand Canyon. As well we visited Los Angeles and San Francisco.

In the ensuing years we have travelled extensively but not so much for personal pleasure. We have been involved in conferences and missionary work again and again. But of course when we venture to the other side of the world for a conference we add some sightseeing to make the most of it.

I am so thankful to the Lord that, though he denied me the opportunity of travel at age 20 he still gave me the desires of my heart included in my service for Him. And, typically of the Lord, he gave me more than I would have been able to do if I had worked to my own plan.

I want to share some of the old/ancient (and not so old) man-made and God-created marvels I have had the privilege to see.

In the United States and Canada –
- Long-abandoned Red Indian homes carved out of tall cliffs
- The Niagara Falls, majestic and powerful
- The Great Lakes
- New York's Times Square
- The hundreds of miles of mountain ranges inland from California

In the UK –
- The famed Loch Ness (didn't see the monster)
- The beautiful Lakes District
- London's Big Ben
- Dover's White Cliffs
- The Christian Retreat Centre of Ffald-y-Brenin in Wales

In Europe –
- Beautiful, well-planned Paris with its Eiffel Tower and the Arc de Triomphe
- Mediaeval towns with their delightful architecture
- The snow-capped Alps from the air
- Switzerland's lovely lakes area
- The countless castle ruins atop hills all along the rivers where toll was exacted from the sailing captains who used the river. In those former times, chains were slung across the waterway so the toll had to be forthcoming
- The Budapest Parliament Building which must be one of the most beautiful buildings in the world, especially when the early morning sun breaks through a slashed cloud cover right above it

ANCIENT WONDERS

The Mediterranean –
- Italy's and Greece's ancient ruins – Pompeii, in particular. The Parthenon
- The colosseum in Rome where faithful Christians were set upon by lions as an audience watched on, and a less damaged one further North in Italy
- The sun-drenched Isle of Capri
- Several Greek Islands with their famed blue domed churches and picturesque homes jumbled together in delightful disarray on hillsides overlooking the Aegean
- The cave on the Isle of Patmos where Jesus' disciple, John, wrote the amazing book of Revelation, the last book of the Bible, as dictated to him by the angel
- Lakes formed from the blown out cones of volcanoes
- The Old Walled City of Jerusalem surrounded by an ever expanding modern city. I've travelled by bus from Tel Aviv to Jerusalem seated next to an Israeli soldier armed with rifle
- The Dead Sea where people float on their backs while reading a book because of the extremely high salt content of the water
- The skeleton of an ancient boat dug up from the mud of the Sea of Galilee which was called The Jesus Boat because that's how long it had been buried and lost and only found because of receding water through drought
- Herod's ancient castle atop Masada with grain storage rooms, etc.
- The towering pyramids of Egypt and the Sphinx pock-marked from gunshots
- The cliffs of Jordan's Petra where the buildings were carved into the rose coloured stone and steps ran up the edge of the cliffs to allow access between homes. We found the fossil of a small fern on top of one of these cliffs

- People lined up with jugs and buckets to secure some of the melted snow running via a pipe from the rock ledge at the side of the road on the Island of Cyprus
- Being invited to share a simple meal with a little old wizened citizen of Cyprus who picked us up in his miniscule utility and harvested the cucumber and tomato from his garden and bought the meat freshly from the market in the nearby town high in the Trodos Mountains where range after range recede in ever paler shades of blue

Asia –
- The Great Wall of China where you can ascend to it via cable car and choose to descend either by cable car or a giant slide which zigzags down the slope
- The Terracotta Army of Xian – the thousands of full-sized clay figures of soldiers, chariots and horses made two and a half thousand years ago and buried in underground channels in the false hope that when the Emperor awoke in the next world he would be accompanied by a powerful army. They were discovered when some farmers were digging a well to water their crops. They began unearthing ceramic fragments and as they say the rest is history
- We were shown through a lady's home in China which had been formed as terracotta clay was removed from a hillside. She daily made pasta for her lunch and used a long piece of dowelling to shape it. She had papered some of her rooms as far as she could reach with pages from newspapers. One room had a kang – a bed made of bricks and hollow underneath so that a fire could be lit which warmed the bed before she retired for the night
- The mile-long footpath night food market in Shanghai selling skewers filled with such culinary delights as crickets, seahorses, beetles, snake, even snake skins

- which are cooked in hot woks while you wait. I formed the impression that anything that moves would be eaten in this overcrowded country
- The fabulous resort island of Pangkor Laut in Malaysia where it is usually celebrities who holiday and hide away there but we were there at the invitation of the owner for a conference
- The milky atmosphere of Hong Kong with its skyscrapers jostling for attention and its silk markets
- The competing small shops of Singapore, and its superb bird park where an amazing variety of birds are kept without cages, except for the parrots
- Japan's Mount Fuji – only the lower half could be seen because of cloud cover until I was flying out and saw the upper half above the clouds

New Zealand –
- The innumerable water features – waterfalls, cataracts, gushing streams, lakes
- The fascinating thermal region of Rotorua with the smell of sulphur permeating the atmosphere and steam rising from the ground and hills. The hot springs where the Maori cook their vegetables in mesh bags hung in the water. The gushing geysers which shoot water metres into the pungent air
- The lovely Bay of Islands

Australia –
- Beautiful Sydney Harbour
- Brisbane's South Bank man-made beach right opposite the city centre
- The Bungle Bungle Range from a mini helicopter with doors removed made for two people but with the two of us plus the pilot barely fitting in
- The Devil's Marbles where huge boulders have been tossed around, some balancing precariously on others

- The magnificent Twelve Apostles along the Ocean Road. These rocky projections from the ocean are gradually wearing away and disappearing. One of them had the form of a bridge arching over the waves and someone had to be rescued from the far end of the 'bridge' when it crashed to the ocean below
- The world's largest monolith, Uluru, deep in the Red Centre which famously changes colour during the hours of the day
- Derby on the North West Coast which has only one high and one low tide daily. The jetty has been built many metres tall to allow for the enormous rises and ebbs of the tide, the second highest in the world

Why have I enumerated so many of the wonders I've seen? Because I want to underline the greatest two wonders of all…

- Firstly, the One who created this entire universe and who has watched all the civilisations come and go, and their achievements rise and be ruined………loves…….me…
- Can I say that again? The Creator of everything knows me with all my weaknesses and sins yet loves me enough to suffer to gain me as a member of his family. Nothing can come near to that wonder… And of course that refers to you as well as it does to me.
- Now for the other great wonder, and this time man had a hand in it… That ancient wonder, The Word of God. Yes, God was the divine author but he gave men the privilege of writing it down so that we could know God, what he is like, how he deals with men and women and what he wants of us. Have you paused to consider that we can so easily hold the very Word of God in our

hands, read it in our own language and meditate upon it so that it becomes part of who we are? That is the second true wonder.

62

FURTHER EDUCATION

Travel has been so much of my education. It gives us a broader understanding of the world and of people. But there are so many other things to learn as well.

This is just a little chat between you and me, not a vital piece of wisdom. But as I'm ageing, I wish I had studied more when my brain was younger. John and I both wish we had studied geology and archaeology because as we move around we see such mysterious, intriguing formations of rock and we try to work out how they have been formed. And we would love to go on digs in ancient areas to find something which would be one of the pieces in the jigsaw of history.

I would recommend to you that you never stop learning. If you wish to have a richer life, if you want to have more topics of conversation that you could take part in, if you would like to be a more interesting person, then broaden your information base. Of course, I'm not suggesting that you become a know-all who annoys people.

You could take a course in subjects of interest but this involves money outlaid. That may be your choice but it isn't absolutely necessary. Reading provides an accessible means of self-education.

If you are young, you may be asking what you should study. Well, of course that depends on your particular personality. But some of the things which we have found enlightening and entertaining are now listed in this chapter. For instance, we have a book on Australian trees. So as we travel in our homeland we can recognize some of the vast array of beautiful trees we have here. We are intrigued by the leaves, the bark, and sometimes the girth. And the grains of the individual timbers are so wonderful. Learn to recognize the beautiful ribbon effect of Maple or the ripple of Silky Oak. You will learn which trees' fruits can be eaten. You'll begin to notice the burls which grow like a swelling on the sides of trees and which are loved by crafty men who like to remove them, hollow them out and polish them to make beautiful bowls.

While mistletoe has been romanticised it really is a parasitic plant which kills its host. Birds carry the seeds of it and begin its growth in another tree. It has a nice shape but eventually you will see a dead tree with these isolated patches of Mistletoe hanging from the lifeless branches. By knowing about this, you are armed to rid your property of Mistletoe before it can do its dastardly deeds.

We notice too that trees can indicate the fertility and type of the soil. For instance, in sandy areas you often notice paperbarks which look as though their fine bark is peeling. They are sometimes spindly because there isn't much water retention in sand and not much nourishment but arty people collect bark from these trees to make bark pictures as there are subtle colour changes in it. I heard a farmer's daughter say once that red gum trees are a sign of poor soil, so I filed that away in my mind as a good piece of information.

Birds are another wonderful subject for your interest. We always keep our book of Aussie birds nearby and when a winged stranger visits our garden or we spy one in our travels we can quickly check out what it is and something about its habits. The varying nests that different birds build are quite fascinating. The Sun Bird which we've seen in North Queensland for instance builds a lovely little basket with a 'handle' threaded over a branch, etc. whereas a plover makes its nest on the ground. We've had peewees build mud nests in one of the trees in our yard and in a couple of places we have small splatters of mud on our outer walls where they have apparently lost some of their mouthfuls of mud. It is a real joy if you have a bird feeder in your garden and you can watch chattering lorikeets or squawking cockatoos if they are in your area, and depending on what kind of seeds you provide.

As we drove through one area we noticed small parrots which sounded as though they were saying 'twenty-eight, twenty-eight'. When we checked them in our book we found that they are often called Twenty-eights for that very reason.

If you want to be truly gob smacked, buy a telescope and study the heavens. To see the rings of Saturn or the stripes around Jupiter is breathtaking, especially if you have a good sized telescope. And the full moon is like a silver Christmas tree decoration. (If you want to be blown away by something which few people know about the stars, read the final chapter of Section Four which is already in my mind. It's Further Evidence for the Accuracy of the Bible and perhaps the greatest proof of all.)

You may be artistic so you may like to try sketching or painting and even painting has many levels – still-life, portraiture, seascape, landscape, or abstract; comic, photo-realistic or impressionistic; using oils, acrylics, watercolours or pastels. If you go to art classes, you will learn not only the lessons taught, but also you will pick up tips from others who have been painting longer than you. If you are not interested in trying your hand, you may find studying the works of the great artists more to your liking.

If you are a handy kind of person, you may like to learn renovation. You could have a lot of pleasure in achieving in your spare time. You would save money in the process.

If you like to cook, why not buy a cook book of the types

of food you've never tried? If all you can do is boil water, why not sign up for some basic lessons? We all need to eat.

How about sewing? Knitting? Crochet? Playing an instrument? Water skiing? First-Aid?

Perhaps you would enjoy learning another language. I have found that even knowing snatches of other languages aids us when travelling. Not only can it help in understanding signs on shops, etc. but it is a compliment to the locals when you thank them in their own language for instance. You may discover that you have a talent for languages and perhaps could enjoy a job as an interpreter. Of course, this wouldn't happen overnight. You would need years of familiarity with a language before you would perceive the nuances, otherwise you could easily misinterpret. (We recently found an amazing app for John's 'phone called Word Lens. Using the app, if you hold your 'phone over printed words in one language it can translate them into the language you have set it at. Very handy for signs in a foreign country.)

What about history? Now before you renege on this one because you think it is boring, take another look at it. Yes, if you are just learning dates and battles as you may have had to in school it could be pretty uninteresting. But if you were to buy a book which gives an overview of history you may be surprised at the changes that have taken place in our world over the centuries and even millennia. When travelling through parts of Europe I was intrigued to learn how the borders of many countries have changed and changed again. Powers have come and gone and the lives of the people of other generations were altered by historical events. Sometimes a people group is overtaken and its lands have been handed to others. What would you have done in such circumstances? History should be a living thing in our minds. We are living within a period of history now. Should this world go on after my time, what will future generations think of what we did with our patch of history? Is God calling us to be history changers?

Hand in hand with history goes geography. Oh I know, maybe you thought this was boring at school too. But it can be fascinating. Don't just look at a map and learn names and borders, see if the library has something on particular countries or continents and find out about those places. Maybe you will decide to visit some places so that the people of those areas become real to you. And if you understand some of the history of those people, it will help you to understand their attitudes and customs.

All these things are parts of our education. It may be that you will decide to have a diploma on your wall when you've completed an official course or perhaps you will be satisfied to keep on educating yourself. You will be enriched even if there is no piece of paper on the wall to testify to it.

On top of these suggestions, I'll mention volunteering. Volunteers help make the world go round. There are all kinds of help needed from volunteers and it would be a rewarding experience and as you meet with more people, you will pick up many ideas to enlarge your own perception of life.

Whatever you take on, and wherever you go, just remember to take your Christian principles with you so you don't get dragged into a lifestyle you wouldn't have chosen...

63

FURTHER EVIDENCE OF THE BIBLE'S AUTHENTICITY

In each of this book's Sections, you've seen that I devote the final chapter to evidence for the Bible record. In Section One, we looked at Exhibits A and B, the astounding accuracy of God's words in Job referring to the unusual behaviour of the Orion nebula and the star cluster, Pleiades. In Section Two, I presented Exhibit C – Dr J. E. Shelley's article – enlarged by Pastor Paul Camac – on The Flood of Noah with amazing evidence for it to have happened just as presented by the Bible.

Now for Exhibit D, I want to mention something I've never heard anybody but my husband John speak about. It is an obscure verse in the Old Testament book of Judges. Strangely, the verse I'm referring to is from the lengthy song sung by Deborah and Barak. The song details marvellous deeds of the Lord, especially as Israel had to fight against its enemies. There in the midst of this song are these strange words: Verse 20 of chapter 5… "From the heavens the stars fought, from their courses they fought against Sisera." Now an unbeliever could be forgiven for thinking surely this is the stuff of myths and legends. Stars fighting against an enemy leader? But let's remember that this is poetry in the form of a song, based on fact.

My husband strongly believes in the accuracy of the Bible, as do I, and he was not content to leave it at that. So, knowing the date of the battle with Sisera, he went searching. There were historians in those far off days who recorded events in plain language. And when he looked up the records of Josephus, a well-known historian who wrote reports of that time he found that during that particular battle, there was a meteor shower, earthquakes and a lava flow which killed more of the enemy combatants than the Israelites did. So, the stars fought against Sisera! No wonder they sang praise to God.

I am including these chapters of evidence of the Scriptures so that not only will you be encouraged in your belief, but you will have information to make other people stop and think if they are mocking the Word of God. If you can give someone another viewpoint it may be a link in the chain which draws them to follow the Lord.

PART FOUR

Introduction

This is the Fourth Section of this book which somewhat surprises me as I began writing thinking I was penning only a short book. How it all began was that my husband John and I boarded our motor home two or three years ago and not long after John had sung the words 'On the Road Again' which he often does when we are setting off, I thought of a subject I would like to address. I reached for my notebook and pen to jot it down so I wouldn't forget it and settled back for a relaxing drive. Within five minutes there was another niggle at my brain with another subject dear to my heart. Again, I jotted it down. I thought they might be good subjects if I was asked to give a talk. This continued to happen every few minutes so it wasn't long before I was sure the Lord was prompting me to write a book.

I became excited at the prospect of writing a book as it was clear that these subjects were chapter headings. I have always enjoyed writing though I hadn't done anything so ambitious before. The subjects were things I would love to hand down to younger folk, things perhaps I had known as far back as I can remember as well as lessons learned in the school of life. I thought it would be such a privilege if I could pass on some of these things to those who hadn't lived so long, so that they could be better armed for life. And I was thankful to those who had been teachers to me.

Previously I had written a few children's story books which I had never submitted to a publisher but one of them we had printed ourselves. A friend who taught Religious Instruction in school had ordered copies of that to give to her pupils as Christmas gifts. Otherwise, I had written Bible Studies for classes I headed up as a Pastor's wife, and when I travelled I usually wrote long, descriptive emails to our family so that they could share our experiences in the 'third person'. For a few years I presented a Christian radio programme and that had given me the opportunity to share little bits and bobs of wisdom or challenge between songs. (The only other book I have written is the story of my life, strictly for our family to read, which includes the story of John's life and as much as we could assemble of our family history. John has done a lot of delving into our family tree so a record of ancestors is included in that book.)

I thought that I would keep this book short and to the point so as subjects kept coming to me I intended to have a series of short books. But I soon realised that some of the chapters in the later 'books' were a progression of things discussed earlier. Hence the Sections in the book, rather than separate books.

I shall have to be content in the hope that you will be blessed by the words which follow. I do believe that God has inspired me to write but that doesn't mean that what I write is sacred in the sense that the Word of God in the Scriptures is. So always check me out that what I say does not contradict the Bible. Why not make yourself comfortable now and settle in for a little read of Section 4…

64

TERROR ALERT!

It is September 2014 and all types of media are abuzz with news – of terrorists and their ghastly activities which they film and release to set hearts all over the world thumping; that Australia's risk of terrorist activities has been raised from moderate to high; that there have been plans in the minds and hearts of home-grown Aussies to slaughter innocent people as well as specifically target politicians.

All sorts of measures are being undertaken to apprehend potential terrorists before they are able to carry out their plots. Men have been arrested then released because of the insufficiency of current laws. Laws are being enacted to give more power to those whose job it is to protect us.

Up until now, our physical isolation from the rest of the world has given us a measure of protection. But the world has become more of a global village and what is happening overseas is soon on our doorstep as well. We have to be aware that life as we have known it has gone forever. True, we came close to warfare in the Second World War, with enemy submarines managing to travel as far as Sydney and Brisbane. And, though it wasn't publicised at the time, the Northern Territory was subject to enemy raids. But compared with Britain and Europe we escaped 'with minor scratches' on home soil. Our men who travelled to the war fronts of course paid a heavy price. But those at home mostly suffered because of scarcity of everyday goods and foods.

So how are we feeling about these new developments?

Many hearts are either angry or aflutter with fear. Some folk are speaking with bravado because they don't want to live scared. So where does that leave you and me?

As with most things in life, the choice is ours. If our foundation is on a rock, we can stand firm. If we have built our lives on sand we are liable to sink when storms hit. I have chosen to build my life on *obedience* to Jesus Christ, which is the Rock in the parable of building on rock or sand in the New Testament. In the Old Testament narrative, the Rock was a foreshadowing of Jesus himself. What has your choice been? If you are also on the Rock, we have many assurances in the Word of God. God has said he will never leave us, never forsake us. (Hebrews 13:5) That gives us encouragement, comfort and courage. With God on our side, we really can face anything which comes our way.

When trouble circles us, we can dig into the Lord. We read his word, we talk things over with him, ask for his wisdom in what our attitudes and actions should be. We all have a circle of influence composed of our friends, relatives, workmates, church brothers and sisters and even casual acquaintances. Our attitudes and words can help them to form solid attitudes and actions which are pleasing to the Lord. When others are alarmed we can give a balanced viewpoint. But this can only happen if we are firmly anchored on that Rock.

When we boil it all down, we realise that our real citizenship is not in this world. We are citizens of Heaven and we look forward to heading there eventually. So, in the very extreme case of our life finishing earlier than we were expecting, things actually get better for us. With this understanding, we can face the future unafraid. This brings to mind the 23rd Psalm "When I pass through the Valley of the Shadow of Death I will fear no evil for Thou art with me. Thy rod and thy staff they comfort me." (That's how I memorised it from the old King James Version which was the most common version used when I was young.)

Okay, that's the extreme. Now, what about the everyday facing of possibilities that could go against us? Well, here is a gem for us... One of the Names for Jesus is The Prince of Peace. This is not referring to World Peace but the peace which Jesus can plant into the minds, hearts and spirits of those who look to him in everything.

The Bible speaks of balm. What is balm? It is a fragrant, oily substance from certain trees used to heal or ease pain. If you are feeling fearful, I want you to reach out to God and in the Name of Jesus, ask him to pour his healing, easing balm all over you so that it flows from the top of your head to the soles of your feet, also seeping right into your very core. When Jesus was preparing to leave this life, his disciples were about to be thrust into difficulties and even persecution and this is what Jesus said to them: Peace I leave with you; my peace I give you. I do not give to you as the world gives. Do not let your hearts be troubled and do not be afraid. (John 14:27)

Why was Jesus' peace different from the world's? Because peace in the world comes from absence of difficulties or persecution, but Jesus offers us peace *in the midst of trouble*. Also, the Hebrew word for peace is *'shalom'* which could be seen as harmony – harmony with God, harmony with our neighbours and harmony within. Isn't that a lovely picture?

If you have chosen to align your life with the Lord, you have access to this peace which doesn't depend on circumstances.

We have been forewarned in the Scriptures that there is coming a most dreadful time before this world comes to an end. But, though everything will look grim during that terrible time, the eventual and ultimate victory will go to God, and thus to his people.

Though we need to know what is going on in the world

so that we can pray intelligently about it, our focus needs to be on Jesus, the author and finisher of our faith. Then our hearts will not fail us for fear. We will be able to stand firm in the midst of any circumstances. So reach out to him right now...

65

JESUS IS ALWAYS NEAR

Because we've been speaking of terrorists and risks to security, I want to share something very special with you to reinforce God's words about never leaving or forsaking us.

First of all, let me draw your attention to one of the early disciples, Stephen. This was after Jesus had returned to Heaven and the early church was establishing itself. Persecution was rife and the chief of the persecutors was Saul of Tarsus, later to become the Apostle Paul whom God commissioned to spread the Gospel among the Gentiles in the then-known world. Saul was travelling to any area where there were Christians and dragging them off to jail or letting his henchmen kill them because at this time he believed that they were following a false teacher.

One of his victims was a beautiful godly man, Stephen, 'full of God's grace and power' who did 'great wonders and miraculous signs among the people'. As so often happens, when a good man is doing wonderful deeds, opposition arose. Because those who didn't want to accept his Gospel message could not beat him in debating, they brought false witnesses to say that he had been speaking blasphemous things against God and Moses. Bear in mind the Jewish community was a religious community with laws based on God's laws. However, many Jews were not sincere followers of God but put on a good show publicly. As a result of his arrest, Stephen was taken before the Sanhedrin, the parliament of the time. (Even today, the parliament is known as the Sanhedrin though Israel is no longer a totally religious community.)

In response, Stephen addressed the rulers, going back over the history of the Jews and the way God had dealt with them. He concluded his defence with a charge against them that they had murdered the One God had sent, (Jesus) and telling them that they had received the Law that was put into effect through angels but 'have not obeyed it'.

This so incensed them that in their fury they gnashed their teeth at him. Stephen must have known that he was now in deepest trouble in the midst of these men of power but the Bible tells us that he looked up to heaven. "Look," he said, "I see heaven open and the Son of Man standing at the right hand of God."

Can you imagine the melee this caused? Those he had charged actually covered their ears and yelled at the top of their voices. They rushed at him, dragged him out of the city and began to stone him, a practice even today in some of the Middle Eastern countries, though no longer in Israel.

Those taking part laid their outer garments at the feet of Saul. "While they were stoning him, Stephen prayed, 'Lord Jesus, receive my spirit.' Then he fell on his knees and cried out, 'Lord, do not hold this sin against them'." With this, he died. And Saul was there, giving approval to his death. (To read the full story of Stephen, look up Acts 6:8 - 7:60)

If you can place yourself there, perhaps up a tree where you can view the lovely face of this righteous man, Stephen, what comes to your mind? Are you overwhelmed by the barbarism of his treatment? Or are you stunned by his composure *plus the fact that in the face of death he is pleading with God to forgive his murderers?*

Does this bring someone else to your mind? What about Jesus who, from his agony on the cross, asked forgiveness for those who were causing his suffering? Stephen experienced an awful death but in the very midst of the dust stirred up by the furious feet of his oppressors, not only was he thinking of the eternal welfare of others but he was very definitely aware of the presence of his Saviour, Jesus, with him in his final hour as at every other hour of his life as a believer.

Who won in that scene? Certainly, the stoners achieved their goal – the silencing of a man who had become a tormenting conscience to them. But was Stephen really a victim? I don't believe so. I believe, not only was he in control of himself and unafraid but he was achieving God's purpose for him as well. You might ask how on earth this could be so. Well, it is obvious that God could have saved Stephen if that would have served his best purpose. But who was watching all of this drama played out? Not you, as you weren't really up in those tree branches, but Saul was watching. He would have seen the victorious attitude of Stephen and even though this didn't bring him to his knees in repentance at that time, I can't help but think that it would have played a part in Saul's later willingness to endure many persecutions himself for the sake of Jesus – beatings, stoning (almost to death), shipwreck, deprivation.

Just as God allowed Jesus to suffer *for the sake of all human beings who would accept that suffering as payment for the forgiveness of their sins,* so God will sometimes allow us to suffer *for the sake of others, that they may be brought to belief that will gain for them eternal life.*

But the main thing I want you to take from this story of Stephen is that he was not alone. Jesus was with him in his suffering, not passively witnessing it but allowing Stephen to see that he was aware of what was happening to him and he was waiting to welcome him into his company in heaven or Paradise.

Now to get round to my special story… About 30 years ago, a woman from a church in a neighbouring suburb to us in Brisbane flew to New Zealand. When a storm began to toss the plane around the sky with accompanying lightning, the passengers were, not surprisingly, perturbed. This lady noticed another woman praying in tongues so she went to her and joined her in prayer. After some time, she decided to take a photo of the amazing lightning from the window of the heaving plane. The plane landed safely in Auckland, New Zealand and eventually she took her film to be processed (in the days before digital cameras). She left her contact details with the photo processor and received a call from him some time later, saying that her photos were ready and asking her to ask to speak to him when she picked them up.

When she went to him, there was just one photo he was interested in. He showed it to her and asked her how she came by it. He knew it was a genuine shot because he was the one who developed it. When she looked at it, she too was surprised. It was the one she had taken from the plane. But the photo wasn't simply a snap of a storm, it was easy to see the form of a person like fire, complete with flowing robe with a sash round the waist, hands held out. She explained the circumstances and that she had been praying because of the fierce storm and said that it was obviously Jesus who was present during her danger in answer to her prayers.

As a result the film developer and others were saved. And the woman gladly shared copies of her photo with many people so they would be assured that God's people are never alone. He doesn't leave them when things get dangerous.

(See back cover for the following photo in colour.)

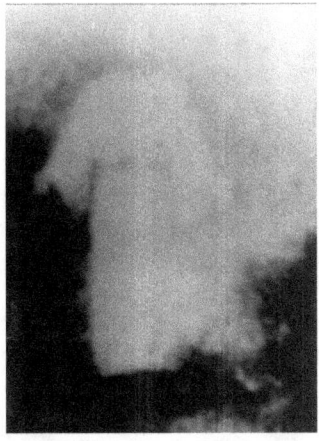

There are a couple of postscripts to this story. Firstly, some time earlier I was not very well and a friend had come to visit and was praying for me. Up at ceiling level in the room I saw a vision of Jesus and he was in the exact position of the photo (above) referred to in this story. So I have no doubt about the story being factual. (I am sorry that the photo has to be printed in black and white in this book to keep the cost within your budget, but my copy of it is in colour.)

Secondly, we have been told another story about a storm many years earlier during a Christian man's flight. In this story, the plane crashed and all lives aboard were lost. When the man's family were given his possessions which had been retrieved from the wreckage, they decided to have the film in his camera developed to relate to what he had been experiencing before the fatal flight. There in one of the photos, in black and white – as this was before the time of coloured film – was the form of Jesus in a flowing robe, sashed at the waist and with hands extended. So, as the Bible says, God does not leave his people, he does not abandon them even as they are unexpectedly reaching the end of their lives. May his Name be praised...

66

A TIMELY REMINDER

When we are young, some of us are rather casual about things. We feel as though tomorrow is soon enough to do things; we cruise along. But I would urge young people to smarten up a little if that is their current attitude. It is great that you usually don't have the stresses and time deprivation of older adults but that is the very reason to make sure you use your time well. When you are older, you may not have the time to choose what you do with your time. It may be all mapped out because of your circumstances and responsibilities.

So, I am urging you to study your Bible regularly. After all, it is the manual for your life so it is the most important book you will ever study, bar none. You don't need to pore over it for hours each day but read it every day – as much as you have time for or as much as you can digest. Then, as you are walking, riding or driving meditate on what you have read so that you work it into the fabric of your thinking. And the more you read, the better overview you will obtain. I know I have already written about studying the Bible, but let's look at it again, perhaps from a different angle. You don't want to be concentrating on battles fought in the Old Testament without balancing it out with the words of Jesus in the New. In fact, one way I would recommend if you are just beginning to read the Bible is to start by reading right through the New Testament before you go back to the more ancient interaction of God with earlier man. After all, we are now living under the New Covenant (or New Testament), but the Old Testament gives great insight into how God's involvement with man developed. And we can learn God's principles from the Old as well as the New. Yes, I know I've spoken about that before, but some things need repeating…

Having said all that, the point I am making here is again in relation to the developments in our world at this very moment in time. As I said earlier, we need to know what is going on in our world but we don't want to be depressed by any bad news we hear. There is one particular Scripture portion which comes to my mind in this regard and it is Philippians 4:4-9. This is a precious gem from the Word of God. I'll print it out so you can come back to it whenever you need to do so:

Rejoice in the Lord always. I will say it again: Rejoice! Let your gentleness be evident to all. The Lord is near. Do not be anxious about anything, but in everything, by prayer and petition, with thanksgiving, present your requests to God. And the peace of God, which transcends all understanding, will guard your hearts and your minds in Christ Jesus.

Finally, brothers, whatever is true, whatever is noble, whatever is right, whatever is pure, whatever is lovely, whatever is admirable – if anything is excellent or praiseworthy – think about such things. Whatever you have learned or received or heard from me, or seen in me – put it into practice. And the God of peace will be with you.

The Apostle Paul wrote those words to those he had introduced to God and they are such good advice. After all, the Bible also says that a man is what he thinks, so it makes sense that we should not be concentrating on dark matters or they will pull us down into anxiety or depression. And I will mention that Paul wrote this letter from prison. Don't those words have extra impact when you consider that the author was himself suffering heavily because of his faithfulness to the call of God upon his life?

Because I have been walking with the Lord for many years I find that Scripture usually comes to me readily at the time I need it. I give thanks to God's Holy Spirit for prompting me. What a wonderful aid to life that is. I want you to have the same help and reading your Bible regularly will do it for you. If you don't normally have good retention of information and learning, ask the Father to improve your memory. (Look back at chapter 5 in Section One for hints on reading your Bible.)

67

ARE YOU MINDING THE SUPPLIES?

Let's have a complete change of subject now... I can remember something I learned from the Bible right back in Bible College and it has stayed with me ever since. It warms my heart and I think it might do the same for yours.

We're going right back in time to when David of Israel was not yet king. His life was in great danger from King Saul who was unbalanced in mind. David had served him faithfully as a court musician as well as being a brave soldier in his wars. When Saul was troubled in mind David would play for him to calm him. But when David's popularity with the population became glaringly obvious Saul wanted to put an end to him. (This is not the heart-warming bit).

As a consequence David had to leave the palace so he set out on his own. Because he was so well known many men and their families joined him and they travelled the countryside but were based at a town called Ziklag. At one time, an enemy army raided Ziklag while the men were away and not only burned the town but carried off the women and children along with the loot.

Of course David and his men set off to avenge this outrage and to retrieve their loved ones. Along the way, some of the men became exhausted so they were left with the responsibility of minding the supplies the group had been carrying. David and the remaining men found the Amalekites scattered over the territory, eating, drinking and revelling because of all the plunder they'd taken in their raids. There was an ensuing battle and David's band of men secured all that had been stolen from them including flocks and herds and of course their loved ones.

When they returned to where they had left the men with their supplies, some of the band claimed that those who had been left with the supplies should not receive an equal share with those who had been actively fighting. But David replied: "'No, my brothers, you must not do that with what the Lord has given us. He has protected us and handed over to us the forces that came against us… The share of the men who stayed with the supplies is to be the same as that of him who went down to the battle. All will share alike.' David made this a statute and ordinance for Israel from that day to this." (1Samuel 30:24, 25)

I found this really encouraging. The principle is that, whatever position you hold, whether upfront or in the background, you share in the rewards. (I am not implying that in heaven every person will receive exactly the same rewards.) In our situations today how would we apply this principle? Well, firstly, I think of those who are unable for one reason or another to be actively involved in projects and missions but who stay and faithfully pray for those who are. When we think of Daniel of the Old Testament praying for 3 weeks, we learn that from the time he began to pray the angel of the Lord set out to accomplish the victory for which he was praying. But the 'Prince of Persia' – obviously a spiritual entity with a stronghold over present-day Iran – had held him at bay. So it was important that Daniel continued to pray. Wouldn't it be interesting to know just how many victories over the Devil are won more by the pray-ers in the background than by those who are active participants by preaching, etc.?

When John and I were in England 2 or 3 years ago we visited a museum and in the gift shop we found some things that were quite interesting to us. There were recruiting posters from World War 1 featuring Lord Kitchener who happens to have been John's Great-Great-Uncle. You may have seen them – Lord Kitchener and his substantial moustache, with raised hand pointing straight ahead and captioned "You are the man I want". (A similar idea was later used by the Americans and theirs featured 'Uncle Sam'.) We bought a tea towel and apron featuring the poster. As well, John bought a book showing postcards from World War 1.

One of the postcards showed two elderly men working in a field. One is wiping his brow, garden fork in hand. The card says 'The allotment holder. *Too old to fight, but doing his bit to beat the Uboats.*' I take it to mean that food was scarce and the men who couldn't be fighting in the trenches were nevertheless doing their bit to supply the food needed.

This ties in perfectly with the Scripture about the men minding the supplies during David's time thousands of years earlier. What does it matter what kind of work you are able to do? All kinds are necessary. When men go to war, work at home still needs to be done. During the Second World War, many women took over men's jobs so that industry could keep functioning. The country would suffer because of the war but not as much as if nobody did those jobs. 'Everybody doing their bit' was brought home when photos were published showing the present Queen Elizabeth II in overalls and working on a car.

So, to bring this up-to-date, what are you doing? What are you doing by way of a job? What are you doing in your spare time? What are you doing for the Lord? Do you feel second-rate because you don't have an '*important*' position? Do you look at others and wish you had their talent? Do you envy them their opportunities? Well, let me assure you that the backroom jobs are every bit as important as the spot-lit ones.

Where would rulers be if they didn't have bakers and butchers, maids and secretaries, even speech-writers? They wouldn't be able to get on with their jobs if others didn't do what they don't have time (and perhaps talent) to do.

I make it my business to every so often say a word of thanks to those at church who man the teapots and kettles for morning tea after church or at other functions. Without them, there wouldn't be the ambience for people to stay around and chat and have good fellowship with one another. These times are immensely important because there could be people who have visited the church to investigate Christianity and who knows, this may be the very time they will be encouraged to trust God with their lives. It is not only by preaching that people are won to the Lord, but also by friendship and caring.

I believe that we will be surprised to find how valued some people's contributions have been to the Lord, when we arrive in Heaven. As we have mentioned before, Jesus commended the poor widow who gave her last two small coins. He raised to life the son of a widow. He also raised to life Dorcas who had done sewing for widows in need. Jesus chose very ordinary people as his disciples and these were the ones he invested his life in and who were to be the leaders in the infant church. As said before, some were fishermen, one a tax collector. Is that who you would have chosen? One of the reasons God likes to work with ordinary people is so that others will give the glory for achievements to the Lord and not glorify the people themselves. That is not because God is self-centred but because when people recognize that he is at work in the world they know that he is alive and he cares. If he used only super-intelligent, super-talented people, those watching would just give them kudos and go on their way unaware that God is at work and loves them.

Now I want to share with you a story that is 'hot off the press'. Just this morning in church one of the young men who regularly attends shared a testimony. He said that last week he didn't feel like going to church but was encouraged to go along by his wife. He had always found it difficult to fully take part in the worship, as though his emotions were not involved.

There he was in church during the worship last week and he opened his eyes and spotted a young mentally and physically disabled girl looking straight into his eyes. She had been standing in the aisle near her grandmother enjoying the music herself and raising her hands but at this time apparently she had turned to look directly at this sad man. He felt as though God's eyes were looking straight into him and he felt very emotionally effected by the experience. Nearly 12 hours later that night he was still quite emotional. But God had not finished with him yet...

During the ensuing week issues in his life surfaced and he began to deal with them. One of them was the feeling of insignificance. Over the years when he would have liked to be a major contributor in church life it seemed that he was always passed over. Progress was being made in ironing out this man's issues, and it was confirmed when he had a chat with his mother. She doesn't live in the area so she had attended another church and she told her son that her pastor had spoken on the subject of – you guessed it – 'Insignificance' and she had thought of her son.

This lovely young man has had some battles during the week dealing with this matter but this morning he was able to take part in the worship wholeheartedly and when I spoke to him after the service he said that it no longer matters to him whether he is given a job to do or not. He will continue to look to the Lord and share his faith as he has the opportunity. He will not allow himself to feel *insignificant* any longer.

But there is another amazing aspect to this story... Did you notice just who the Lord used to touch this young man's heart? It was a dear little girl who is very frail, who walks with bent knees and cannot speak. Who would ever think that she would be useful to the Lord? Without a word, she spoke into this man's heart and a healing began which had been needed for years. That little girl is not often in church with us because she comes only when she is having a sleepover at her Gran's. But God's love drew the main two people in this story together at the very time it would bear fruit in the young man's life.

All of us need humble hearts whether we have a public position or not. As a matter of fact, the person in the public view needs to stay humble perhaps even more so than others or they could become a stumbling block instead of a stepping stone to God.

On a slightly different tack, it delights God when we seek him out privately and talk with him, not making a show for others to see and admire us.

So, in light of all these things, check up with the Lord as to what job he has for you to do and (as a well-known brand of sports clothes says) just do it!

Work is honourable.
God says that if a man will not work he should not eat.
Of course, that does not apply to someone who is seeking work but cannot find it.
In that case, however, we need to look for ways we can be useful to someone who could do with our help, even if it is unpaid work.
Laziness is not honourable.

68

DO YOU HAVE ITCHING EARS?

I'm not trying to be too cheeky, but do you have itching ears? No, I don't mean are people talking about you. The Bible has a different meaning for the phrase. When it speaks of itching ears it is referring to people always wanting to hear new and exciting things, things pleasing to the ears.

It isn't just that we shouldn't enjoy hearing new and exciting things, the emphasis is on whether there is truth in them. If we are easily bored and always chasing something new and exciting we run the danger of chasing after things which are false, and holding them close to our hearts to our cost. And running after new things often means that we are not being faithful to the things we are already committed to.

Women, particularly, are prone to do this with the latest fads in fashion. I find fashion fascinating, but I don't take it too seriously. I don't slavishly follow fashion because then the item becomes dated so quickly and you need to buy the next 'latest thing'. I like to find something which doesn't look old-fashioned but isn't right on the cutting edge either so that it can be worn for some time and still look fresh. (Mind you, I think men these days are also aware of what's in and what's not in the way of their fashion as well...)

But I'm more concerned with more serious matters. There's always some new 'guru' telling us how to eat well, how to overcome personal problems, how we should exercise, how to find peace, etc. etc.

I would stress to you, if you feel you'd like to try something you read about, please try to check the background. Is it in any way related to religion, particularly Eastern religion? I have been very troubled to see many people following things like karate and yoga. I am not saying that they have no good ideas involved in them but if they have their beginnings in false religion, they could be spiritually dangerous. Sometimes people are naïve about the sounds they have to make or the bowing of the head when they take part in these regimes. I believe that the bowing of the head practised in some cultures is bowing 'to the god in that person'. Well, excuse me, but I won't be bowing to any false god. And, if you are ever told to empty your mind when you are taking part in an exercise or self-defence course, withdraw from it.

An empty mind invites the wrong spirits. When investigating a new thing, we need to '*keep our wits about us*'.

A fellow from a Brisbane church my husband John used to pastor was a keen karate man. He was sure there was nothing untoward in it. But as he was doing so well he was invited to take part in a seminar given by a visiting sensei (teacher) from Japan. During the session the sensei revealed that when exponents make their grunting sounds they are calling out to powers to give them the strength they need (or something to that effect). I'm glad to report that at that point our young man withdrew from karate.

Of course, we can extend the 'new things' to a new preacher or a new church. If you are not satisfied with your preacher or your church and feel that you need to find something better, ask the Lord to guide and protect you in the process. And if you hear a new exciting preacher, remember to check him out by lining up his theology with the Scriptures. If you can't find the principles he is teaching in the Bible, it likely is just his own idea and as such, quite useless and time wasting.

DO YOU HAVE ITCHING EARS?

So, be on your guard. Many people have been drawn in to cults and sects just by having '*itching ears*'.

69

HAVING TROUBLE WITH PRAYER?

At its simplest, prayer is simply a conversation with our Heavenly Father. Do we ever speak to others? Then we know how to pray... But sometimes we feel as though we really don't know how to begin, or how to end, or perhaps how to go deeper with prayer.

I don't pretend to be an expert at prayer but there are some helps we can use to get us started or to develop our prayer life.

Firstly, why not begin the way Jesus told his disciples when they asked him to teach them? The Lord's Prayer is given in two places in the New Testament – Matthew 6:9-15 and Luke 11:2-4.

I'll print the Matthew reading here so we can refer to it as we delve into it a little. (Luke presented an abbreviated version, and of course it's possible that Jesus spoke about it to his disciples more than once at different times...)

> "Our Father in heaven,
> Hallowed be your name.
> Your kingdom come,
> Your will be done on earth as it is in heaven.
> Give us today our daily bread.
> Forgive us our debts,
> As we also have forgiven our debtors.
> And lead us not into temptation,
> But deliver us from the evil one.

For if you forgive men when they sin against you, your heavenly Father will also forgive you. But if you do not forgive men their sins, your Father will not forgive your sins."

I don't think that Jesus expected his disciples to parrot this prayer all the time so much as to use it as a model for their prayers. So as well as actually praying The Lord's Prayer, you can do the same.

How does it help us to begin our prayers? *Our Father in heaven, hallowed be your name.* By recognising that the One to whom we are speaking is our God (in heaven) but also our Father. The word 'God' can conjure up in our minds an entity who is fearsome but the fact that we can come to him as our father shows a personal loving connection. In addition, to ask for his name to be *hallowed* is to acknowledge that he is to be respected and his name should not be used carelessly (such as in 'Oh! My God' as we hear so often today or in saying 'Jesus' or 'Christ' as swearwords).

So when we pray it is good to begin with words which praise the Lord for who he is. We might say something like 'Our Heavenly Father we thank you for who you are, that you are King of Kings and Lord of Lords and we honour you.'

Your kingdom come, your will be done on earth as it is in heaven. This can be taken for the present – that God's kingdom will be established in our hearts and lives now; and for the future – when Jesus establishes his kingdom on earth. This is acknowledgment of the authority of the Lord over ourselves and people in general (whether they know it or not) and furthermore, it is asking that God will be bringing about his will on the earth. Perhaps we could phrase it something like this 'Thank you that you have all power in my circumstances and I commit my welfare to you. Help me to fulfil your plan for my life and please be drawing an ever greater number of unbelievers into your family so that your influence on the earth will be multiplied.'

Give us today our daily bread. This is interesting in that it refers only to ***today's*** physical needs. It gives us the clue that our relating to God is to be a daily event. God doesn't want us to go for days or weeks without talking to him. It also shows that we are to see God as our source of supply beyond the work that we do to earn money to provide for ourselves. Let's place ourselves in the time frame which saw Jesus walk the earth. Many folk grew their own food and in the natural they would be at the mercy of the elements. A drought could deprive them of a crop altogether, or a storm could rob them of a crop which was almost ready for harvest. And we all know that a crop takes weeks or months to produce food. So they would have been more aware of their dependence on the Lord than perhaps we are in this day of dashing to the local supermarket to buy any number of goods sourced not only locally but flown in from distant countries. But in reality we are still dependant on the Lord because even today there can come natural disasters such as droughts, floods and diseases to staunch the flow of supply. And in countries like Vanuatu many of the locals still depend on what they grow themselves and they are devastated by tropical cyclones virtually every year.

Perhaps we could pray: 'Thank you Lord for all that I have – a roof over my head, a job and food in my pantry. I acknowledge that without you the sun wouldn't shine and the rain wouldn't fall. So I ask you to supply what I need for today.' (Here we could ask the Lord for things other than food as well. Maybe we don't have a job so that could be on our list...)

Forgive us our debts, as we also have forgiven our debtors. The word 'debts' clearly means 'sins' because in verses 14 and 15 at the end of The Lord's Prayer, Jesus expands on this: *For if you forgive men when they sin against you, your heavenly Father will also forgive you. But if you do not forgive men their sins, your Father will not forgive your sins.* I have made mention of this principle before but it is easy for us to forget in the rush of events in our lives. We are here asking for forgiveness but with the understanding that our forgiveness is dependent on our having forgiven anyone who has offended us. When we pray regarding this we may need to wrestle with a fresh matter. Perhaps we would need to say something like this: 'Loving Father, I want your forgiveness and I realise that I need to have forgiven others. You know that I am having trouble forgiving .... because I am so hurt by what was said/done. Please help me to have a forgiving heart. In fact, Lord, I bless .... and ask that you will work in his/her life and draw him/her closer to yourself. Thank you Lord.' I think you will find that if you make a habit of blessing people whether you feel they deserve it or not, your heart will become softer toward them and you will be able to forgive the hurt they have inflicted.

And lead us not into temptation, but deliver us from the evil one. Here we are asking for help in the attractions, distractions and snares of life. But we are also seeing that some of the snares come purposely from the Devil. And we certainly need to ask for help in defeating him in our lives. Perhaps we could pray like this 'I know I sometimes disappoint you Lord and I ask you to show me when something is a temptation to do wrong. And I pray that you will protect me from falling for a trick and trap from the Devil and from anything which he would send upon my life because I know he desires to rob and destroy your work in my life.'

I would suggest that you finish your prayers always with praising and thanking the Lord for who he is (the Lord, holy, reliable, powerful, loving, forgiving, merciful) and what he has done (providing my needs, allowing trials in my life so that I will develop as his child, giving me direction, etc. etc.)

Now, please understand that I am not trying to improve on The Lord's Prayer but it is good that prayers become real to us, not just a recitation of something we've learned by heart. So I don't want you to adopt the words I've provided in this chapter. They are just suggestions to give you a springboard into your own way of expressing what you would want to say to God. I hope you find them helpful. And always remember, there's no competition in praying. We should never be trying to be the person who prays the 'best prayers'. In reality, the best prayers are simply when you are being real with God and having a meaningful and sincere chat with your Daddy.

I'm not being disrespectful in referring to God as Daddy. The Bible calls him 'Abba' and that is a Greek word for Daddy. A Greek child was seen running after his father calling out 'Abba, Abba' because he wanted to ask his Dad for an ice cream. Prayer is a little like that – 'Daddy, I need your help with …..' (Examples of the use of the word *Abba* in the Bible: Mark 14:36 where Jesus calls the Father Abba. Romans 8:14-16 "…because those who are led by the Spirit of God are sons of God. For you did not receive a spirit that makes you a slave again to fear, but you received the Spirit of sonship. And by him we cry, 'Abba, Father.' The Spirit himself testifies with our spirit that we are God's children." Galatians 4:6 & 7. "Because you are sons, God sent the Spirit of his Son into our hearts, the Spirit who calls out, 'Abba, Father.' So you are no longer a slave, but a son; and since you are a son, God has made you also an heir.")

There is another matter regarding prayer. We can pray on the run when that is all the time we have but to be honest it is important that we learn to stick in there when it comes to how much time we pray. The Bible says we shouldn't repeat words like a parrot thinking that our many words will cause God to hear. (Matthew 6:7, 8) "And when you pray, do not keep on babbling like pagans, for they think they will be heard because of their many words." If we are right with God, he is attentive to our prayers. But there are many situations and people who need prayer on their behalf. Are there aids to being able to pray for longer periods of time? There certainly are...

For instance, you can begin by ***praising*** the Lord for who he is; then ***thank*** him for blessings you can think of in your life or in somebody else's life or generally in the world. Then you can pray for your ***own needs*** – *spiritual, emotional, physical*; then on to the ***needs of others*** – your family, friends, colleagues, church brothers and sisters, the poor. Now pray for ***leaders*** – our parliamentarians and councillors, school masters and teachers, pastors, Bible Study leaders. Remember to pray for the upholders of the law. They need wisdom – policemen, judges, lawyers. And make sure you include those who are ***persecuted and suffering*** in the world – believers who are in prison, refugees. And it would be a good idea to pray for those who are helping others – ***charities and volunteers***. I like to pray for people of other faiths. Jesus died for their sins as well. They need their eyes opened to the truth. I'd suggest you have a list of people to pray for every day. And this should be a flexible list, added to as you come to know of someone in need. People can be erased from the list if you wish as their needs are met. All these items are very important and you can be sure that if you start to pray like this you will find that you will spend plenty of time in God's presence. I would add one more thing in this regard: I find it helpful just to sit silently in the Lord's presence sometimes to have my perspective on life realigned. There is strength to be drawn from being quiet before the Lord. You may have all sorts of circumstances whirling around you and you need to know that there is an atmosphere of faith and peace keeping you calm in the midst of it all.

On this subject, I would like to say one more thing. We often end our prayers with the word 'amen'. The meaning of 'amen' is 'so let it be'; in other words it is asking that what has been said before will be granted. And it is a handy word to be used in prayer meetings so that all the pray-ers can agree with what has been prayed by somebody else. But in the last 30 years or so preachers have adopted the word incorrectly. They make a statement then say 'amen' with a question mark in their voices so that the congregation with also say 'amen' to show that they agree with what has been said. Now that sounds quite okay, but sometimes they have said something negative such as 'now the Devil will try to get at us, amen?' While we may agree with the statement we would hardly want to say 'so let it be'. That is tantamount to asking for trouble. But I have heard this type of thing said so often.

So, could I ask you to watch that when you say 'amen' to something, it is really something desirable.

If the preacher says something negative like that and adds 'amen' to it, you could say 'that's right' rather than 'amen', because what he's saying is true but is not something that you want to invite. Good on you!

70

WHAT SHOULD I PRAY FOR OTHERS?

While we're chatting about prayer, I thought we might extend it to what to pray when we're praying for other people. Good examples can be found in the Bible. Let's look at some of the Epistles (letters) written to various people groups and churches in the New Testament.

The most common blessing announced on the recipients of the letters was 'grace and peace'. In Romans 1:7, Paul says *'To all in Rome who are loved by God and called to be saints: Grace and peace to you from God our Father and from the Lord Jesus Christ.'* In his closing remarks (which go on for some time because he is sending greetings to many individuals) he includes this: *'I want you to be wise about what is good, and innocent about what is evil'*. This echoes a saying of Jesus which I have always liked. He said to the disciples that he was sending them out 'like sheep among wolves'. Then he said *'therefore be as shrewd as snakes and as innocent as doves.'* (Matthew 10:16) Doesn't that conjure up a great picture in your minds? We are not to be naïve when it comes to dealing with evil people but there is to be no guile or malice in us. We will not act as they do but we will be able to be wise, not foolish. And this is what Paul was saying to the Romans as well. Echoes of these thoughts can be seen in Paul's first letter to the Corinthians, (14:20) *'Brothers, stop thinking like children. In regard to evil be infants, but in your thinking be adults.'*

When Paul wrote to the Corinthian church he had these

things to say to them in chapter 1: *'In (Christ Jesus) you have been enriched in every way – in all speaking and in all your knowledge....He will keep you strong to the end, so that you will be blameless on the Day of our Lord Jesus Christ.'* As he was speaking to the whole church, he had this to recommend: *'I appeal to you...in the name of our Lord Jesus Christ, that all of you agree with one another so that there may be no divisions among you and that you may be perfectly united in mind and thought.'*

Can you see that you can take these words of teaching from Scripture and pray them for people and groups you want God to bless or help? It certainly beats 'And God bless.... And God bless....'. We can be specific in what we want God to do because we can see that they are the very things the Lord would love to do for people.

Let's look further. Still in the book of 1Corinthians, in chapter 4:2 we see *'Now it is required that those who have been given a trust must prove faithful.'* So we can pray for a fellow believer that they will be faithful to what they have heard from the Lord. In 6:18-20, Paul speaks against sexual immorality and concludes *'Honour God with your body.'* We can pray purity for someone we feel may be tempted in this direction.

When we look at the first letter of Peter, because it was written during a time of persecution, his first words to them – after saying who it was from and to – were: "Consider it pure joy, my brothers, whenever you face trials of many kinds, because you know that the testing of your faith develops perseverance." When we pray for someone it is tempting to pray for easy times for them. But when we consider this Scripture, we realise that sometimes God allows trials into our lives for the express purpose of developing our character. So it could be wise to ask the Lord to strengthen a person during their trials rather than ask for them to be removed. I make a point of asking the Lord for wisdom on how to pray sometimes because he knows what is best in each situation.

James says in chapter 1:19, 20: "Everyone should be quick to listen, slow to speak and slow to become angry, for man's anger does not bring about the righteous life that God desires." I guess most of us need to be reminded of this and can pray it for ourselves. But also, if you know someone who tends to speak rashly or blow their top easily, pray for them that they will be more concerned for others than their own interests, that they may be able to be kinder under all circumstances, or something along those lines.

I don't think I need to say anything further in this regard. You get the idea. So as you read through the Bible, as you see something which God desires in his people, pray that thing for yourself and for anybody else you can see needs it. You don't necessarily have to tell them you are praying something specific for them or they may be offended that you think they need praying for, although most people are pleased if they find out someone cares enough to pray for them.

71

GOD'S SECRETS

Christianity is at once very simple and very complex. And therein lay its treasures.

Why do I say that? Well, the Gospel is quite simple – as David Pawson says in his wonderful book 'The Normal Christian Birth', there are four main steps to beginning to walk the way of salvation – Repent toward God the Father, Believe in the Lord Jesus Christ, Be baptised in water and Receive the Holy Spirit. I surrender to God and he forgives my sin and makes me worthy to live for him here on earth and live with him in heaven. That is so simple that even children can understand and take part in it themselves. In fact it is so simple that clever people try to complicate it. They just can't accept the simplicity of it. But there it is.

However, because God is so majestic, all-powerful, all-seeing, and has greatness unmatched, there is so much depth in the Gospel and its working out that we can be learning more all our lives. I remember my High School English teacher saying that Shakespeare was great literature because it can be read over and over again and each time you discover something new in it. I thought at the time that the Bible is great literature because we discover more and more gems within it the more we read it. And that is because there are aspects and depths of God which can only be appreciated over time and from experience. This further knowledge greatly enriches our lives. I've been following the Lord for as long as I can remember, and I keep having more revelations of the ways and grace of the Lord.

Deuteronomy 29:29 had this to say: "The secret things belong to the Lord our God, but the things revealed belong to us and to our children forever, that we may follow all the words of this law." So at that time, long before Jesus had come to earth, God related to his people via the laws he gave them to live by.

Did you notice *the secret things?* God has things which he alone knows, and surely we would say that that is reasonable. After all, he *is* God. But there is another verse in the book of the Old Testament prophet Jeremiah – in chapter 33, verse 3: "Call to me and I will answer you and tell you great and unsearchable things you do not know." Now we have to be careful about taking a verse out of context and making a rule of it. I don't believe that anybody at any time can just decide to call to God and expect to be told things which nobody else knows but God. But this verse does tell me that it is possible for a human being to be given secret understanding *at the right time*.

Why am I mentioning this? Because I find that sometimes I ask God for understanding about something specific and I learn the answer – sometimes God just gives me a *knowing* in my spirit, at other times I hear the answer in a conversation or perhaps a news item. I'll give you a tiny example – this is nothing earth-shattering, but just an indication of what is possible between God and his children.

This happened perhaps 15 years ago. I had heard people say that a particular brand of Cola drink was bad for you but I had never heard why. As I thought it was delicious I asked the Lord would he show me whether this Cola was bad for me or not. A simple question – not really one of *the secret things* of God – but the very next evening there was an item in the TV news saying that Cola drinks (no specific brand) had a particular acid in them which was believed to be harmful to our bones. I thanked the Lord and from that time on I have had only an occasional mouthful of Cola when it is on offer at a get-together. Never again did I hear anything mentioned on that subject until about a week ago when – again on the news – it was said that *soft drinks* had phosphoric acid which is believed to cause Osteoporosis. Osteoporosis is a weakening of the bones so this news was similar to the previous item, only this time it mentioned soft drinks in general, though I don't believe that all soft drinks have phosphoric acid. But can you see why I mention this answer to my prayer? For fifteen years I have been guarding my bone strength by not drinking Cola drinks. Had I not enquired of the Lord, I may have been suffering Osteoporosis by this age which I am not.

There have been many other times when I have asked the Lord for guidance on something specific and I have received that *knowing* inside me. So, walk as closely to the Lord as you can and you will find that you get to know him more and more intimately, not just by your Bible reading but also by asking him questions. This is sometimes called Interrogatory Prayer. I am blown away by the fact that the Creator and Sustainer of the universe invites us to ask him for wisdom and says he will not find fault with us but will grant us the wisdom we seek. (James 1:5)

This reminds me of King Solomon, David's son. When he acceded to the throne of Israel in his father's place, God said "Ask for whatever you want me to give you." After a preamble, Solomon's answer was "…Give your servant a discerning heart (in another word *wisdom*) to govern your people and to distinguish between right and wrong. For who is able to govern this great people of yours?" Now see what God's response was: "The Lord was pleased that Solomon had asked for this. So God said to him, 'Since you have asked for this and not for long life or wealth for yourself, nor have asked for the death of your enemies but for discernment in administering justice, I will do what you have asked. I will give you a wise and discerning heart, so that there will never have been anyone like you, nor will there ever be. Moreover, I will give you what you have not asked for – both riches and honour – so that in your lifetime you will have no equal among kings.'" Now that is an indication of how highly God esteems a request for wisdom. When we ask for wisdom it is not for our own benefit. It is so that we will think and act well and that is God's great desire for us. (You will find this story in 2 Kings 3: from verse 5.)

We began this subject by looking at Deuteronomy 29:29 about the secret things of God, but that verse also speaks about God's laws in the Old Testament. In the next chapter, let's look more closely at that part of the verse...because you can tell a lot about a person by the laws they bring in.

72

WHAT DO HIS LAWS SHOW US ABOUT GOD?

There are many ways we find out aspects of our God. Simply looking at Creation is one of them as I've mentioned before. Reading his Manual for Life, the Bible, has to be one of the greatest ways of getting to know him better.

How about we look at something which is hardly ever mentioned – the laws God gave to his ancient people, the Israelites. These are in the Bible of course but, because we are no longer under the old Law, we tend to ignore it. But we can learn much about a person by the laws he gives. Let's look at some of them…

We could begin with the best known ones, The Ten Commandments. For these, we look at Exodus 20.

You shall have no other gods before me.

You shall not make for yourself an idol in the form of anything in heaven above or on the earth beneath or in the waters below. You shall not bow down to them or worship them; for I, the Lord your God, am a jealous God, punishing the children for the sin of the fathers to the third and fourth generation of those who hate me, but showing love to a thousand generations of those who love me and keep my commandments.

Before we go any further, let me tell you that God later brought in that nobody would ever again be punished for his ancestors' sins. Now let's examine God's motives behind these first two Commandments. God knows that he is the only God so he is guarding his people from being lured into

WHAT DO GOD'S LAWS SHOW US ABOUT GOD?

false religion by warning them against making any idols to worship. You see, we have been created with a natural urge to worship so that we will seek the truth and discover God, even if we have never been taught about him. If you doubt that, look about you at people's lives. I can't help but think of footy fans as my first example. Have you looked at them on TV before any major match? Proudly wearing their idols' team colours, waving their team scarves before the camera, cheering and full of excitement in hope that their idols will win the Premiership or whatever.

Then there are the screen idols – actors and actresses that people go gaga over. And music idols – outrageous prices will be paid for tickets to their concerts then the 'worshippers' will scream and shout so that they hardly even hear the music.

Of course, many of us worship 'self'. We want life just the way we like it, and will do almost anything to see that we get it.

Bearing this in mind, it was important that God gave this law so that his people would not become victims of worshipping wrongly.

Now, I am not saying that all the above examples are entirely wrong. It is just the emphasis that is put on them that is extreme, especially when worship is given to these 'idols' and none to God.

You shall not misuse the name of the Lord your God, for the Lord will not hold anyone guiltless who misuses his name.

If we examine The Ten Commandments as a whole we will see that they are all about respect. Firstly, respect toward God and his name and then respect for others. Let's continue...

Remember the Sabbath day by keeping it holy. Six days you shall labour and do all your work, but the seventh day is a Sabbath to the Lord your God. On it you shall not do any work, neither you, nor your son or daughter, nor your manservant or maidservant, nor your animals, nor the alien within your gates. For in six days the Lord made the heavens and the earth, the sea, and all that is in them, but he rested on the seventh day. Therefore the Lord blessed the seventh day and made it holy.

First of all, we note the kindness of the Lord to include servants and even animals in this enforced rest from work one day per week. On one of my visits to Israel some years ago I noted that Israelis still worked for six days and had one day off. Here in Australia, we used to work five and a half days, having Saturday afternoon and Sunday off. I believe that having Sunday off was particularly so that the population could attend worship services in their churches. This was greatly important, not only to spend time with God but also to be together with loved ones, family and/ or friends, all having the same day off work. (Of course, emergency services have always needed to be available 7 days a week. But by far, most people had the privilege of all being off work together.)

Now families are split because laws in this land have been brought in that shops should open all sorts of hours and all days. So, to keep a job, people are forced to work various shifts on any and every day. Can you see the splintering of relationships, not only with God, but within families? God's unit is the family. It is the support network that he intends every person to have. We are aware, of course, that it doesn't always work out well, but if we *all* walked closely with the Lord, it would. Our secondary support network is the church which is the Family of the Lord. Here, brothers and sisters in the Lord should offer us love and compassion, kindness and understanding, forgiveness and opportunities to use our God-given gifts.

But, because businesses are kept open so much we are prevented from having the support that God intended. Surely there is something wrong with us if we cannot do all our business in six days. Of course, it is convenient to be able to shop almost any hour of the day on any day, but if we look at the overall effect it cannot be a good one. For instance, people can only buy so many items in any week. By having to stay open longer, business owners have to spread their profits over more working hours. Therefore, they tend to use part-time workers to cover their busier hours and some people are scrambling to have enough paid hours of work to bring in enough income to care for themselves and their families.

Of course, the large supermarkets don't mind because now they are taking the profits that small convenience stores used to glean when the large ones were closed.

I am sharing all this with you so that you will look at overall effects when a law is mooted in Parliament. I believe we need to speak up and contact our local representatives when we can see that a new law is not going to serve us or our community well in the long term. Convenience is not enough reason to bring in a new law. That's enough from me on that subject, so let's look further...

Honour your father and your mother, so that you may live long in the land the Lord your God is giving you.

This is rather intriguing, isn't it? Firstly, it is urging us to show respect toward our parents. And we can see that this is necessary if the family is going to serve as a suitable nurturing nest for us from infancy to adulthood. But did you notice that there was a reward – in this life – for obeying this particular Commandment? Longevity is related to our honouring our parents. And I might add that it is a foreshadowing of our *eternal life* for honouring our heavenly Father.

I wonder if this reward is still one of God's principles? I noticed that my mother and all her six siblings greatly honoured their parents, their mother in particular. She had died at age 59 and they spoke of her almost in awe. She obviously was a little lady who commanded respect. And every one of those siblings lived long. Mum's sister lived only until 70 but considering that she was not expected to live when she was born, that was a good age – and the one the Bible says is the natural span of our lives (before the days of extending life by amazing surgeries and drugs). Mum's 5 brothers all lived into their 80s including the eldest who had been injured at birth because he was such a large baby born to an extremely tiny woman. And my mother died at 92. It just makes me wonder…

Now I am not suggesting for one moment that if a person dies young they have not honoured their parents. Heaven forbid! There are other factors involved in how long we live of course… But it is very interesting that this Commandment was so important in God's plan for our lives that he granted a reward for keeping it.

You shall not murder.

This is pretty straightforward, isn't it? God wants people to feel secure. Note, though, that it doesn't say 'you shall not kill'. God has not forbidden warfare though he doesn't instigate it under the New Covenant. Therefore it is not murder to fight for your country. We are told, however, not to defend ourselves in the New Testament – "But I tell you, Do not resist an evil person. If someone strikes you on the right cheek, turn to him the other also. And if someone wants to sue you and take your tunic, let him have your cloak as well. If someone forces you to go one mile, go with him two miles." (That was Jesus speaking, in Matthew 5:39-41.)

You shall not commit adultery.

Again, we see that God is seeking to protect people, and

their marriage. I mentioned that the Commandments are about respect and here we have respect, not only for people, but for marriage itself.

You shall not steal.

Here we see God is commanding respect, not only for people themselves and their marriages, but also for their property, whether it be money, goods or cattle and sheep.

You shall not give false testimony against your neighbour.

What is being commanded here? Respect for others' reputations. Our good reputation is one of our greatest possessions. It effects how people interact with us (or refuse to interact with us) and can so easily be destroyed by careless words.

You shall not covet your neighbour's house. You shall not covet your neighbour's wife, or his manservant or his maidservant, his ox or donkey, or anything that belongs to your neighbour.

God cared so much for how people should be treated that he now goes into a greater depth. This is not just lying or stealing; this is dealing with the very motives of our hearts. Coveting is different from jealousy. Did you notice in the 2nd Commandment that God said he is a *jealous* God? Jealousy is wanting what is rightfully our own whereas coveting is wanting what doesn't belong to us. There's a lot of difference, isn't there? God is jealous over what is rightfully his – our loyalty to him and his good name. He is not coveting what belongs to someone else. We must watch our deepest motives. We can admire what belongs to others. We may even desire to have for ourselves the kind of thing they have – a nice house, a good job, a good reputation. And we can work to obtain those things for ourselves. But we must watch that we don't begin to desire to have *their* house, *their* job or *their* reputation. We would then be no longer respecting or loving them.

Well, that's a brief perusal of the major commandments God gave to his people under the Old Covenant. What kind of society would we have if everyone lived according to these Commandments even today? It would be one where justice ruled, where mercy was the catchcry, where God was given his rightful place – that first place in our love and honouring. But there are more laws which give us an indication of the kind of God we are honouring…

In these olden days we are examining there were no pension schemes and if a Hebrew (Israelite) got himself into debt, he could choose to 'sell himself' as a servant to pay off his debt. But even in this instance, God put in place a protection. We see in Exodus 21:2 "If you buy a Hebrew servant, he is to serve you for six years. But in the seventh year, he shall go free, without paying anything." Again, we see justice and moderation in action.

An interesting law was that if a man *accidentally* killed another man there was a place of refuge to which he could flee so that vengeance was not gained at his expense. (Exodus 21:13)

These laws were enforced by God for his own people but we note that aliens (strangers to the land) were included in the protection of the law. We saw that in the 4th Commandment regarding the Sabbath rest. Again, in Exodus 22:21 we find "Do not mistreat an alien or oppress him, for you were aliens in Egypt."

The very next verse instructs the Hebrews not to take advantage of a widow or an orphan. God's penalty would be very harsh.

Even lending money was legislated. Let's look at Exodus 22:25 "If you lend money to one of my people among you who is needy, do not be like a moneylender; charge him no interest. If you take your neighbour's cloak as a pledge, return it to him by sunset, because his cloak is the only covering he has for his body."

There were many other items legislated about. Poor people were not to be denied justice in the courts, but nor were they to be sided with just because they were poor. Bribery was forbidden. And how about this beautiful law in Exodus 23:10 – "For six years you are to sow your fields and harvest the crops, but during the seventh year let the land lie unploughed and unused. Then the poor among your people may get food from it, and the wild animals may eat what they leave. Do the same with your vineyard and your olive grove."

Let's look at Deuteronomy 24:21 for another look at God's care for the needy. "When you harvest the grapes in your vineyard, do not go over the vines again. Leave what remains for the alien, the fatherless and the widow." If you read the story of Ruth in the book of the same name in the Old Testament you will see that she, as a widow, gleaned a field after the harvesters had gone over it once.

The Israelites were not to have dishonest scales in commerce. They were even told to build a railing around a flat rooftop so that no-one would fall from it. So we can see that God thought of everything and gave very sound rules for running a society founded on justice and compassion.

So what does that tell us about God himself? Surely it announces loudly and clearly that God is a God of justice, mercy, kindness and compassion. Isn't it surprising what you can learn by reading a list of laws?

There were many more laws and you can read them in Exodus and Deuteronomy if you would like to study them in more depth. Many of them were regarding hygiene and this kept Jews healthy even during the Black Plague in London when others were dropping like flies.

Interestingly, Jesus at once enlarged and reduced the ancient laws by giving us the law of Love. In Matthew

22:37-40, when Jesus was asked which was the greatest Commandment in the Law, these were his words: "'Love the Lord your God with all your heart and with all your soul and with all your mind.' This is the first and greatest commandment. And the second is like it: 'Love your neighbour as yourself.' All the Law and the Prophets hang on these two commandments." (You may notice here that Jesus summed up the Commandments into just two.) So Jesus revealed that God's Law was all about love and if we truly love we will walk God's way. I like to use the word 'respect' because it may seem impossible to love someone we don't really know, perhaps someone we have only just been introduced to. But if we think of it as *respect,* we can do that to anyone. We can respect his person, his belongings, his words (even if we don't agree with them), and his reputation.

Of course, Jesus made mention of other laws as well and went on to point out that it is not just in the *doing* of *actions,* but in our thoughts and motives that God is interested. For instance, in Matthew 5:21 we find these words: "You have heard that it was said to the people long ago, 'Do not murder, and anyone who murders will be subject to judgment.' But I tell you that anyone who is angry with his brother will be subject to judgment." Wow! That's where the rubber meets the road, isn't it? Jesus is saying that murder begins in the heart when hatred brings forth anger. When we consider that this was Jesus speaking, we need to examine our own thoughts very soberly. Of course, we need the help of the Holy Spirit within our hearts to make and keep them clean in God's sight.

So in looking at this matter, we find that God is serious about wanting his people to live truly godly lives, not just to look good on the outside, but to *be* truly pure right in the heart. This is because we are to be a reflection of his lovely and pure character. What a God!

73

IF AT FIRST YOU DON'T SUCCEED...

Have you heard the old ditty "If at first you don't succeed, try, try again"? It comes to me from the mists of time as clearly as if I had heard it yesterday. Yet I can't recall how I came to know it. Was it taught us at school? Did I hear my Mum say it?

Nevertheless, it is worth not only recalling now but also filing away in our memory banks. There must be hundreds of proverbs and sayings in our English language. Some are more important than others. The reason I'm bringing up this one is that I have been astounded at the tenacity of some famous people over the ages. And it happens to be true that if they hadn't 'tried and tried again', not only would they not have succeeded, but neither would they have been famous names now.

Some have been inventors. Some have been orators. Some have been authors or artists. And what they have in common is that it took time for their ideas to be accepted. Some writers have offered their manuscripts to publisher after publisher only to be rejected. When, at last, because of their perseverance, a publisher decided to give them a go, their works became world renowned; perhaps not immediately, but when the world was ready for them.

When it comes to inventions, many hours – even years – and much brain power was utilised to produce the desired product that would be a useful thing to mankind. And most inventions are extensions of what someone else has already made. For instance, Humphry Davy produced light – an electric arc – by connecting carbon to his electric battery. But it quickly burned out. That was in 1800. English physicist, Sir Joseph Wilson Swan persisted in trying to produce a longer-lasting light and in 1878 introduced his paper filament light. He had been working on it for 18 years. Then American Charles Francis Brush had his carbon filament light used to light a town square and some buildings. However, it wasn't widely used. This was in 1877. The inventor **Thomas Alva Edison** (in the USA) (the one we have mostly heard about) experimented with thousands of different filaments to find just the right materials to glow well and be long-lasting. In 1879, Edison discovered that a carbon filament in an oxygen-free bulb glowed but did not burn up for 40 hours. Edison eventually produced a bulb that could glow for over 1500 hours.

Today, and for generations, we have taken electric light for granted and would feel greatly inconvenienced if it was taken from us. Yet, if these men had not persisted with their dream to create a functional enduring light we would still be groping by candle light.

William Wilberforce whom we've mentioned before was 'a voice crying in the wilderness' for some 20 years in British Parliament, trying to secure an end to slavery. He was a frail, small, unattractive man but eventually his godly voice was heard and influential men were themselves influenced by Wilberforce. Slavery for Britain was officially put to an end.

So, what I want to say to you is *if you have a good dream, if at first you don't succeed, try, try, again!* Don't allow yourself to be put down or put off.

Some of the information in this chapter was obtained via Google

74

HOSPITALITY

When I think of the word *hospitality* I think of that similar word *hospital*. I think the two are linked as *hospital* can be traced to a root – meaning *guest rooms*. Of course, a hospital's guest rooms are for the treatment of injury or illness whereas *hospitality* appears to have more to do with a clean bed and meals. But I have a suspicion that the likeness goes deeper than the root meaning.

The Bible urges believers to be *hospitable,* and look what Jesus said in **Luke 14:12-14** ESV

"He said also to the man who had invited him, 'When you give a dinner or a banquet, do not invite your friends or your brothers or your relatives or rich neighbors, lest they also invite you in return and you be repaid. But when you give a feast, invite the poor, the crippled, the lame, the blind, and you will be blessed, because they cannot repay you. For you will be repaid at the resurrection of the just.'"

Just think about what would begin to happen to the poor, the crippled, the lame and the blind if they were invited into homes to be entertained and fed. Because of their circumstances, they quite likely could have issues of self-pity and rejection. Now I'm not suggesting that all people who are poor or disabled have these problems, but it is not an exaggeration to say that some do. After all, many people with disabilities are ignored or overlooked. Sometimes it is simply that folk aren't sure how to handle them. Can you see that by merely being invited to your home they could begin to feel differently about their lives?

I believe there is quite some power in *hospitality* as there is in *hospitalization*. Shall we look at it a little further? I want us to always try to see things from the Lord's eye view. Jesus seemed to have a somewhat different slant on things from his companions. We would probably say it is great to invite people over for a meal. We can share stories, share experiences and share jokes. Well, if that is good for us, how much more good would it do for those whose life is a struggle? I feel sure Jesus was not saying that we should never invite those we love to our homes. Rather, I believe he was showing that it was more important to make sure that those whose life is difficult should be included and made to feel important and significant.

Our problem is that we tend to go with what feels natural and makes us feel comfortable and good. God wants us to think of what makes others feel comfortable and good. And therein lays the difference.

Okay! Now, just so you know that the verse above is not just a one-off, let's see a number of other Scriptures where hospitality is recommended or instructed…

Hebrews 13:2 Do not forget to entertain strangers, for by so doing some people have entertained angels without knowing it.

1 Peter 4:9 Offer hospitality to one another without grumbling.

Romans 12:13 Share with God's people who are in need. Practise hospitality.

It is not just a New Testament attitude. Look here at Leviticus…

Leviticus 19:34 The alien living with you must be treated as one of your native-born. Love him as yourself, for you were aliens in Egypt.

Then in Romans, Paul urges the believers to be kind to

Phoebe, a Christian who obviously is travelling to Rome:

Romans 16:2 I ask you to receive her in the Lord in a way worthy of the saints and to give her any help she may need from you, for she has been a great help to many people, including me.

We don't need to provide a feast for visitors. See what Jesus is reported to have said in the book of Mark...

Mark 9:41 I tell you the truth, anyone who gives you a cup of water in my name because you belong to Christ will certainly not lose his reward.

Another Scripture which shows that our hospitality can be more extensive and for those who are serving the Lord. This from the Old Testament...

2 Kings 4:8-17 One day Elisha went to Shunem. And a well-to-do woman was there, who urged him to stay for a meal. So whenever he came by, he stopped there to eat. She said to her husband, "I know that this man who often comes our way is a holy man of God. Let's make a small room on the roof and put in it a bed and a table, a chair and a lamp for him. Then he can stay there whenever he comes to us." One day when Elisha came, he went up to his room and lay down there. He said to his servant Gehazi, "Call the Shunammite." So he called her, and she stood before him. Elisha said to him, "Tell her, 'You have gone to all this trouble for us. Now what can be done for you? Can we speak on your behalf to the king or the commander of the army?'" She replied, "I have a home among my own people."

"What can be done for her?" Elisha asked. Gehazi said, "Well, she has no son and her husband is old." Then Elisha said, "Call her." So he called her, and she stood in the doorway. "About this time next year," Elisha said, "you will hold a son in your arms." "No, my lord," she objected. "Don't mislead your servant, O man of God!" But the woman became pregnant, and the next year about that same time she gave birth to a son, just as Elisha had told her.

We had friends who did a similar thing. They had a magnificent house on a cliffside overlooking the ocean. We stayed in their home on one occasion. But after a while they decided to build an apartment on top of their garage for those who were travellers serving the Lord. We were privileged to enjoy this comfortable 'home away from home'. Now of course, not everybody has the need nor the finance to do this, but it is a wonderful blessing when it can be done.

3 John 1:5-8 Dear friend, you are faithful in what you are doing for the brothers, even though they are strangers to you. They have told the church about your love. You will do well to send them on their way in a manner worthy of God. It was for the sake of the Name that they went out, receiving no help from the pagans. We ought therefore to show hospitality to such men that we may work together for the truth.

You will note from that verse what we were speaking about in Chapter 4, that we are sharers in the work by supporting those who are on the 'front line'.

We may have spoken about this next verse before but it fits in beautifully in the context of this chapter… The Jews of long ago had been fasting and calling out to the Lord but he hadn't been granting their requests. He tells them that the reason for his not answering their prayers was that their lives were unjust and self centred. He goes on to show what he required of them which included this verse…

Isaiah 58:7 Is it not to share your food with the hungry and to provide the poor wanderer with shelter – when you see the naked, to clothe him, and not to turn away from your own flesh and blood? (i.e. your needy relatives)

Another verse on this line. This time Paul is instructing the younger Timothy about church management. Even the leaders were to practise hospitality.

1 Timothy 3:2 Now the overseer must be above reproach, the husband of but one wife, temperate, self-controlled, respectable, hospitable, able to teach, not given to drunkenness, not violent but gentle, not quarrelsome, not a lover of money.

Just one more quote, spoken by Jesus, regarding the reward for looking after those who are working for the Lord.

Matthew 10:40-42 He who receives you receives me, and he who receives me receives the one who sent me. Anyone who receives a prophet because he is a prophet will receive a prophet's reward, and anyone who receives a righteous man because he is a righteous man will receive a righteous man's reward. And if anyone gives even a cup of cold water to one of these little ones because he is my disciple, I tell you the truth, he will certainly not lose his reward.

So, have I convinced you that there is more to *hospitality* than just a clean bed and some food? I hope so...

75

ANOTHER LOOK AT TEMPTATION

Let's take a moment to look at one special verse. I memorised this one years ago and have been glad to be able to recall it every so often, either for my own sake or for others'.

The verse is 1 Corinthians 10:13. "No temptation has seized you except what is common to man. And God is faithful; he will not let you be tempted beyond what you can bear. But when you are tempted, he will also provide a way out so that you can stand up under it."

Wow! What a verse! What a truth! Did you catch all the implications of that verse? For you? What it is saying is that if we are tempted we don't have any reason to feel that we are more tempted than others, because temptations of all kinds come to all people. It doesn't mean that you will have exactly the same temptations that I will, but it does say that you are not unique in what you are tempted with. What does that truth produce? Well, firstly it makes us feel for others, knowing that they are being tempted too.

What's the next great truth? God is faithful. That is telling us that God doesn't forsake us because we are being tempted. Being tempted to think, say or do wrong is part and parcel of being human.

Now for a truly amazing part: God puts a limit on temptation. The Bible tells us that God doesn't tempt anyone. After all, he is not wanting anyone to do wrong. (However, we are also informed that if people reject God and his ways he will eventually give them over to their evil ways. In other words, he will stop striving to save them. They have made their choices.) When we are tempted, it is either the Devil coming to us as he did to Jesus in the wilderness with enticements; or it is our own foolish or evil inclinations. But isn't it comforting to know that our temptation never need overpower us because the Lord will see to it that we can bear it.

Make sure you always remember the final part of this wonderful verse. God will have a way for you to bear up under the onslaught. Now you know why I have been glad that I memorised this verse. There have been times when I have turned to the Lord and asked him to show me the way out. When I felt hemmed in he was able to show me the attitude to take to banish the temptation.

Do you know why temptation has victory over us? It is because we enjoy it. We need to recognize temptation for what it is. It is not a harmless dwelling on a little bit of naughtiness. It is siding with the enemy against the will of our Lord. It is living at a level that doesn't bring glory to God. It is allowing ourselves to be weakened in our resolve. It is making a fool of ourselves.

Being tempted is not a sin in itself. It is what we do with the temptation that decides whether it 'gives birth to sin'. If we pull up a chair to enjoy the temptation, we have already slipped from one to the other.

I should mention the couple of verses which precede our wonderful verse. Paul was referring to events which happened to the Israelites, God's people of the Old Testament. Then he continues in verses 11-12 of 1 Corinthians 13:

"These things happened to them as examples and were written down as warnings for us, on whom the fulfilment of the ages has come. So, if you think you are standing firm, be careful that you don't fall!"

So, though we have all the great provisions of verse 13 as

believers, it is clear that we need to treat temptation seriously and guard our hearts against taking it too lightly.

May the Lord give us all great wisdom in this regard.

76

THE CUPS OF THE LORD

Jesus himself recommended that we get together regularly to eat and drink 'in remembrance of Him' as we've touched on before. Of course, we are to remember his sacrifice, but If we are to remember him, we need to know what he is really like. So let's look at another aspect of the Lord. Bear in mind that when a woman came to Jesus for healing, he addressed her as 'daughter'. So, though he is the Son of God, he shares the Father heart of God.

Growing up as an only child, my parents were strict with me. I had to be obedient and when you are an only child you can't blame anybody else so it's pretty obvious when you have misbehaved. But my parents loved me. They weren't rich by any means and when I began work at 15 I paid part of my meagre wages as board to them which is very fair. However, I didn't realise that they were keeping my board money – either all of it or part of it I can't remember now – in a separate bank account and when I turned 21 that money was given back to me to give me a good start in life.

As it turned out, the Lord called me into Bible College full time for 2 years round that time so the money was handy to pay my College fees. I did a couple of weekly cleaning jobs as well to stretch it out.

So my parents demanded obedience from me but their whole intention was that I should grow up to be a good, useful citizen so they could entrust blessings to me.

When I think of that, it seems to me that they really did

fulfil God's will for parents in that regard. [I am not saying that all parents should give board back to their children. There are many ways of blessing our children and money is only one of them. And in the wrong hands, money may not be a blessing at all...]

Do you know why I think that my parents fulfilled God's will for parents? Because that concept is an echo of our Father God's ways with his children. And we know that Jesus is the human form of God.

May I share a verse from the book of Isaiah which illustrates this point? Chapter 58:10 has this to say: "..if you spend yourselves in behalf of the hungry and satisfy the needs of the oppressed, then your light will rise in the darkness, and your night will become like the noonday." So there is just one of the verses that show us that, as we fulfil God's will, we find that we are ourselves blessed by God. As we look after others, light will dawn on our circumstances. Wisdom and aid come to us.

God said to Moses that the fear of God would keep his people from sinning. So when we are told to fear God it is for our own good.

Generation after generation in the Old Testament, God called men to be prophets to his people. Their job was usually to call the people back to God so that God could bless them. How many times is the word 'bless' or 'blessing' in the Bible? It seems to me that is the chief aim of God - to bless. But he cannot bless sin so he calls us to live lives that are pleasing to him and he makes his Holy Spirit available to us so that we *can* please him.

So, as we approach Communion, let us see Jesus as one who wants to bless our lives, not just in a selfish way but so that we in turn can be a blessing to others. Blessing makes us joyful, firstly in the receiving, then in passing it on.

Before we take the bread and the cup, let us always take

time to check up on ourselves. Is there anything coming between God and us? If so, let us put it right so that we have the right to eat and drink in remembrance of the one who is the greatest blessing to the whole world...

As the bread represents the broken body of our Lord Jesus and the cup stands for the shed blood – and the Bible says there is no forgiveness without the shedding of blood – we are affirming that we have received the redemption paid for by the Lord. We are entering again into 'communion' with our Lord by partaking 'in remembrance of Him', as he instructed.

I want to look at another 'cup' in Scripture. Let's visit the Garden of Gethsemane with Jesus. He had just shared the last meal with his disciples before going to the cross, and had given them the instruction to eat and drink in remembrance of him. He knew the time had come for his arrest and death, so he went with some of his disciples to this quiet garden outside the old city walls of Jerusalem, on the side of the Mount of Olives. He was there to pray to his Father. In Matthew 26: from verse 38, he said to his disciples "'My soul is overwhelmed with sorrow to the point of death. Stay here and keep watch with me.' Going a little farther, he fell with his face to the ground and prayed, 'My Father, if it is possible, may this *cup* be taken from me. Yet not as I will, but as you will.'" It was such a hardship to him that Jesus repeated the prayer.

What was this *cup* he was talking about? If you don't know, take close notice because it will explain why his soul was overwhelmed with sorrow to the point of death. This pure Son of God who maintained such close communion with his Father God was about to drink – in a figurative sense – the *cup of God's wrath* – on our behalf, so that we could be forgiven all our sins.

I don't believe we will ever completely comprehend

just how dreadful that was for Jesus. As he was taking the world's sins upon himself, he would feel the wrath he didn't deserve. When he was later on the cross he cried out "My God, my God, why have you forsaken me?" Crucifixion is one of the cruellest forms of punishment. Because hands (or wrists) and feet are nailed to the wood, there is constant pain. Then, because hanging like that makes it difficult to take a breath, the person would push up on their feet which would again increase the pain in the feet. As the body again sagged, the arms would be gut-wrenchingly aching, the lungs again were seared with pain as they could hardly take in any air and so it was a seesawing of pain in so many areas of the body. Sometimes the legs were eventually broken by a soldier to hasten death. This didn't happen to Jesus as he had already dismissed his spirit and having no bone broken fulfilled an ancient prophecy.

Crucifixion has happened to many people but they had mainly the physical ache and pain to bear. But Jesus had a spiritual pain to bear which we can only try to imagine. To be disconnected from his beloved Father must have been almost more than he could bear.

Yet in the midst of all this horror, Jesus prayed for the very people who had brought about his pain and asked forgiveness even for them. That emphasizes to us that the whole purpose of this suffering was **so that we would never need to drink of the *cup of God's wrath.***

When we consider all these things, I think it makes the cup of Communion and the bread all the more special and precious. Don't ever tire of having Communion regularly. It really is what Christianity is all about – Jesus taking our punishment so that we need not.

So, if you have not yet surrendered to God and accepted Jesus' sacrifice for the forgiveness of your sins, please don't put it off any longer. Not only is it a doorway into a life of real purpose and joy and peace, but we can never be sure how long any one of us has here on earth.

The other point in all this - *Is there someone you should be sharing these things with? Does your family know the wonderful Gospel of God's forgiving grace? Do your friends? Why not share the truth with them?*

77

THE DIAMOND

I have discovered over the years that God often doesn't look at things or people the same way we human beings do.

Twenty-five or thirty years ago I was at one of our church camps. The speaker was talking about our service to the Lord. We sang the lovely chorus: *Jesus, Take Me As I Am*. It was by Dave Bryant and taken from Scripture in Song Volume Two. Some of the lyrics say:

> Make me like a precious stone,
> Crystal clear and finely honed;
> Life of Jesus shining through,
> Giving glory back to you.

After singing those words the speaker invited us to close our eyes and hold out our hand. We were to ask the Lord to show us what kind of a precious stone he saw us as. I did so, expecting to see a rough, dirty, unpolished cheap gemstone. To my amazement I had a vision of a large, multi-faceted beautiful diamond. I thought that was quite ridiculous and it must have been a trick of my imagination. But then the Lord said to me that it was my availability that made me like that to him.

As you can imagine I was greatly cheered by this message. So I want to pass it on to you. It is not really your *ability or abilities* that God is looking for. After all, he can build those into us any time he wants. He is looking for our *availability*.

THE DIAMOND

That's what he can use to achieve whatever he wants.
So what are you waiting for?

Music has the amazing ability to transport us
But we need to ask
'where is this music taking me?'

78

HUMANISTIC RELIGION

If we look at the very word *religion* it is a system devised to connect human beings to God. Now, because there is only one true, living God we can easily understand that the Christian religion is the only system devised by God himself. Other religions are man's attempt to reach out to a god of their own making.

These other gods have been imagined in the form of serpents, bulls, elephants, cats, monkeys and in human form. Isn't it interesting that the true God doesn't want us to worship an image at all? He wants us to think of him as far greater than any image. After all, images fall, shatter, can be exploded by enemies etc. etc. And the Lord knows that human beings have a tendency to begin to worship the image rather than the Lord himself.

I have mentioned before that Christianity has often been said to be a *relationship* rather than a *religion*. But it is a religion in the purest sense of the word. However, with other religions worldwide they are always a quest to *do enough* to appease their god (or multiple gods). As far as I know there is no real assurance in any other religion. As I've said in China I saw people lighting incense sticks, placing them on a stand outside a temple, and seeking to brush the smoke from the incense over themselves. They wanted a blessing. And don't we all want blessing in our lives? If only they had known that the true and living God just wants to bless them without the incense stick because he has done everything necessary to procure the forgiveness that invites blessing into our lives. As a matter of fact, the forgiveness of sins is the greatest blessing and the peace that comes from knowing forgiveness is the second greatest blessing.

So God doesn't want any intermediary to come between us and him. He wants us to know that his Spirit is *with us* whether we are in church or elsewhere.

Now, let me get round to what is really troubling me about the Christian church in general these days. Bearing in mind that we are the only ones with the truth (which doesn't mean we are know-alls), we should be a shining light to the rest of mankind. This is our duty as well as our privilege. We should be able to show what it means to have God and his will and his ways at the forefront of our minds and hearts and behaviour. But what are we finding so often? We are seeing acted out humanistic religion *within so-called Christian churches and Christians individually.* What is humanistic religion? It is one where human ideas are central. I have tried to lay out before you in chapter after chapter things that God has made clear by his Word. And sometimes these things aren't popular with the world because they don't make them feel comfortable. But is it the duty of the church to make people feel comfortable? Most of us need to feel uncomfortable about our way of life before we will seek God who can 'calm the troubled breast'.

It seems to me that many church people and even church leaders are seeking to be popular so they water down – they dilute – the clear word which God has given to us. In other words, their main aim is to please people rather than God. This is humanistic religion. It is based on how human beings feel, how they view things. And God's ways are much higher than our natural ways. Isaiah 55:8 & 9:

"'For my thoughts are not your thoughts, neither are your ways my ways,' declares the Lord. 'As the heavens are higher than the earth, so are my ways higher than your ways and my thoughts than your thoughts.'"

Well, that's something we need to understand. We, as humans, may think we have some lofty thoughts and noble deeds but if they are not in line with the way God sees things, we are fooling ourselves.

Again, this is why it is important to know the Word of God. That is where we gain our basic understanding of what is important to the Lord, and what is not pleasing in his sight.

So, if you are seeking to follow the Lord, watch that you don't make popularity your first aim when dealing with others. Of course, I do not mean that you should be careless of how others are feeling. But with grace and respect, you can gently mention what God has to say about the matter and then it is up to the person to decide whether to go God's way or their own. And many of us are selfish enough to decide to go our own way even when we know it is not God's way.

Years ago, I spoke to a relative of mine about the Lord and her response was 'I am far too selfish to let someone else rule my life.' I continue to pray for her and I think she is softening toward the Lord in her older age. But, as always, the choice is hers. But at least I gave her the chance to know the truth.

When a contentious issue arises in the media, they often seek out church leaders for their comment. And sometimes my heart sinks as I listen to compromised answers. Of course, we don't want to be offensive, but it is our responsibility to make the truth known and if we hide behind a cloak of popularity we may have many people follow us but we won't have done our job for the one who matters most. The world is crying out for reality and power in people's lives but they will stop and applaud a leader who serves up something easy on the palate. Don't let people die needing the truth. The very least we can do is pray for church people and their leaders and for the people who are 'dead in their sins.'

What the world needs most is not just love, as the song says, but they need the truth about God's love and people who have a God-centred religion.

Some years ago I was confronted with a prickly situation. I was visiting a friend, and her sister who had lived in France for many years was visiting her too. I had a chat with the sister and she told me something of her way of life. She was living with a man who had not yet been divorced. She was also teaching at a church school in France. One day, as she was speaking with the priest at the school she mentioned her 'husband' then said that he was not really her husband. The priest had replied 'Of course he is your husband'. Now the priest obviously knew that she was living with the man and they weren't married but instead of taking up the opportunity to influence her toward God's way, he wanted to please her and make her feel comfortable.

What was I to say in that circumstance? If I said nothing, it would be concluded that I agreed with the priest. So, taking my courage in hand, I *very gently* said something like "And what do you think God thinks?" Well, she left my side pretty quickly and my friend later told me that she had gone to her room fuming. When she later emerged she had told her sister how *intolerant* I was. Now consider what I had said to her. I had merely tried to turn her to what God felt about her situation. Interestingly, she wasn't back in France very long and she had married her de facto. Now, I'm not saying that that would have been my solution to the situation as I don't believe in remarriage after divorce, but nevertheless it said to me that she needed to hear what I said and probably acted in the way she thought God would want.

That priest had aided and abetted her sin by being so humanistic. And she needed to be faced with the seriousness of her situation. It doesn't matter if 99% of the population were living in sin, she needed to face up to what God says about it.

So, you can see that siding with God is not necessarily the way to win friends, but then again, Jesus wasn't always popular either, was he?

79

TRACING REDEMPTION THROUGH THE OLD TESTAMENT

We are stepping up a gear in some ways in this chapter. We are seeking to see what many people miss out on because they don't look deeper into the Word of God. I figure that if you are still reading this book you are wise enough to want to study a bit more deeply. And it is my pleasure to open up to you what I have hardly ever heard anybody teach.

I want us to see proof that Christianity was not a new religion which began with the coming of Jesus to the earth. Rather, it was the fulfilment of what had been in the heart of God since time began.

God chose Abraham to be the Patriarch of a family which would grow into a family of nations through his promised son Isaac, and other nations via his son Ishmael. Let's check up on some of the things God said to Abraham (at that time called Abram). And bear in mind that at this time Abram and his wife Sarai were old and had no children. (Sarai was renamed by God Sarah.): Genesis 17:3-8...

"Abram fell facedown, and God said to him, 'As for me, this is my covenant with you: You will be the father of many nations. No longer will you be called Abram (meaning exalted father); your name will be Abraham, (meaning father of many) for I have made you a father of many nations. I will make you very fruitful; I will make nations of you, and kings will come from you. I will establish my covenant as an everlasting covenant between me and you and your descendants after you for the generations to come, to be your

God and the God of your descendants after you. The whole land of Canaan, where you are now an alien, I will give as an everlasting possession to you and your descendants after you; and I will be their God.'"

Now let us look a little further on, Genesis 18:18:

"Abraham will surely become a great and powerful nation, and all nations on earth will be blessed through him."

How could *all nations* be blessed via Abraham? Surely because out of Abraham's descendants would come the very son of God, Jesus, to be Saviour of those who would accept him from across the whole world.

That is just a small clue, but it shows that God's intentions were already for Jesus Christ to be born centuries and centuries from that time.

Now we turn detective and look for traces of blood. Oh! So it's a murder mystery? Well, of a kind.

The very first book of the Bible, **Genesis** (which means *beginnings*) traces the beginnings of the human race, starting with Adam then Eve. They were pure in mind and were naked without being mindful of their nakedness. However, once they had been enticed by the Devil, they now had a sin problem. And once they had lost their innocence, they were aware of their nakedness. (This is why nakedness is no longer acceptable. We have all lost that innocence.) Adam and Eve's solution was to join fig leaves to make a covering for their bodies. But God had another way. Of course we know that leaves would have been too fragile to make lasting clothing, but I believe that God had another reason for making coverings of skin for them. To obtain skin, an animal/s had to shed its blood. So we have the first blood shed on the earth. God has said that there is no forgiveness without the shedding of blood so it is not stretching the imagination to say that this was the first sacrifice for sin. I am not making this a solid piece of theology, please understand. But it would seem to make sense that in this first book of the Bible we see one living thing losing its life on behalf of others.

Once Adam and Eve had a family we see their two sons making sacrifices to the Lord. Cain was a farmer so he brought to God some of his crops. Abel kept flocks so he brought fat portions from some of the firstborn of his flock. Even as far back as this in the mists of time, we see that the sacrifice that required blood was acceptable to God whereas Cain's offering was not. At a cursory glance this may seem unfair. Surely each man brought what he produced. But again we are looking at what seems all right to man over against what God knows. I don't believe there was anything unfair about this situation because of what God said to Cain: Genesis 4:5-7...

"So Cain was very angry, and his face was downcast. Then the Lord said to Cain, 'Why are you angry? Why is your face downcast? If you do what is right, will you not be accepted? But if you do not do what is right, sin is crouching at your door; it desires to have you, but you must master it.'"

Now, it seems to me that God had already instructed the brothers on what was required but Cain thought he knew better. (Humanism on display.) And of course his ego was at stake. He was offering what he had grown himself. To offer an animal he would have had to go to his younger brother Abel to procure one. But the very fact that God asked *If you do what is right, will you not be accepted,* shows that either Cain already knew what was acceptable or all he had to do was to offer another sacrifice, this time the one required, and he would have been right with the Lord. But instead, as you probably already know, he chose to get rid of his brother, the first murder in the new creation.

Aside from the personalities involved, we see again a sacrifice of blood in an offering was required by God. And the sacrifices - which later formed a major part of the Law of God for his people (the descendants of Abraham), - were in evidence right back here soon after the original pair, Adam and Eve, had been banished from the Garden of Eden. (I should add that when later books were written in the Old Testament they listed the kind of offerings which were acceptable, and while everybody needed to offer an animal sacrifice for their sins, they could also offer grain offerings as a fellowship offering.)

Let's stay a little longer in Genesis which is full of interesting stories of our first ancestors. Still focussing on Abraham, we'll take a look at the well-known event when God told Abraham to sacrifice Isaac – his promised son. Isaac was born to Abraham when he was very old and Sarah was past the age of bearing children. So he was a miracle from the beginning. Now, when he was a grown man, his father is told to kill him on Mount Moriah as a sacrifice to the Lord. A man of less faith would have been railing against God – perhaps saying 'but this is the son you promised me. He is the only son still with me. He is the miracle. We are now *far* too old to produce another son. And you told me you would bless me through this son.' Abraham had laughed when told by the angel that he would have this promised son. But because of his experience with God his faith had grown and he believed that if God required him to offer his special son as an offering now, he was able to raise him to life again. We learn that from the account in the New Testament. Let's take a peek at Hebrews 11:17-19...

"By faith Abraham, when God tested him, offered Isaac as a sacrifice. He who had received the promises was about to sacrifice his one and only son, even though God had said to him, 'It is through Isaac that your offspring will be reckoned.' Abraham reasoned that God could raise the dead..."

Those few words show us the situation Abraham found

himself in. God had given him a miraculous son and had promised that it was through this promised man that many descendants would issue. Now he was being asked to sacrifice this very son. Yet, because he reckoned that God had given him this son in the first place against the human impossibility of its happening, God could raise Isaac back from the dead. In this rather more sophisticated age this seems very strange to us, but try to place yourself back in this much more basic civilisation. (Just a little side issue – I mentioned that God does not tempt us. In the verse quoted above it mentions that God *tested* Abraham. Tempting is prodding toward sin, testing is prodding toward God's will to see if the person will be obedient.)

In any case, the short story is that Abraham intended to go ahead with God's requirement. He, Isaac and 2 servants travelled some distance to Mt. Moriah, carrying wood and fire for a sacrifice. When Abraham could see the place in the distance, he told the servants to wait for them and they would worship the Lord and then return. At this stage, Isaac didn't realise that he was to be the sacrifice. He eventually asked his father where the lamb for the sacrifice was. Abraham gave the cryptic reply that 'God himself will provide the lamb for the burnt offering, my son'.

Eventually they reached the place God had specified and Abraham built an altar and arranged the fire wood on it. Then he bound his son and placed him on the wood. He took the knife he had carried with him ready to kill Isaac when the angel of the Lord cried out to him "'Abraham! Abraham! Do not lay a hand on the boy. Do not do anything to him. Now I know that you fear God, because you have not withheld from me your son, your only son.' At that, Abraham looked up and there in a thicket he saw a ram caught by its horns. He went over and took the ram and sacrificed it as a burnt offering instead of his son. So Abraham called that place *The Lord Will Provide*. And to this day it is said, 'On the mountain of the Lord it will be provided.'" (Genesis 22:11-14)

I want to now show you the next thing the angel of the Lord said to Abraham as a result of his obedience... Genesis 22:15-18...

"The angel of the Lord called to Abraham from heaven a second time and said, 'I swear by myself, declares the Lord, that because you have done this and have not withheld your son, your only son, I will surely bless you and make your descendants as numerous as the stars in the sky and as the sand on the seashore. Your descendants will take possession of the cities of their enemies, and through your offspring all nations on earth will be blessed, because you have obeyed me.'"

Now before you get the idea that God is likely to tell you to kill someone, let me assure you that God never ever had it in mind that Abraham should kill his son. It was a test because he had an important role for Abraham to play. And Abraham passed that test and was able to receive great blessing as a result. God sometimes checks up on us to see if he can trust us with the blessing and responsibilities he has in mind for us. But I can tell you categorically that he will not ever want you to kill someone - because of something he said to Jeremiah the prophet. Let's read that now:

"'The people of Judah have done evil in my eyes, declares the Lord. They have set up their detestable idols in the house that bears my Name and have defiled it. They have built the high places of Topheth in the Valley of Ben Hinnom to burn their sons and daughters in the fire – something I did not command, nor did it enter my mind.'" (Jeremiah 7:30, 31)

So please be assured that if you ever feel like killing somebody on behalf of the Lord, it will be your own imagination. In the Jeremiah reading we hear something of the anguish that God feels over his own people. In this instance, the Jews had adopted a god of the people around them – Molech. Part of the worship of Molech involved the sacrifice of children. Not only is God disturbed that his people have turned to other gods (which of course are false gods), but how can he bear the thought that his own people would prefer a worship system which demanded the sacrifice of their children – something which he would not even think about demanding. Hence, we see that, though the Jews had to fight wars at times, it was when the surrounding people had sinned so much that God had said *enough is enough* and he allowed his people to kill their enemies as God's punishment. But that was under the Old Covenant. We are no longer under that Covenant. We are under the Covenant of Grace. Grace has been extended to people and it is not the job of believers to judge those who are unbelievers. God will do that himself at the right time.

I felt it important to make all that clear in case there is a reader of this book who gets the wrong idea. Now I want you to take your magnifying glass and take a closer look at Mt. Moriah and that scene with Abraham and Isaac. Who are the players in this drama? There is a father. There is a miraculous only son. There is a ram wearing a crown of thorns (caught in the thicket by his head). I have seen thorny branches growing in Israel and the thorns are long spikes and would easily hold a woolly lamb. The ram is sacrificed in place of a human being. Does this strike you as a picture of something which took place long afterwards? Will it help if I tell you that another name for the place on Mt. Moriah is Calvary? That's right, this all occurred at the same place that Jesus Christ was crucified centuries later. Jesus, the miraculous son of the Father, with blood streaming from the place where a crown of thorns had been jammed on his head. He died in place of you and me.

So, there again in Genesis is a picture of redemption way back in the beginnings of our human history. It was a way of God writing his signature on the books of the Bible. It was also a way of enabling us to *connect the dots* and see that Christianity is a fulfilment of all that went before.

But before we leave the book of Genesis, we can take a look at Noah. Once the flood had subsided Noah and his wife and family were able to set foot once more on the earth. What was the first thing Noah did? He built an altar and offered on it some of the creatures which had travelled with him in the ark. So as you can see, we are following the traces of blood… (The reference for this is Genesis 8:20.)

Now we move on to the book of **Exodus**. Here we see a picture where the emphasis is somewhat different. At this time, the Israelites – who had gone in a previous generation to Egypt because of a terrible famine in their own land – had grown in such numbers in their adopted land that the Pharaoh of the time was unsettled. He was afraid that they could rise up against him. Do you remember that originally Joseph, an Israelite, had been sold by his brothers as a slave and ended up in Egypt? There he had shown himself to be such an extraordinary man that he had been eventually promoted to governor of Egypt with only the Pharaoh above him. But over the succeeding generations – after Joseph's family had joined him in Egypt because of the famine in their own land – they were made slaves to stop them from rebelling against a later Pharaoh.

God raised Moses to be their leader and – at the Lord's instruction – he went before this Pharaoh to ask that the Jews be allowed to go out into the wilderness to worship their God. Pharaoh would not let them go and each time he refused Moses' pleas, God unleashed upon the Egyptians a plague of something regarded as a god by the Egyptians. It took 10 of these terrible plagues before Pharaoh relented and let them go. Thus we find the Israelites gathered on the shore of the Red Sea. Before them is the sea, behind them is the Egyptian army with their horses and chariots as well as all of Egypt's troops, because Pharaoh had again changed his mind and determined to keep them captive. Now we see a miraculous deliverance.

You know the story of the exodus. It was even made into a film. But there are some things that a film misses out on. As we look at them, we notice an enormous cloud in front of them. It was a gift from God to guide them. Exodus 13:21 says that 'the Lord went ahead of them in a pillar of cloud.' But in Exodus 14:19 it is clarified as the 'angel of the Lord'. By night the cloud became a pillar of fire so that they could see to keep on travelling. The cloud would be stationary when it was time to camp for a while.

But here they are on the edge of the water. How would you have felt in that situation? They hadn't had to think about anything for a long time because they were so burdened with work as slaves that there was nothing else in their days. Now, they were out in the wilderness. While slavery had been dreadful, with the quota of bricks they had to produce raised without giving them help in finding the materials to make the bricks, there was a measure of security in it. At least there was food for them to eat. But now, here they were between 'a rock and a hard place' we might say, and all they could see in their corner was this enormous cloud. Terror filled their hearts as they saw Pharaoh's troops marching toward them and they cried out to God.

They immediately turned on poor Moses railing at him for bringing them away from Egypt, saying 'it would have been better for us to serve the Egyptians than to die in the desert.'

Moses assured them that the Lord would deliver them and they need only be still. With that, the Lord told Moses to stretch out his staff over the sea 'to divide the water so the Israelites can go through the sea on dry ground.' Are you still watching in your mind's eye? You will note that the pillar of cloud goes from in front of them to the rear to protect them from the Egyptians. More than that, the cloud brought thick darkness to the Egyptians on the one side, while it shone light on the Israelites.

When Moses stretched his hand out over the sea, the Lord blew with a strong East wind all night and caused the waters to bank up on either side of the Israelites as they walked across on dry ground. When the Egyptians tried to follow, the banked up water dumped on them and they were swept under and drowned.

Now while this is a fascinating story of adventure and miraculous deliverance, we find that it also has spiritual significance. You see, when we look into the New Testament we see that there is more to this than we would normally notice at a quick reading. 1Corinthians 10:1-4:

"..I do not want you to be ignorant of the fact, brothers, that our forefathers were all under the cloud and that they all passed through the sea. They were all baptized into Moses in the cloud and in the sea. They all ate the same spiritual food (Manna, supernaturally provided by God each day) and drank the same spiritual drink; (water which came from a rock when it was struck by Moses on the instruction of the Lord) for they drank from the spiritual rock that accompanied them, and that rock was Christ."

So, while this particular part of the story is not bloodstained, it contains a picture of Christian baptism and our partaking of the spiritual food and drink, the 'body and blood' of Jesus, as we do in Communion. When we read the Gospel message in the New Testament, we see that to be saved we are to *believe and be baptised*. Moses believed in God's promise to deliver his people so the people were figuratively baptised into Moses so that his faith covered them. This was in the early days when each person was not able to have the Holy Spirit within them teaching them and empowering them and God seemed to make allowance for their ignorance and helplessness on many occasions.

Before I turn from 1Corinthians 10, let me show you a few words from verse 11.

"These things happened to them as examples and were written down as warnings for us, on whom the fulfilment of the ages has come."

Did you grasp that last clause? We Christians are those who have received the *fulfilment of the ages*. This is what I am wanting you to fully comprehend – Christianity is not 2000 years old. It began in the Garden of Eden when God began to interact with mankind whom he had just created. But it wasn't *fulfilled* until Jesus came to earth to complete the work of redemption.

Are you aware of what redemption is about? It simply means *to buy back*. There is a sense within it that there is something to be lost if payment is not made. So our great redemption was paid by Jesus on the cross. You see, in a sense, we were already God's because he was the Creator of mankind. So he owned us. But we handed over the rights to our lives to the Devil when our first parents obeyed him instead of God. Hence, each one of us is *born a sinner*. What was God to do about this situation? Our punishment was clear. *The soul that sins, it shall die.* If God didn't want us all to die spiritually, and suffer eternal separation from him, he had to pay our punishment on our behalf.

That is why you will sometimes hear Jesus referred to as The Redeemer. He bought us back – he paid the ransom for us – so that we could again live in the Kingdom of God instead of that of Satan. We are *the redeemed*. Entry into God's Kingdom is through his pure Son so by believing (trusting) in him and being baptised into his death via the action of baptism then being raised to new life as we rise out of the baptismal water, we are aligning ourselves with God and his right to be our Lord. We are no longer the slaves to sin and self (as the Israelites were slaves in Egypt) but we have *passed through the water, eaten and drunk of spiritual food, and have taken the benefits of the fulfilment of the ages – what God had planned all along*.

If you think I am labouring the point, I can assure you that is my intention. And this is the reason. Many people are flocking to other belief systems. These have originated at various times, and this means that before someone started the systems, they didn't exist. Surely this should make us suspicious of them. But Christianity in its foetal form was there in the Garden of Eden. It is just that the dealings of God with us have gone through stages *as God chose*.

If we follow this thought through, we see that when Jesus walked the earth he chose 12 Jews to be his disciples. A disciple is one who learns the disciplines of the person discipling him. Note they were all Jews. They had had the Holy Scriptures and God's prophets all through their long history. But many of them were expecting their Messiah to come as a military figure. Remember the story of Jesus' entry into Jerusalem days before his death? He was riding on a donkey (as the Scriptures had predicted that he would). That should have warned them. Had he been coming as a military leader, he would have chosen to ride a horse, not a humble donkey. The people hailed him, even throwing their cloaks and palm fronds down on the ground in front of him so that they cushioned his ride. But then he did the 'wrong thing'.

What did he do? They expected him to turn toward the right to the Roman headquarters to overthrow the ruling powers over their occupied land. But instead, he turned left, toward the temple. More than that, his intention was to purify the temple of the traders who had it overrun with animals etc. They were selling goods for the people to offer as sacrifices at the temple. But Jesus drove them out with a whip – the very thing they thought he would do to the Romans. And he said that his Father's House (the temple) was meant to be a House of Prayer for All Nations. There we have it again – the difference between man's thinking and God's. The Jews wanted to be free of their overlords but God wanted them to purify their hearts and honour him in their daily lives. He wanted them free in their hearts, to be all that he planned for them.

What happened next? Now the plots thickened. There had been Jewish leaders who had wanted to be rid of Jesus because he was like their conscience haunting them day after day. Now they plotted in earnest, called men to tell lies against him, had him arrested and shouted to the very Roman leaders they hated, to have him crucified. Of course, this was all part of God's plan so that Jesus could be our Redeemer, but it didn't make it right for these so-called spiritual leaders to bring it about.

In a nutshell, Jesus died, was put in a borrowed tomb and rose 3 days later. He then spent the next 50 days mixing with his followers, all Jewish people. It is a sad fact that the majority of the Jews missed the whole point and as a consequence they are still awaiting their Messiah though he arrived 2000 years ago. But we need to acknowledge that it was Jewish followers who carried Christianity to the entire world. Those who had eyes to see realised that this Christ-centred religion was the fulfilment of Judaism that they had been awaiting for several thousand years. As a matter of fact, all but one of the writers of the New Testament were Jews.

Subsequent persecution drove the Jewish believers ('completed Jews' or 'Messianic Jews') out into the corners of the world. And this was part of God's plan too because wherever they went they carried the truth of Jesus with them and made more disciples, firstly from synagogues of Jews then from the general Gentile populations as well. So, though we now look at Christianity as a Gentile religion, there are many people of Jewish origin who are numbered among the believers. And the fact that Jews carried the gospel all over the world is a fulfilment of the promise that God made to Abraham so very many years ago; that, through him, all the nations of the world would be blessed.

Please don't lose sight of this. We almost never hear this sort of thing actually spelled out but it is an assurance for us that we have not believed some new-fangled religion but we have followed the design of God right from the beginning of time.

Having said all that important stuff, let's go on to **Numbers**, another book of the Old Testament, where we shall see something quite different... Numbers 21:4-9...

"They travelled from Mount Hor along the route to the Red Sea, to go around Edom. But the people grew impatient on the way; they spoke against God and against Moses, and said, 'Why have you brought us up out of Egypt to die in the desert? There is no bread! There is no water! And we detest this miserable food!'

"Then the Lord sent venomous snakes among them; they bit the people and many Israelites died. The people came to Moses and said, 'We sinned when we spoke against the Lord and against you. Pray that the Lord will take the snakes away from us.' So Moses prayed for the people.

"The Lord said to Moses, 'Make a snake and put it up on a pole; anyone who is bitten can look at it and live.' So Moses made a bronze snake and put it up on a pole. Then when anyone was bitten by a snake and looked at the bronze snake, he lived."

Remember that we are tracing redemption through these

old events. Can you see the picture? Well, for illumination, let's look at a reference to it in the New Testament... John 3:14, 15...

Jesus speaking: "Just as Moses lifted up the snake in the desert, so the Son of Man (Jesus) must be lifted up, that everyone who believes in him may have eternal life."

It seemed a strange antidote to the venom of the snakes in Numbers didn't it? To fix a bronze replica of a snake onto a pole so that anyone bitten could look at it and be saved? How can we make sense of this? My hubby John teaches that the bronze snake represented the people's sin and as they 'owned' their sin (perhaps a picture of confessing their sin as they had done when they said so to Moses) they could be forgiven. And that seems to fit when we tie in what Jesus did on the cross. He 'became sin for us' as it says in 2 Corinthians 5:21, and as we identify with Jesus lifted up on the cross we can be saved from our sin too. You can be sure there is a good reason for whatever God does whether our feeble minds can comprehend it or not.

I'd like to take a look at just a couple more instances in Old Testament books – differing aspects of the Gospel of Jesus echoing in the ancient scrolls... Firstly, we have a spy story as told in the book of **Joshua**. Let's look at chapter 2...

"Then Joshua son of Nun secretly sent two spies from Shittim. 'Go, look over the land,' he said, 'especially Jericho.' So they went and entered the house of a prostitute named Rahab and stayed there.

"The king of Jericho was told, 'Look! Some of the Israelites have come here tonight to spy out the land.' So the king of Jericho sent this message to Rahab: 'Bring out the men who came to you and entered your house, because they have come to spy out the whole land.'

"But the woman had taken the two men and hidden them. She said, 'Yes, the men came to me, but I did not know where they had come from. At dusk, when it was time to close the city gate, the men left. I don't know which way they went. Go after them quickly. You may catch up with them.' (But she had taken them up to the roof and hidden them under stalks of flax she had laid out on the roof.) So the men set out in pursuit of the spies on the road that leads to the fords of the Jordan, and as soon as the pursuers had gone out, the gate was shut.

"Before the spies lay down for the night, she went up on the roof and said to them, 'I know that the Lord has given this land to you and that a great fear of you has fallen on us, so that all who live in this country are melting in fear because of you. We have heard how the Lord dried up the water of the Red Sea for you when you came out of Egypt, and what you did to Sihon and Og, the two kings of the Amorites east of the Jordan, whom you completely destroyed. When we heard of it, our hearts melted and everyone's courage failed because of you, for the Lord your God is God in heaven above and on the earth below. Now then, please swear to me by the Lord that you will show kindness to my family, because I have shown kindness to you. Give me a sure sign that you will spare the lives of my father and mother, my brothers and sisters, and all who belong to them, and that you will save us from death.'

"'Our lives for your lives!' the men assured her. 'If you don't tell what we are doing, we will treat you kindly and faithfully when the Lord gives us the land.'

"So she let them down by a rope through the window, for the house she lived in was part of the city wall. Now she had said to them, 'Go to the hills so the pursuers will not find you. Hide yourselves there three days until they return, and then go on your way.'

"The men said to her, 'This oath you made us swear will not be binding on us unless, when we enter the land, you have tied this scarlet cord in the window through which you let us down, and unless you have brought your father and mother, your brothers and all your family into your house. If anyone goes outside your house into the street, his blood will be on his own head; we will not be responsible. As for anyone who is in the house with you, his blood will be on our head if a hand is laid on him. But if you tell what we are doing, we will be released from the oath you made us swear.'"

That was rather a long excerpt to print for you but it is a rather exciting tale of intrigue, don't you think? Now, where is the blood? Why, in the scarlet cord of course. I see it as an echo of that amazing story of the final plague sent upon the Egyptians – the death of the firstborn of all humans and animals. This was back when the Jews were slaves in Egypt and the Jews were instructed to kill a lamb and to sprinkle its blood on the doorframes, top and sides, as a sign to the death angel. On seeing the bloodstained entrance to the homes, the death angel would *pass over* that home without taking the life of the firstborn. This was the origin of the Passover Feast that Jews keep even up until now. And it was certainly something to celebrate, that a sacrificed lamb saved their lives...

Now, you're not going to tell me that that isn't a picture of redemption are you? Well, now back to Rahab and the scarlet cord. She tied the cord in her window where it would be seen as the Jewish army approached the city gate. Although she didn't know it, it was a symbol of the blood which Jesus would shed which would bring salvation to those who were on the Lord's side. Rahab proved that she was on the Lord's side and she – and her family – were saved. Interestingly, she became an ancestor of Jesus. God does these things so that, no matter what you have been in your earlier life, you can be sure you can be saved if you trust in Jesus.

Well, I really sneaked in an extra example there in the Passover, didn't I? Now for just one more.

For this we turn to **Isaiah** chapter 53. I don't want to print out the whole chapter as you can read that for yourself. But I will just jot down a few references that you will see were prophecies regarding Jesus himself. Again, we see God's signature here and there all through the Scriptures...

"He had no beauty or majesty to attract us to him, nothing in his appearance that we should desire him. (Jesus was born poor and walked the dusty paths speaking the words of God. He was not born in a palace but in a stable.) Surely he took up our infirmities and carried our sorrows, yet we considered him stricken by God, smitten by him, and afflicted. But he was pierced for our transgressions, (a Roman soldier ran a sword into Jesus' side) he was crushed for our iniquities; the punishment that brought us peace was upon him, and by his wounds we are healed. He was assigned a grave with the wicked, and with the rich in his death, though he had done no violence, nor was any deceit in his mouth. (He died as a criminal though he had committed no crime and he was buried in a tomb provided by a rich man, Joseph of Arimathea.) Yet it was the Lord's will to crush him and cause him to suffer, and though the Lord makes his life a guilt offering, he will see his offspring and prolong his days, and the will of the Lord will prosper in his hand.

You can read the whole chapter. Everything speaks volumes about the work Jesus would fulfil so long after these words were penned.

Before we leave this subject, I want to show you a different fingerprint of God right at the beginning. During the confrontation with the Devil in the Garden of Eden, God forecast a future event. Can you think what it was? Speaking to the Devil, (Genesis 3:15) God said 'I will put enmity between you and the woman, and

between your offspring and hers; he will crush your head, and you will strike his heel.' Did you notice that the word 'offspring' is obviously not referring to all of her descendants because it goes on to say what 'he' will do. So God was referring to one male descendant in particular. Who could that have been but Jesus himself whose work of redemption thousands of years later 'crushed the Devil's head'? So now we can be sure that Christianity was never at any time a 'new religion'. It was in the heart of God right from the beginning of time.

I think that is enough on that subject. As you read right through the Bible, see if you can spot other references to the redemption that Jesus would accomplish. It can be like a different kind of treasure hunt or detective 'sleuthing', looking for the traces of blood in the 'murder' that brought us life everlasting.

> "Rise in the presence of the aged,
> Show respect for the elderly
> And revere your God.
> I am the Lord."
>
> (Leviticus 19:32)

I have included that piece from the Old Testament book of the Law because I notice that many young people in this age have lost respect for the older generation. This is a shame and it is to their own loss as the elderly have 'been there, done that' and often have some wisdom to share.

80

KNOWLEDGE TO BE GAINED WHEN WE FEAR THE LORD

Back in Section 3, I promised you a couple of examples of how you can gain knowledge when you fear (or reverence) the Lord. So, here they are...

When we trust in the Lord, we sometimes have to swim against the tide of popular opinion. We can look foolish to others because we don't accept what the majority believes. That's just the price we must pay to be on 'God's Team'.

I recently met a man and had a wonderful conversation with him. His name is David and he is a retired medical chemist. Because of his reverence for God, he pursued a certain line of study for his PhD during the period 1998-2004. I'll let him tell his experience in his own words:

"The existing opinion of most of the medical world at the time was that the purpose and function of urinary proteins produced by the kidney was unknown. I believed that they had a fundamental purpose in kidney stone prevention (as there is a purpose in everything that God has made).

"My PhD research was to discover the role and function of urinary proteins produced by the kidneys. Some proteins attach themselves to the surface of urinary crystals thus preventing aggregation (like charges on the crystal/protein surfaces repel each other).

"However, the discovery that other urinary proteins actually get into the crystal framework upset quite a number of medical people. They could not believe that proteins could enter the crystal matrix. I verified this by Field Emission

Electron Microscopy (UWA and Curtin) and Synchrotron x-ray crystallographic techniques (Japan) coupled with Rietveld computer modelling analysis. I was then able to show that naturally occurring enzymes in urine will only break up those crystals with proteins in them (intracrystalline proteins). We believe that people lacking those particular urinary proteins at a certain stage of their life (either by gene switching them off or by other means) have a higher propensity to form stones. It is an interesting fact while 10% of the general world population develop kidney stones, African Negroes don't suffer from stone formation."

Now this is going out on a limb, isn't it? When you believe something simply because you know that God is a practical God and doesn't do something whimsically...

And by the way they say that passing kidney stones is the cause of the greatest pain there is. So learning about their formation is very important. I'm thankful that there are people like David who pursue a line of investigation for no other reason than that *they believe in a practical God*.

David is a very intelligent man but, let's face it, without his reverence for God he would have gone along with the current medical opinion regarding these proteins and the knowledge he gained would never have been available.

The second example features my darling husband. John was a hospital chaplain at 2 hospitals for 11 years during his time as a pastor in Brisbane many years ago. Because he respects God he asks for his wisdom and listens for his guidance. The Lord told him to speak to people in comas as though they could hear because they can. He passed this information on to others visiting the sick, warning them not to say negative things and express worries in the presence of the sick one because they may hear.

You would agree that this is of utmost importance, wouldn't you? After all, the last thing a gravely ill person needs is to hear people discussing their medical problems and pronouncing hopelessness over them. More than that, it means that a believer visiting a patient can read helpful Scripture or other devotional material to encourage and comfort the sick person. They can give the gospel to someone who may pass into eternity without knowing Christ otherwise.

As we were driving home from the prayer meeting this morning the car radio was featuring two men – one had been a comatose hospital patient and the other had been his Intensive Care nurse. The patient was relating how he was aware of what the nurse was saying even though he could not reply. The fact that comatose patients can be aware of what is happening around them is now more widely known than it was back in John's chaplaincy days. While he was in the coma, the nurse wisely told the patient where he was, briefly what had happened to him and that he was in a safe place, all things to reassure him.

John smiled as he heard the radio session and said 'God told me that years ago.' So these are just two examples of the knowledge and wisdom that can come to those who 'fear the Lord'. After all, as I've said before, fearing the Lord isn't just about trepidation but also about acknowledging that he is the Creator and Sustainer of all things and does all things well.

81

GOD-INCIDENCES

We sometimes talk about coincidences and we're happy when they fit in with our plans. But I want to speak to you about God-incidences. This is when things happen at *exactly* the right time and it could only have been God engineering it. When we are believers we should trust God in every avenue of our lives and this can result in some truly remarkable God-incidences.

Firstly, let me share a Scripture with you which reveals something about God which you may not have yet realised. Let's look at Matthew 6:7 & 8.

"...When you pray, do not keep on babbling like pagans, for they think they will be heard because of their many words. Do not be like them, for your Father knows what you need *before you ask him*."

Isn't that both exciting and comforting? Our Father knows what we need *before* we ask him. He really does keep an eye on us, doesn't he? While we're thinking of his care for us, let's briefly check on a couple of other Scriptures...

Matthew 10:29-31. "Are not two sparrows sold for a penny? Yet not one of them will fall to the ground outside your Father's care. And even the very hairs of your head are all numbered. So don't be afraid; you are worth more than many sparrows."

Now I don't know about you but that thrills me so much particularly because the number of hairs on my head is constantly changing. No parent could match that kind of watchfulness. If you did not have a happy childhood be strengthened by knowing that God is the most amazing Father. If you have been adopted into his family you will never again be alone.

Then there is that other well-known Bible passage, 2Chronicles 16:9. "For the eyes of the Lord range throughout the earth to strengthen those whose hearts are fully committed to him."

With those 3 Scriptures in mind, let's look at some things which have happened to real people which can only be seen as God-incidences.

Years ago I heard a story involving Dr. Helen Roseveare who ran a clinic or hospital for women in Africa for many years. I am not aware whether she is still there or not. Minor details may not be accurate but the general story is. The doctor also had orphaned children in her care.

One night a woman died in childbirth and the little premature baby needed special care. Though they were living right on the Equator, because it was an elevated position it could be very cold at night. So a local nurse ran for their one hot water bottle to try to save the little girl. As the nurse began to fill the hot water bottle she found that it had become perished and was useless. So they wrapped the infant as best they could, put it where it would get some heat from the fireplace and a nurse lay between the door and the child to shield her from draughts.

The following morning Dr. Helen spoke to the children in her care, telling them about the poor little child and her two-year-old sister who was also orphaned. They gathered together to pray for them. One little girl laid it straight on the line to God. She said that they needed a hot water bottle and they needed it straight away. She added a little postscript to her prayer: asking the Lord for a doll for the older sister so that she would know that He loved her.

I don't know what must have run through Dr. Helen's mind at this because there was nowhere within range of their medical station to buy such things and she wasn't in the habit of receiving parcels from anyone.

Later that same day, a car pulled up outside one of the buildings and soon after pulled away again. Dr. Helen went to see what had been happening and found a box that had been left for her. As the children gathered around her she opened the box and found bright little items of clothing suitable for the orphans. Then, as she reached into the box once more, her hand picked up – of all things – a hot water bottle! The little girl who had prayed rushed to the box and said something to the effect that if God had sent the hot water bottle he would have sent the doll as well. And there it was at the bottom of the box – a doll as requested from a loving heavenly Father.

When we think of the circumstances, there are marvels on several levels. Firstly, who would ever think of including a hot water bottle in a parcel to someone on the Equator? Secondly, Dr. Helen was in an out of the way place and didn't receive parcels. Again, it was found to have been sent from England and it had left five months earlier! A co-incidence? No. A God-incidence!

I hope that encourages you. It certainly does me. I have another true story which also took place in Africa. Perhaps these God-incidences happen more often in countries and times when there is no other means of help – no mobile phones etc. This story involves my husband John. He was on the Australian board of an African Mission Society and was visiting mission stations including the one where his sister and her husband, Ruth and Jon Allan, were serving as medical missionaries.

John was behind schedule, partly because his luggage had been misplaced on his flight from Europe then also because the train he was taking toward their area had been held up. The train had stopped at a washout – railway lines were missing for a stretch. Men from the train trooped to the back of the train, took up a stretch of lines they had already passed over and transferred them to in front of the train, and the train continued on its journey. Consequently, John was a day late and when he arrived at the station, Jon and Ruth were not there to meet him. He decided to take a taxi and asked the driver to take him to the nearest hotel/motel where there would be white people. Five African men also jumped into the car and John was wondering about their motives. On the way, they approached a service station and John noticed a Hillman car being filled with fuel. He knew Jon and Ruth had a Hillman and asked the driver to stop. Sure enough, in the middle of nowhere, there were Ruth and Jon – who also had suffered hold-ups and were a day late. An ordinary co-incidence? I don't think so!

You can imagine how thrilled they were to know that God had brought them together and then Dr. Jon shared something which had happened to him not long before...

Dr. Jon Allan, our brother-in-law, was often called upon to meet medical needs which he hadn't experienced in Australia and sometimes had to operate, using a manual during the operation, because it was an emergency and there was no specialist available anywhere near. But on one occasion, he was confronted by an African man with a particularly badly injured leg. He was examining the injury and thinking he really needed an orthopaedic surgeon (a bone specialist). Just then, a white man stuck his head round the door saying that he was an orthopaedic surgeon from America and was visiting mission hospitals to see how things were set up. Well, you can imagine Dr. Jon's elation. He happily handed his patient over to the specialist for expert treatment. Just a coincidence? No, another God-incidence!

But, as they say in the TV commercials, there's more!

This next story is more an outright miracle than a God-incidence, but I'll include it to encourage your faith as it has done mine. This happened in the islands of Vanuatu over 20 years ago. John and I, along with our youngest daughter Angela and a young musician from our church were on a visit and at night we showed a 16mm Christian film. That went well and some of the locals asked if we could show it to another village further on. We said that we would need fuel for the generator and they agreed that they had fuel there. However, when we arrived, the fuel they had was diesel and quite useless for our purposes.

John felt God challenge him to trust him, so when the projector and lights were set up, he pulled the starting cord and the generator purred into action. Villagers from up the mountain also wanted to see the film – news travels fast by the grape vine in the islands – so night after night for a week God continued to power the projector and lights without any fuel in the generator. On the final night, we hopped into our makeshift beds then realised that the lights were still glowing. John called to our local pastor to 'killem lights' (pidgin for turning off the lights) when the generator slowly droned to a stop – without anyone touching the switch. God is certainly watching his people to *strongly support* those whose hearts are fully committed to him.

We need to know that these God-incidences do happen in our own land so two more stories, this time in Australia. John knew it was time to fly to Vanuatu for another mission so he booked his flight even though he didn't have the money to pay for it. He was trusting that God would supply it in time. He had secured a reduced fare – on condition that it be paid by a particular Friday. Friday came and went and John was thinking he would now need to have more money to pay for the normal fare.

On the Saturday, the church held a fete which they did yearly. During the morning service at the church the following day, one of the women of the church asked John if she could make an announcement. She went on to say that the women had made some money on their stalls and they had decided they would like to give it to John for his forthcoming trip to Vanuatu. They were not aware that he didn't even have money for his fare. And when John saw the amount of money the women donated, it was just what he needed for his *reduced* fare. Then, early on Monday morning, an anxious airline worker rang John to say that she should have reminded him the previous week that his fare needed to be paid by Friday if he was to enjoy the discount. She apologised profusely and said if he could possibly be in their office early that day, she could extend the discount for him. Praise the Lord! More God-incidences!

On another occasion, when John was pastoring in a more rural area, he had agreed to go to the church without a set salary as they were struggling. We were short of funds and decided we would have to go without meat. The following morning, a dairying couple whose daughters were attending the church turned up on our doorstep with the equivalent of half a slaughtered beast - steaks, mince, sausages. We would have beef which we didn't usually buy in any case because chicken was cheaper. Just a coincidence? Hardly! These lovely folk weren't even attending our church at the time.

I could share more God-incidences but I think I'll leave it to you to so follow and trust the Lord that you experience your own...

Faith is contagious
So is fear
Live by faith

82

FAITH MEANS RISK

Sometimes we have the seed of a truth within us but we've never put it into words. Then someone comes along and speaks it out clearly and we feel a *'Yes'* resonate deeply within us. Well that happened to me just a few days ago as I was listening to a message from that great Bible teacher David Pawson. David was speaking about faith and he was pointing out the difference between believing that the stories about Jesus are true and actually *living by faith*. I had thought about this kind of thing before but this time David mentioned the word *risk*.

We might believe what the Bible says. We may have believed it for years. But until we risk something, we are not actually *living by faith*. Jesus said that if we are ashamed of him, he will be ashamed of us before his Father. Now, that should make us look into this more deeply, surely.

How can I illustrate this principle? Let's look at some of the people mentioned in the book of Hebrews in the Bible... In my Bible, chapter 11 is headed "Faith in Action". And that is what I am getting at. This chapter is so well known as the 'Faith Chapter'. It begins with a general 'we' in verse 3: By faith we understand that the universe was formed at God's command, so that what is seen was not made out of what was visible. Okay, so that is a case where we have what we might term *mental faith*. We accept that the world did not come about by some cosmic accident but was designed by a Creator.

Let's move on to verse 4: By faith Abel brought God a better offering than Cain did….. So now we have moved from abstract belief to an action *motivated by faith*. Abel brought an offering which was the kind God wanted. Perhaps we could call this *obedient faith*.

Verse 6 has something interesting to say: Without faith it is impossible to please God, because anyone who comes to him must believe that he exists and that he rewards those who earnestly seek him. Earnestly seeking God can be the beginning of our walking with God but it can also speak of our *continuing* walk with the Lord as we seek to know his will in all that we think and do.

Verse 7 is where it begins to warm up. "By faith Noah" it begins. Now this is where risk is involved. By faith Noah, when warned about things not yet seen, in holy fear built an ark to save his family. By his faith he condemned the world and became heir of the righteousness that is in keeping with faith. What did Noah risk? Well, he risked looking awfully stupid in the eyes of his neighbours. Here he was building this huge ship. It would have taken him many months of hard work to build and, although we are not told what his neighbours' attitudes were, it's not hard to work out that he would have been subject to ridicule from these people given to wickedness. Let's face it, it is not easy to stand in the face of ridicule and continue to do the thing which God has said, even in small things. But when you are doing something which is going to be obviously stupid if God doesn't 'turn up', we are risking much. This was exactly Noah's position. If God didn't send the rain and the bursting forth of waters of the deep to float this huge 'marine zoo' together with Noah, his wife, their 3 sons and their wives, they were going to have to eat humble pie, and how! Now that's risk! And that's *living by faith*. It's moved from just *mental faith* to *obedient faith with risk!*

For the next few verses we are looking at Abraham and Sarah and they lived by faith in a number of ways. By faith Abraham, when called to go to a place he would later receive as his inheritance, obeyed and went, even though he did not know where he was going. By faith he made his home in the promised land like a stranger in a foreign country; he lived in tents, as did Isaac and Jacob, who were heirs with him of the same promise. For he was looking forward to the city with foundations, whose architect and builder is God. And by faith even Sarah, who was past childbearing age, was enabled to bear children because she considered him faithful who had made the promise. And so from this one man, and he as good as dead, came descendants as numerous as the stars in the sky and as countless as the sand on the seashore. Let's pay special attention to the next part: All these people were still *living by faith* when they died. They did not receive the things promised; they only saw them and welcomed them from a distance.....They were longing for a better country – a heavenly one. Therefore God is not ashamed to be called their God, for he has prepared a city for them.

Wow! Did you take that in? God is not ashamed of us when we are *living by faith*. It may take risk, but we have our eyes on that distant shore, that heavenly one.

Let me stay on Abraham and Sarah a little longer. I left out a few words in the above quote – If they had been thinking of the country they had left, they would have had opportunity to return. That's a sentence we could easily pass over but I want to draw your attention to what they had left behind. It's not common knowledge that Abraham and Sarah, living in tents in the land designated for them by God, had left behind a city – Ur of the Chaldees – where the homes had hot and cold running water and many of what we would call 'mod cons', modern conveniences. God called Abraham and he followed – to a country he didn't know, to live among people who were strangers to him, and *in tents*. Now that's quite a challenge and risk, wouldn't you say? But God commends them. AND is *not ashamed of them*.

So it's pretty clear that to *live by faith,* risk is sometimes involved. If we want to please God, we need to not only have a mental assent to the facts of the Bible, we need to have an *obedient attitude,* and we need to recognize that sometimes we will be called to a degree of risk in our actions.

How about we look at verse 22… By faith Joseph, when his end was near, spoke about the exodus of the Israelites from Egypt and gave instructions concerning the burial of his bones. I love the stories of Joseph in many ways. They are the stories of a man who lived by faith from first to last. The fact that he foresaw the exodus of his people from Egypt in the distance and asked for his bones to be taken back to the Promised Land was almost a small post script to a life *lived by faith*.

Do you remember that God had given Joseph a couple of dreams while he was quite young? In both dreams, the interpretation was that his family would be doing homage to him. I suppose it's not surprising that he was 'rubbished' by his brothers for telling them these dreams. After all, he was younger than ten of them, so who did he think he was asserting that they would bow down to him? And I know some people think Joseph was naïve or stupid for telling his family about the dreams. But I see a young fellow who already trusted God, with a pure heart, and he expected that they would see things as he did.

Of course, all it did was breed jealousy and malice in their hearts because they were already aware that their father favoured Joseph. Have you known someone like Joseph? They have a purity of heart and they don't foresee wickedness in others. I've mentioned some of the story previously, but to put it in a nutshell, the brothers sold Joseph as a slave to a caravan of Ishmaelite traders who sold him on when they arrived in Egypt. The brothers took the special coat his father had given him, dipped it in the blood of a goat they slaughtered, and showed it to their father when they arrived home, knowing that he would assume that Joseph had been attacked by a wild animal.

So his story begins with tragedy and we would think it could only get worse. But remember the dreams? God was still with Joseph. He became a slave to Potiphar, captain of Pharaoh's guard. Joseph did all things well and Potiphar was impressed and made him his attendant. Potiphar actually put him in charge of his household and knew that all was in good hands. But there was more for Joseph to endure along the way to the fulfilment of his dreams...

I didn't mention that, as well as being pure in heart and with ability, Joseph was also handsome and well built. Alas, Potiphar's wife noticed this and tried to seduce him. He explained that her husband had entrusted everything into his hands and he would be sinning *against God* if he took advantage of her advances, but she persisted day after day.

One day this situation came to a head. And in this story there is a good piece of advice for anyone caught in a situation of attraction – run for your life. In this instance, Potiphar's wife was alone in the house with Joseph and she caught at his cloak to make sure she drew him close to her. Rather than be caught up in this sin, Joseph left the cloak behind and raced from the house. What's the old saying, 'hell hath no fury like a woman spurned'. And so next we find Potiphar's wife telling her husband that Joseph had tried to force himself on to her and she had his cloak as 'evidence'.

Joseph then finds himself in prison along with the king's prisoners, as a result of her treachery. Yet even in prison, God had not forsaken Joseph and he was soon in favour with the prison warden. Joseph was given the responsibility for all the running of the prison.

To shorten the story, two of the king's prisoners whom Joseph attended, revealed to him dreams they had had. Joseph interpreted them correctly because he relied on hearing from God. One was killed, the other restored to his former position. Although Joseph asked the one to be restored to remember him and to mention him to Pharaoh for leniency, the fellow forgot until two years later – yes, two years later – when Pharaoh had two dreams which no official could interpret. Joseph, as a result, was called and he was able to tell Pharaoh that there were going to be 7 years of plenty followed by 7 years of famine in the land. In doing so, he gave the glory for the interpretation to God.

Joseph encouraged Pharaoh to seek a wise and discerning man to oversee food storage during the first 7 years to see the country through the following lean years. Pharaoh perceived that Joseph had the 'spirit of God' in him so he appointed Joseph to the task and consequent honour.

Joseph was given charge of the whole of Egypt. To signify his authority, Pharaoh took his own signet ring from his finger and placed it on that of Joseph and had him dressed in fine clothes with a gold chain – probably the chain of office such as we see on mayors of cities these days. (Now we begin to see the fulfilment of those two dreams of Joseph from his youth.)

Joseph managed very well and Egypt was saved from starvation. Now comes the really intriguing part of the drama... Because the famine affected the Israelite land as well, Joseph's brothers were sent by their father Jacob to seek food supplies from Egypt. This brought them in contact with the man in charge of the food, their long-lost brother Joseph. There would have been a number of reasons they didn't recognize him. He was no longer a stripling youth, perhaps as an Egyptian official he would have been clean-shaven though Israelites wore beards, he was dressed in Egyptian style, and of course, there was no way that they were thinking of their brother who, as far as they knew was slaving away in some distant place. As visitors from a 'foreign' country, seeking relief from famine, they probably hardly let their eyes meet his as theirs was the humble position.

But Joseph knew *them*. And how did they greet him? They bowed down to him with their faces to the ground. (Now there is the fulfilment of the dreams of his youth, given by God, who foresaw all that the future would bring.) Joseph spoke harshly to them as he didn't at that time want them to recognize him. Rather, he wanted to find out more information.

We could go on with more of this amazing series of dramas but I will leave that to you to follow up in Genesis, from chapter 37 onward.

What we want to take from this is that Joseph didn't just believe in God, he *relied on him, he trusted in him*. In other words, he *lived by faith*. If he hadn't, he may have given in to defeat and depression and remained a slave all his life. So, while we need to take risks, the life of living by faith is a life of achievement and victory.

Let's leave Hebrews 11 there, even though it numbers many more who lived by faith. I'd like to bring this subject more up to date...

I don't think I've shared a couple of stories with you about my husband John's experiences. We've had so many adventures with the Lord over the years, and many of them in the islands. But I try to keep the stories to the theme of the chapters.

Keeping in mind the theme of living by faith involving risk, let me tell you about one time John was travelling to the airport with our son Dan to fly out to PNG. On this occasion, money to pay for the flight had not eventuated so John was risking looking very foolish when he got to the airport. He believed God had called him to visit PNG with a small team at this time to erect a building for village translators who spent 5 days a week with the missionaries aiding them in translating the Bible into their own language, then returned to their home village at the weekend. So there they were driving toward the flight time. John had received a call asking him to call in on a friend on his way so he had left home in time to include this short visit.

You guessed it! The friend said that he believed that God had told him to give John money and it was enough to pay for both John and Dan's fares. Praise the Lord! Living by faith... means <u>acting</u> as though God is going to supply what you are trusting him for, in another word – risking.

There was an uprising in the New Hebrides in 1980 which resulted in much turmoil, ending up with the islands being renamed Vanuatu. John arrived for the first time during this turmoil. Jimmy Stevens, a chief, was the figurehead leader of the rebellion and, along with many others, was in the Luganville prison. John had the privilege, along with a friend, Phil Dunk, of ministering to Jimmy in prison and leading the prisoners into a time of repentance.

Our church had purchased a red utility to be used as a taxi by a local church to help them finance their work. And this utility was handy when it came time to visit Jimmy Stevens' village, as they felt the Lord wanted them to do. So far, so good. However, when they arrived at Jimmy's village, they saw 'taboo leaves' outside the fence. These are the leaves of a particular plant, placed one over the other in an 'x' formation and they signify that to pass that point is to invite death. *Now that was just the time for risk to be calculated...* Once John believes that God has called him to do something he doesn't allow anything to put him off, so, though the local men with him were fearful of the taboo leaves, they rushed behind him once they saw that John and Phil didn't drop dead once they passed the leaves. BUT...they were instantly surrounded by several village men wearing the briefest of native clothing and fierce expressions, *and with bows and arrows raised and pointing at their chests.*

Well, I'm pleased to report that God had gone ahead, and just then some picaninni (children) ran up to the archers saying 'hemi fren blong papa' – he is Dad's friend. These were some of Jimmy's many children – not surprising as he had 18 wives - who had been at the jail during John's visit. With that, the weapons were put away and grass skirted girls brought out lemon juice and conversation was underway.

So, when I speak of *risk,* there is the risk that you may look foolish, but there is also risk *to life.* So you can see why I needed to speak to you about the fact that living by faith is far more than mere mental assent to the facts of the Bible...

One more story. This took place about 5 years ago. John had had heart trouble for 12 years and had experienced 4 heart attacks. He was told that he was having a heart attack when checked by an ECG, but after the attack there was never any further disabling of the heart. But there were frequent attacks of angina pain because some of his smaller blood vessels would collapse under stress. There was no operation which could help as his arteries were not involved.

Then came a time when he was called upon by a young man to pray for his wife, in Tasmania. When he asked the Lord for wisdom John received a word for the woman which really needed his presence with her to work through. He received another 'phone call from Tasmania inviting him to a farewell barbeque for this man and his wife as they were leaving for England. John decided to combine the two, attend the barbeque and counsel and pray for the woman and her husband. He was due to fly very early on Saturday morning. But on the day before, John had a couple of momentary blackouts, was taken to hospital by ambulance and was told that he had had another heart attack. He was kept in hospital all day with blood tests taken and being monitored.

As it was a small hospital and he had settled down, he was released for the weekend on condition that he visit a cardiologist on the Monday. John agreed, returned home and packed for his flight to Tasmania the following morning. (He hadn't mentioned at the hospital that he intended to fly over the weekend obviously.)

He had a great time ministering to several people over the weekend in Tasmania and a number of young men whom he had mentored over the years along with the late Rev. Tom Jewett anointed him with oil and prayed for him when they heard of his visit to the hospital so soon before flying down. I picked him up at the airport round 11 o'clock on the Sunday night. We arrived home round 1am. Later that morning he was faithfully in the heart specialist's rooms. As it was 12 years since his original angiogram had been done, the doctor ordered another one. On Wednesday, John fronted up for the results. The Christian cardiologist held the two results, taken 12 years apart. His comment was something to the effect that somebody must have been praying for John as he said the angiograms were not of the same heart; and there was nothing wrong with John's heart now. He was to be off all medications.

Before I go any further, I would stress to you that we do not recommend that people go flying after suffering a heart attack. It would be foolish indeed unless you had heard from the Lord. But John knew he was to deliver that special word to this woman, so his *risk* was based on God's faithfulness. And I must say that John is willing to die at any time if that is the will of the Lord.

So, have I exercised your minds and hearts enough to

encourage you to understand that living by faith involves risking all sorts of things – if God were not to turn up? Isn't that a wonderful adventure that God has called us to? Don't try to tell me that the Christian life is a dull one.

I want to make one more comment. I mentioned in a chapter way back in this book that it is often necessary to put our feet 'in the water' before God blows the waters apart to let us through. I believe that sometimes healing doesn't come until we act in faith. Think about that…

I had a chat with a man recently.

He had been an atheist for nearly 60 years before he had an encounter with God.

Now he wants to talk to the man in the street about God.

But one of his comments about general attitudes on the street was this:

People say they came from monkeys but they hope to go to heaven when they die.

Can you see any logic in that?

I can't.

83

THE FOREIGNER AND THE KINSMAN REDEEMER

There's a little story tucked away in the Old Testament – just four chapters long – that has become a favourite with quite a number of people. But if you are not familiar with the Bible you may have missed it completely. So let me fill you in...

These events took place before there were even any kings ruling the Jews. Instead they had judges to whom they went with any problems. A man named Elimelech, with his wife Naomi and sons Mahlon and Kilion lived in Bethlehem – the town where Jesus was born generations later. However, as there was a famine in the land the family moved to neighbouring Moab. Sadly, Elimelech died in Moab and Naomi and the two boys were left.

Mahlon and Kilion married two Moabite girls, Orpah and Ruth. Within a few years, both husbands also died so Naomi, Orpah and Ruth were all left widows.

News filtered through to Naomi that the famine was over in her country so she decided to return to her late husband's property. When she broke the news to her daughters-in-law, they loved Naomi so much that they wanted to accompany her to make a new life for themselves with her. However, Naomi felt she had nothing to offer the girls so she recommended that they return to their parents' homes where they might find new husbands. After much persuading, Orpah did return to her home. But Ruth was determined...

Naomi said something very intriguing in my estimation. She said to Ruth "Look, your sister-in-law is going back to her people and her gods. Go back with her." Was this a challenge to Ruth about her faith? Now listen to Ruth's reply: "Don't urge me to leave you or to turn back from you. Where you go I will go, and where you stay I will stay. Your people will be my people and your God my God. Where you die I will die, and there I will be buried. May the Lord deal with me, be it ever so severely, if anything but death separates you and me." Wow! I have heard most of that reply used in wedding ceremonies. But did you notice that Ruth was already a believer in Israel's God, the one true God though she came from pagan Moab? Naomi related everything to God, whether good news or ill, and obviously Ruth had come to have faith in Naomi's God.

When the two women returned to Bethlehem, their arrival caused a stir and news spread of their bereavement and Ruth's faithfulness to Naomi. Of course, they needed food, so Ruth went out into the fields to glean as it was at the beginning of the barley harvest. It so happened that she chose a field owned by a close relative of her late husband. His name was Boaz, a man of honour in the community.

We see something of the kind of man Boaz was when we read that when he returned to his property he greeted his workers "The Lord be with you!" and their reply: "The Lord bless you." Boaz noticed a stranger in his field so he asked who this was and was told it was Naomi's daughter-in-law Ruth. He had heard of her reputation so he went to her to show her kindness. It wasn't always safe for young women gleaning so Boaz instructed his workers to look after her and told her to stay behind his servant girls so she would not be alone. We note that Boaz was older than Ruth and called her 'daughter', not sister.

I noticed a nice little detail. Ruth at first had asked to be allowed to 'gather among the sheaves'. I suspect that this was not what the law required. I remember reading that the law said that the farmers were to leave the borders of the fields unharvested to allow poor people to glean those areas. Ruth wouldn't have known the law and possibly was harvesting further into the field. We see that after Boaz had provided her with food and drink for lunch, he told his workers "Even if she gathers among the sheaves, don't embarrass her. Rather, pull out some stalks for her from the bundles and leave them for her to pick up, and don't rebuke her." Don't you warm to a man with a heart like Boaz's? Naomi picked up on his kindness when she saw how much grain Ruth brought home to her.

Ruth continued to glean in Boaz's fields during the wheat harvest as well. The time came when Naomi wanted to provide a home for Ruth with a husband who would provide well for her. She hatched a plan. She knew that Boaz, being a close relative, could be a Kinsman Redeemer. That's not something we hear about today but in these faraway times people's lives were ordered differently. As a matter of fact, even in these days, people have vastly differing customs in different countries.

In Israel at this time when Naomi, Ruth and Boaz lived, land was very important to them. It was not just wealth. It was their very livelihood. And God had given the land of Israel to his people, the Jews. It had been divided according to the 12 tribes of Israel. So each tribe had an area and each family within that tribe had a share of that area. Inheritance came through the sons usually (although there is one story in the Bible where, when their father died, his daughters applied to gain his land as he had no sons) and daughters relied on their parents until they married. Because of this arrangement, people kept their ancestry recorded so they could prove their entitlement to their parcel of land. So what happened when a man died without children, such as was now the case with Elimelech? To protect the ownership of his land, and keep it within the tribe, they had the 'Kinsman Redeemer' custom.

The closest relative of the dead man had the right and responsibility to redeem his land. But, though this may seem strange to us today, with that responsibility came another one. If there was a widow involved, you were expected to take her as your responsibility as well, and if she was a young woman, you would marry her to raise children to maintain the name of her deceased husband. So here was Naomi's plan.

She told Ruth to go to Boaz's threshing floor after dark when he would have finished work. She was to secretly note where he lay down for the night. Then, when he was asleep, she should lie down at his feet and spread the corner of his cover over her. I should mention that Naomi also made sure that Ruth washed and perfumed herself so she was doing all she could to make sure this turned out right. (Don't you love the personal touches?)

Ruth did as she was instructed and during the night, when Boaz was startled by something, he became aware of the presence of someone at his feet. As it was dark, he had to ask who it was, and Ruth then asked him to spread the corner of his garment over her because he was a Kinsman Redeemer. Boaz was delighted that Ruth had chosen to ask him as he was older than she and she could have gone after a younger man. He could see that in everything, Ruth acted according to Jewish custom though she was a foreigner.

But there was a snag... There was another relative who had a closer connection so he had to be given first opportunity to take over the property. Boaz told Ruth that he would settle the matter that very day.

Boaz, true to his word, positioned himself at the city gate and eventually saw the relative coming. He also called for ten of the city elders to be witnesses and made the offer to the man. The man at first was interested in buying Naomi's land but when he realised that there was a widow involved, he felt that she could harm his interests – perhaps by her future children further dividing his estate?

They had another interesting custom in those days. To provide proof of a deal done, one man gave his sandal to the other and at the end of discussion, Boaz had the other man's sandal. Boaz was the Kinsman Redeemer. Ruth and Naomi – and their inheritance – were secure in the hands of this man.

So there was a happy ending to their story. Later, Ruth gave birth to a son, Obed, and Naomi's joy was full as she loved playing the part of baby sitter.

I haven't told you this lovely story just to give you information. I want to draw your attention to the parallel with Jesus as a Kinsman Redeemer. Just think about it for a moment... We human beings, as God's creation, had an inheritance of eternal life in the Garden of Eden. But because of our own foolishness and sin, we lost touch with that inheritance. The only way to pay for sin was by death. The old King James Version of the Bible says it poetically – The wages of sin is death. All work earns something. If we work at sin our wages are death. If I am to attain my inheritance, I need a Kinsman Redeemer, someone human – and without sin – to pay the wages I had earned as a sinner.

More than we could ever have hoped for, Jesus, the very son of God, became a human being so that he could be our Kinsman Redeemer. Because he was sinless, he could pay the penalty for our sin. He was named 'Jesus' because he was to save us from our sins.

Now it is up to human beings to go to Jesus and ask him to cover us with his garment so that we become his 'bride' and share in the inheritance of eternal life.

If we so link up with Jesus by repenting of our sins, are baptised in water for the washing away of our sins and are filled with his Spirit we are secure in Him for he is a kind and honourable Kinsman Redeemer.

I hope this warms your heart as it does mine.

84

EVEN MORE EVIDENCE FOR THE BIBLE'S AUTHENTICITY

You know that I have been presenting 'exhibits' as evidence of the truth of the Bible in the last chapter of each section of this book. Well, be prepared to have your mind blown now. I am so excited about what I am going to share with you now that I wish I could shout it from the rooftops. And I want you to share it with everyone in your circle of influence as well. Every earthling needs to know that God loves them so much that he wrote his Good News (which is what the word 'gospel' means) right across the sky. No kidding! Here's Exhibit E:

"The heavens declare the glory of God; the skies proclaim the work of his hands. Day after day they pour forth speech; night after night they display knowledge. There is no speech or language where their voice is not heard. Their voice goes out into all the earth, their words to the ends of the world." That is a quote from Psalm19:1-4, and in case you thought that the psalms were simply poems sometimes set to music, remember that Jesus referred to the psalms so he was giving his stamp of approval to them.

You may have read the above psalm and felt it was a poetic way of saying that God had 'done a good job' of creating the beautiful sky full of millions of shining stars. But there is much more to it than that. Did you notice how it says that the skies *'pour forth speech'* and that *their voice is heard everywhere?* That is intimating more than majestic beauty…

I have mentioned to you that my hubby John is an

amateur astronomer. He has a good sized telescope (for a private person that is) and we have enjoyed looking at the rings around Saturn, the coloured stripes round Jupiter, the amazing mountains and valleys of the moon as well as smaller moons which circle some of the other planets. It is a thrilling hobby and one which gives us the opportunity to share the beauty and majesty of God's creation with others. But because of John's interest in the universe he came across books which shared something even more stunning.

You know how I have referred to the sunrise and sunset as God's signature on the beginning and ending of each day, well he wrote much more than just his signature in the sky. We have all seen small planes in the sky trailing a sign behind them or those that write a message by looping round and leaving a vapour trail which then is blown away. But did you know that God wrote a whole story in the sky which won't disappear until he rolls up the heavens ready for the new earth and new heavens?

Firstly, let me make sure that you understand that I am not speaking of astrology where people say that the position of stars at the time of your birth determine your destiny. No! Definitely not! That is part of the New Age nonsense which actually hides the truth. I am not meaning to criticise astrologers. I feel sorry for them for they have been misled and are missing out on something far greater...

Right back at the beginning of the Bible we are told that Adam was given the privilege of naming the animals that God created. But in Psalm 147:4 it says that God *named and numbered the stars*. He determines the number of the stars and calls them each by name. This is echoed in Isaiah 40:26 Lift your eyes and look to the heavens: Who created all these? He who brings out the starry host one by one, and calls them each by name. Because of his great power and mighty strength, not one of them is missing. Sometimes a few words say more than a mouthful. Those words are crucial, and here is why. When we research we find that back in the early ages, though different languages existed such as the Chaldean and Babylonian, the names of stars had the *same meaning* in each language. This gives credence to the fact that it was God himself who gave the stars their names. An example is with the constellation which we call Virgo. We call it The Virgin. The Romans called it Virgo and the Hebrews called it Bethullah. Each of these words means exactly the same thing.

We have heard stories from various places in the world that when Christian missionaries originally went to those areas and told the Gospel story about Jesus, the local people said that they knew the story from the sky. They just didn't know his name. Isn't that truly awesome? And doesn't it tell us that God wants everyone to know how much he loves the people he has made and wants them to be right with him?

You probably know that *astrology* uses 12 signs of the Zodiak. Well, those 12 signs are genuine. ('Zodiak' is a Greek word. In the Hebrew language, the word Mazzaroth refers to all the constellations along the path of the sun including the 12 most well-known ones, **so I will continue to use the Hebrew name so that you remember that what I am saying is nothing to do with astrology**. In the original language of the Bible, the Hebrew word Mazzaroth is found in Job 38:32 which is translated in the New International Version "Can you bring forth the constellations in their seasons?") It's just that astrology gives them a twisted meaning so I want to show you God's intention. (**One of the Devil's weapons to deceive people is to hide the truth by counterfeiting what God has done, but with a twist. The one positive to be taken from this is that, if there is a counterfeit, there must be a very significant original.**

Only great things rate counterfeiting.)

The ancient Israelites, God's people, were instructed that when they camped for a time they were to set up, with the tabernacle (the enormous tent for the worship of God) at their centre and with their 12 tribes arranged round it, 3 tribes on each side in the same order every time. And that order represented the order of the 12 major signs of the Mazzaroth. Each tribe had an ensign which represented their constellation sign. Even today, groups carry a flag which is their 'label', whether it is the countries represented at the Olympic Games or a protest group in the streets. I believe this order and the representative ensigns had a much nobler purpose. They were relating the gospel of Jesus to the Hebrew people *long before Jesus came to earth.* We know that Jesus' purpose in coming to earth was to save people from their sins, in other words to allow forgiveness and full reconciliation with the Creator God. What was the basis for this relationship between the Hebrews and God *before Jesus came?* Everything in their lives spoke of the future work of Jesus even though the people themselves couldn't have realised that. But God was able to view his people as righteous because they obeyed his Laws which put in place these representative things which spoke of Jesus and the work of redemption that he would do.

Can you see the picture that my mind's eye paints for me? Mentally, I position myself above the tribes of Israel. I see the Tabernacle of God at their centre. I see the representations of the constellations which speak of the One who would come to earth to bring salvation. And I feel that when God looked down on that scene he could see the 'stamp' of the Gospel on his people and he could thus accept them as right in his sight, that wondrous word *righteous*. None of us can be *righteous* of ourselves. It is only in Christ that we have the covering of his righteousness.

I see this type of thing repeated in us in modern times when we first accept Jesus' sacrifice and are baptised for the washing away of our sins. We are like babes, having no real idea of all that God is doing for us. But we simply obey his Word, and he does the rest. As time goes on and we grow closer to the Lord and learn more from his Word, we marvel at his generous grace toward us, at the way he goes out of his way to mould us into the likeness of his Son.

What did the Creator himself say was the reason for the heavenly bodies? Genesis 1:14 – And God said, "Let there be lights in the expanse of the sky to separate the day from the night, and let them serve as signs to mark seasons and days and years...

Bear in mind that there were no punctuation marks in the original Bible. The first thing we note is that this is referring to the sun, moon and stars. Then we see that they were to serve *as signs*. They were to mark *seasons, days and years*. A rudimentary knowledge of astronomy shows us how the heavenly bodies mark seasons, days and years. But how do they serve as signs?

Another Scripture to bring in here is Romans 1:20 – For since the creation of the world God's invisible qualities – his eternal power and divine nature – have been clearly seen, being understood from what has been made, so that men are without excuse.

The first star sign is Virgo the Virgin so right at the beginning we have a virgin woman who plays an important part in God's story. You're not surprised at that, are you? The last star sign is Leo the Lion heralding Jesus' second coming to earth as the Lion of the Tribe of Judah. (Judah was the tribe into which Jesus was born and the name 'Judah' means praise.)

You are probably aware that the constellations are represented by shapes in star maps. The shapes themselves are not able to be seen in the sky at this time. Whether they were originally visible to our first parents and have now 'faded' or whether God instructed ancient man how to represent each group I don't know. There is a legend that Seth and Enoch first illustrated the shapes. But when you hear about some star names, you will realise how it all falls into place in the story.

Now let's look at some of the meanings of star names. When we look at the constellation of Virgo, it obviously represents a pure woman. Virgo is represented by the shape of a woman with a sheaf of wheat in one hand. The meaning of the star in that sheaf is 'seed'. Do you remember how God called Abraham to look at the sky and told him that his offspring would be as numerous as the stars? Well God did that with Abraham more than once, and one of those times he used a different word and it meant 'take a census of the stars'. Now a census is not just a numbering, it also records something about the thing. When we fill out a census form it is not just to say we are still alive on earth, we also have to give information about our circumstances. Well, it is not difficult to believe that on that occasion Abraham was to look at the constellations and see the life of his 'offspring' Jesus written in the stars. If you think I am stretching the truth here, check out – in the New Testament - Galatians 3:16 The promises were spoken to Abraham and to his seed. The Scripture does not say "and to seeds", meaning many people, but "and to your seed", meaning one person, who is Christ. 'Seed' in olden times was a word used for a child who would be born to you or to one of your descendants, or one who had already been born to you. It was usually used of men and was similar to the way we think of sperm now – the makings of a child are already within us but still in 'seed' form.

Now we look at another star name within Virgo, with the

Latin name Coma. Old drawings show this star as a little boy in the lap of the virgin. Now who but God would have a child in a virgin's lap, written in the stars?

One of the more spectacular parts of the story involves what is commonly called The Big Dipper. Its name is more correctly Orion and it is The Warrior. The figure of The Warrior is of a man armed with a sword hanging from his belt and a club in his raised arm. He carries in his other arm the head and skin of a lion. This is great news for us when we think of the reference to the Devil as a 'roaring lion seeking whom he may devour' as we've spoken of in an earlier chapter. There is a star in Orion's belt with the ancient meaning of 'wounded'. Does that ring a bell with you? Jesus certainly is a warrior waging war against the Devil. Do you recall when Jesus was on the cross that a Roman soldier came to him and drove his sword into his side? Well that was already recorded in the stars millennia earlier.

We look again at this Warrior and we see that one foot is raised and the star in that foot has the meaning 'the foot that crushes'. The full significance of that comes to us when we look in Genesis where God said: I will put enmity between you (the Devil) and the woman, and between your seed and hers; he will crush your head... So God not only said it, but he wrote it in the stars that although there was a struggle between humankind and the Devil, one 'seed' or offspring would crush the Devil's head.

Other bright stars in the shoulders of Orion are Betelgeuz meaning *the coming,* and Bellatrix meaning *quickly coming or swiftly destroying*. These are self-explanatory. In his leg is Saiph meaning *bruised,* and we are told in Isaiah chapter 53 that Jesus was wounded for our transgressions, He was *bruised for our iniquities*. We could also link it to the Scripture which says that the devil would bruise his heel.

Let's move on to Leo the Lion, another of the constellations. This is a picture of a pouncing lion and underneath him is Hydra the Serpent. You probably know that the Devil is depicted in Genesis as a serpent so here is another stellar portrait of the victory of Jesus over our arch enemy the Devil.

There are many other references to Jesus and his work in the God-given star names but I think I have given you enough to assure you of God's majesty, power and love and that he will bring all to the culmination he has promised in his Word. (There are a number of books on this subject if you would like to follow up on it though you may have to search for them. Some of them give a simple explanation, others go into more scientific detail.)

I have one more Exhibit for you, just a small one, Exhibit F: Do you remember how the formation of Eve was described? Here it is: ...the Lord caused the man (Adam) to fall into a deep sleep; and while he was sleeping, he took one of the man's ribs and closed up the place with flesh. Then the Lord made a woman from the rib he had taken out of the man, and he brought her to the man. We are familiar with the idea of cloning in these days but normal cloning would have produced another man. So this was a miracle but it seems to me that God often works within the laws of his own creation. I have learned an astonishing fact from an article by Dr. J. Shelley about ribs. The rib is one of the few bones of the body which, if removed while leaving its sheath intact, will fully grow again. So where else would God have taken some of Adam's DNA? Isn't God wonderful? And isn't his Word factual? The answer has to be a resounding Yes!

www.ingramcontent.com/pod-product-compliance
Lightning Source LLC
Chambersburg PA
CBHW071114080526
44587CB00013B/1340